Christology in Context

Christology in Context

*The Earliest
Christian Response to Jesus*

Marinus de Jonge

The Westminster Press
Philadelphia

Book design by Gene Harris

First edition

Published by The Westminster Press®
Philadelphia, Pennsylvania

PRINTED IN THE UNITED STATES OF AMERICA

9 8 7 6 5 4 3 2 1

Library of Congress Cataloging-in-Publication Data

Jonge, Marinus de. 1925–
    Christology in context : the earliest Christian response to Jesus
/ Marinus de Jonge. — 1st ed.
        p.   cm.
    Bibliography: p.
    Includes indexes.
    ISBN 0-664-25010-6 (pbk.)

    1. Jesus Christ—Person and offices—Biblical teaching. 2. Bible.
N.T.—Crtiticism, interpretation, etc. 3. Jesus Christ—History of
doctrines—Early church, ca. 30–600. I. Title.
BT198.J64 1988
232'.09'015—dc19   87-30878
                                                            CIP

Contents

Contents 7

Foreword

In the earliest Gospel the demons know exactly who Jesus is, but his closest disciples are mystified. Even when they appear to have used the correct words to name him, they turn out to misunderstand completely. This disturbing irony ought to have stood as a warning against the confidence with which, through the succeeding centuries, orthodox and heretic, conservative and modernist, outsider and insider have thought to define precisely who and what Jesus was or is.

Can we avoid the demonic pretense of certitude without lapsing into the comfortable suspension of conviction that we so often dress up as academic objectivity? In this book, at the same time cool and quietly passionate, Professor de Jonge shows us a way. He begins neither with unanswerable and pretentious questions about Jesus' "self-consciousness" nor with generalized titles, offices, or roles, but with the responses to Jesus by those who followed him directly or mediately. This is not a completely novel approach, for often in recent years scholars have framed their inquiries about the historic identity of Jesus Christ in ways that implied such a focus upon the symbolic productions of the responding communities. Consequently de Jonge is able to use the best of historical scholarship in our century, and not the least of the merits of this book is the way he has brought together the results of an enormous number of specialized studies and incorporated them with deceptive simplicity into his narrative. However, what we have here is more than the sum of up-to-date scholarship, for de Jonge is pursuing his own clearly defined goals. Throughout he keeps firm hold on the central questions, presents the evidence squarely and plainly, weighs and judges the arguments of his predecessors, and invites us to share his decisions. Thus we feel that we are being led by a master detective, who does not merely announce his conclusions when the case is closed, but invites us from the outset to join in the search. It is clear on every page, moreover, that we are in the hands of a skilled exegete and historian, with long experience in the decipherment of manuscripts and the editing of texts, thoroughly acquainted with the currents of thought and the symbols of religion in the Greco-Roman and the Jewish cultures of antiquity.

Still, though de Jonge rigorously and honestly confines himself to a description of what is historically probable, it is obvious that his inquiry into the earliest responses to Jesus has more than historical interest for him and for us. His approach has significant theological and more generally human implications. The decision to focus upon the responses to Jesus' life does not result from a counsel of despair, as if it were a consolation prize for our inability to find out the "real" identity of Jesus. On the contrary, it implies a profound rethinking of what "identity" is. Some of the most provocative thinkers of our time—as disparate in cultural setting and specialty as Mead, Piaget, and Bakhtin—have argued that a person's identity is not a given essence with which one begins, but an open-ended, continuous trans- action between self and others, between individual and community. If that is true, then traditional Christology must be rethought. As historians we have slowly grasped the truth that there is no meaning without context; no statement or text does its proper communicative work except in dialogue with its own language community and its own extraverbal situation. All the more, the meaning of a person's life is to be found not by abstraction from the historical situation but by understanding the person's interaction with that situation and the engagement of those who follow after with the memory and effects of that prior transaction. Personal meaning transcends the particular not by stripping it away but by deeply engaging it in a dialogue that unfolds toward the future. Thus we must learn to hear in new ways the testimony of the early followers of the Christ that he was not known from the beginning but becomes known only in continuing, mutual responding, and will be fully known only at "the end."

WAYNE A. MEEKS

Preface
and Acknowledgments

This book is an attempt to describe and analyze the great variety of ways the earliest followers of Jesus responded to him. It also tries to relate those various responses to the circumstances in which the early Christian communities lived. Anyone who is aware of the nature of the sources we must depend on for our knowledge of first-century Christianity will realize that this is a hazardous undertaking.

I have opted for an inductive approach. Starting with the oldest written sources at our disposal I have asked what they reveal about earlier stages of Christological reflection. I have tried to describe the Christology of the earliest writings themselves and have compared the most important elements in their response to Jesus with those found in the writings of later groups and authors. A long chapter has been devoted to terms and concepts applied by Christians in their response to Jesus. Finally, the question is asked, In what respects does the earliest Christian response to Jesus reflect Jesus' own views on his relationship with God and his fellow human beings?

Many studies have been devoted to early Christian Christology, and to the Christology of individual writings in the New Testament. No one can write on this very central subject without touching upon discussions and debates on almost all major problems to which modern New Testament scholarship has paid attention. I know myself indebted to many of my colleagues of the past and the present. In order to keep the analysis as sober and as concise as possible, however, opinions of other scholars are only referred to in cases where their insights were of great assistance in reaching certain conclusions.

A word of warm thanks is due to Wayne A. Meeks for inviting me to undertake this work, for helping me in mapping it out in the course of a long "conversation by letter," and for much support and constructive criticism while the chapters were being written. He and the readers of The Westminster Press assisted me in clarifying my thoughts and put me right in matters of vocabulary and idiom. Finally, I want to thank Mrs. T. C. C. M. Heesterman-Visser, the first critical general reader of the book, who typed out an often barely legible manuscript and looked after many corrections at later stages.

Quotations from the Bible and the Old Testament Apocrypha are from the Revised Standard Version unless otherwise noted. Translations from the works of Flavius Josephus were as a rule taken from the edition and translation of the works of Josephus by H. St. J. Thackeray, R. Marcus, A. Wikgren, and L. H. Feldman, published in the *Loeb Classical Library* (London: W. Heinemann/Cambridge, Mass.: Harvard University Press), nine volumes, 1926–1965.

MARINUS DE JONGE

Leiden, 1 April 1987

Abbreviations

AB	Anchor Bible
ATANT	Abhandlungen zur Theologie des Alten und Neuen Testaments
BETL	Bibliotheca ephemeridum theologicarum lovaniensium
BZ	*Biblische Zeitschrift*
CBQ	*Catholic Biblical Quarterly*
DJD	Discoveries in the Judaean Desert
E	English (where numbering differs from the Hebrew)
EKKNT	Evangelisch-katholischer Kommentar zum Neuen Testament
FRLANT	Forschungen zur Religion und Literatur des Alten und Neuen Testaments
HNT	Handbuch zum Neuen Testament
HNTC	Harper's New Testament Commentaries
HR	*History of Religions*
HTKNT	Herders theologischer Kommentar zum Neuen Testament
HTS	Harvard Theological Studies
ICC	International Critical Commentary
JBL	*Journal of Biblical Literature*
JJS	*Journal of Jewish Studies*
KEK	Kritisch-exegetischer Kommentar über das Neue Testament
NedTTs	*Nederlands theologisch tijdschrift*
N.F.	Neue Folge (new series)
NIGTC	New International Greek Testament Commentary
NTA	*New Testament Abstracts*
NTS	*New Testament Studies*
OBO	Orbis biblicus et orientalis
par.	parallel(s)
SBLMonS	Society of Biblical Literature Monograph Series

SBLDS   Society of Biblical Literature Dissertation Series
SBLSBS   Society of Biblical Literature Sources for Biblical Study
SBS   Stuttgarter Bibelstudien
SNT   Studien zum Neuen Testament
SNTSMS   Society for New Testament Studies Monograph Series
ST   *Studia theologica*
TDNT   G. Kittel and G. Friedrich, eds., *Theological Dictionary of the New Testament*, 1964–76
WMANT   Wissenschaftliche Monographien zum Alten und Neuen Testament
WUNT   Wissenschaftliche Untersuchungen zum Neuen Testament
ZTK   *Zeitschrift für Theologie und Kirche*

Introduction

Christology in Context

Early Christology is not simply a set of ideas about Jesus held by early Christians, or a part, however important, of early Christian doctrine. Early Christology must be viewed in the context of the dynamics of the first hundred years or so of church life. All beliefs about Jesus were expressions of faith in him and trust in God. But in what ways did Christians respond to Jesus, and to the message about him? How is the great variety in their responses to be explained? Believing was by no means a matter of abstractions; the statements about Jesus were born as answers to vexing questions and existential needs. That the believers' responses were influenced by the life of Christian groups and individuals will become apparent in the chapters that follow.

In this book the emphasis will be on Christian groups and their ways of life in Roman-Hellenistic society. This is not to deny that early Christianity had important leaders who were theologians ·in their own right. The writer of the oldest Gospel, Mark, did a remarkable thing by creating a coherent picture of Jesus' public life from the perspective of Jesus' cross and resurrection. He thereby made a significant contribution to Christology. The same applies to the composers of Matthew and Luke. The latter even added to his Gospel a survey of the developments in the life and mission of early Christianity. This came to be called "The Acts of the Apostles." We may also mention "the beloved disciple" (John 21:20–24), who was the central authority for what we now call the "Johannine" communities. These communities had their own very articulate and advanced views about Jesus and his relation to God and to believers. And then, of course, Paul was a powerful missionary to the Gentiles and an equally powerful thinker. He called himself "the least of the apostles" but was at the same time convinced that his gospel was essentially the same as that of his colleagues (1 Cor. 15:1–11). He is the one who thought out the consequences of the gospel in preaching it to non-Jews. Particularly in his letters to the Galatians and to the Romans, Paul explains the implications of Jesus' death and resurrection, both for non-Jews and for Jews, with great consistency and penetrating insight.

Granting the individual elements in these compositions, we should immediately also stress another side. Our present Gospels all incorporate much traditional material current in the Christian communities for which they were written. As collectors, their authors were exponents of the groups in which they lived and which they served. They brought together as much relevant information about Jesus as they could find and presented it in a meaningful framework. One cannot read a Gospel properly without continually asking what situation its author (or, perhaps, group of authors) wanted to address in the interplay between the tradition and his own composition, henceforth called a "redaction." One also asks what the common belief and common practice were in the groups for which the Gospel was written, and which particular aspects the author wished to emphasize.

The same questions apply to Paul. Paul developed his theology while dealing with certain often difficult situations in the individual Christian communities he addressed. He answered questions, reacted to reports by visitors, reflected on his own situation—and he did so in the community in which he worked, on his travels, while in prison, in debate with bearers of a false message, and in other circumstances. Paul's theology is not theoretical, but eminently practical; it was developed in response to definite needs and challenges (see chapter 1 on Galatians and 1 Corinthians). And because Paul was writing to fellow Christians, he constantly stressed the beliefs and practices he had in common with them. He encouraged them, warned them, and sometimes reproached them. He made his own particular points, but he did so on the basis of a common faith. Time and again, for instance, he clearly referred to short formulas in which his fellow Christians expressed their faith ("confessional formulas"), to hymns, or to parts of the formulas recited at baptism or when believers sat together at the communal meal. Paul as an individual thinker shared, and purported to expound the consequences of, the message that is authoritative for all Christians.

This book seeks to describe patterns of belief in the context of patterns of life[1] but concentrates on the former. It will refer to other studies when necessary to illustrate the life of the Christian communities. The book tries to show how the earliest Christian responses to Jesus interacted with the Christians' responses to the needs experienced in their own lives, and to the challenges of the outside world. Christology presupposes certain views of God's dealings with humanity in general and Israel in particular. It is therefore also concerned with the situation of individual men and women, and with the relations of the Christian community to Israel and to the whole of humanity. What one believes about Jesus is closely related to what one regards as the meaning of life and what one hopes for the future. Christological statements correlate with aspects of early Christian self-understanding. We shall have to bear in mind, however, that self-understanding and ideas about salvation may not be narrowed down to *individual* self-understanding and the response to longings for personal salvation. In asking how a particular group of Christians views Jesus, we shall have to take into account the terms and expressions it uses to identify itself with respect to God and its fellow humans. Christology is always "Christology in context."

The Proper Approach to the Subject, and the Limitations of Our Knowledge

The earliest Christian response to Jesus is known to us from the earliest Christian documents. We have to rely on the writings that eventually became part of the authoritative collection called the New Testament.[2] Of these writings the letters of Paul, written in the period between A.D. 50 and A.D. 60, are the oldest. Among these letters, the one to the Romans, the two to the Corinthians, those to the Galatians, the Philippians, and Philemon, and the first letter to the Thessalonians are generally considered to have been written by Paul himself. The others (Ephesians, Colossians, 2 Thessalonians) are regarded as "deutero-Pauline"; that is, coming from followers of Paul trying to answer later questions in his spirit. The so-called pastoral epistles, 1 and 2 Timothy and Titus, form a separate group.

Next in importance are the Synoptic Gospels (Mark, Matthew, Luke), and Acts. New Testament scholars have reached certain general agreements, which I follow in this book without feeling the need to set forth all the evidence: Mark is the oldest Gospel, and it was used in some form by the authors of the Gospels of Matthew and Luke. The latter two Gospels had still another common source, generally called Q, mainly consisting of sayings of Jesus and other teaching material. Acts reflects first of all Luke's view of the history of early Christianity. It no doubt used and incorporated older material, but it is difficult to delineate earlier written sources with any degree of certainty.[3]

The Gospel of John and the Johannine epistles stem from a distinct group in early Christianity, often called "the Johannine

School." It has some material in common with the other three Gospels. In this case also (contrary to the opinion of some scholars), I do not think it possible to reconstruct a source that contained a number of stories concerning significant acts ("signs") performed by Jesus and that had a Christology of its own.

The Fourth Gospel and the letters are important because of the very clear and consistent views found in them of Jesus Christ as the Son sent and authorized by the Father. They also enable us to trace certain developments in this Christology in the Johannine communities.[4] But they can hardly be considered to represent the *earliest* Christian response to Jesus.

Of the other, so-called catholic epistles (James, 1 and 2 Peter, and Jude), 1 Peter is of particular importance, because it reflects traditional Christological thinking in relation to a situation of discrimination and persecution which the communities addressed were facing. There are some clear links with Paul's letters; as in the deutero-Paulines, 1 Peter can be used as proof for the viability and persistence of a number of earlier Christological answers to the problems confronting early Christians.

Quite apart stands the book of Revelation, both in its imagery and in the situation of violent persecution and severe crisis it addressed.

Not all these sources can be analyzed in detail. I shall concentrate on the genuine letters of Paul, on Mark and Q (the common source behind Matthew and Luke), and on all further relevant material that corroborates and supplements the evidence found in these earliest documents. I intend to follow an *inductive* approach and to read these documents as means of communication between the author and his audience. This is obvious in the case of Paul's letters and, as was argued in the preceding section, must also be taken into account in the case of Mark and Q. We should not only list the elements that are peculiar to the author concerned, but also look for those elements which the author and his audience clearly had in common. Finally, there were views circulating within the communities addressed, or threatening to influence them, that were opposed by the author. We shall have to study the documents as the outcome of a very complicated interplay of ideas. There are methods that enable us to discover with some clarity the common traditional material (see below). But the author's reaction to this, and his assimilation of it in his own story, is often clearer than the function and meaning of that material in different, earlier contexts. Further, the reconstruction of the views of opponents whom we know only from what is said against them is notoriously difficult.

This book studies the documents of the New Testament with the purpose of detecting the earliest Christian response to Jesus. It tries to explain the meaning and background of the various forms of this response and to sketch the continuity and development in the later stages of Christological thinking. It does not attempt to give a synthesis of *the* Christology of the New Testament. Neither does it present a comprehensive picture of the Christology of different groups and individuals within early Christianity. This is partly because of a shortage of space, which has led to concentration on the earliest stages and allows only a general view of later developments. It is also because we simply lack sufficient evidence to give an overall reconstruction.

Recent attempts at an overall view of early Christian Christology have often concentrated on the use of the so-called Christological titles (Christ, Son of man, Son of God, Lord, the Word, etc.). These attempts have usually distinguished between the views of Jesus himself, of Palestinian-Jewish Christianity, of Hellenistic-Jewish Christianity, and of Hellenistic-Gentile Christianity.[5] But, apart from the problems connected with an approach via Christological titles (see below), we may well ask whether a distinction between the various types of Christian communities is any more than a theoretical exercise. Some years ago, N. A. Dahl[6] remarked that it may be helpful to distinguish between Palestinian-Jewish, Hellenistic-Jewish, and early Gentile Christianity in clear cases, but that the borderlines were fluid. He stressed the great variety in Christological vocabulary and ideas about salvation within the various Christian communities and remarked: "There is no evidence and little reason to think that there ever existed communities that had a pure form of Christology, characterized . . . by one type of preaching and one Christological title." Dahl added that he doubted whether the early Christians mainly used fixed formulations about Jesus; in his view they used a less standardized language than is found in the written texts.

In any case the letters of Paul and the Acts of the Apostles picture a variety of Christian communities connected in a network. But Paul with his assistants, and other missionaries and leaders, were not the only ones who traveled a lot. Ordinary Christians visited the churches, sometimes on business trips but also sometimes with special mandates. Paul and others made many journeys along different routes between Corinth and Ephesus (mentioned in 1 and 2 Corinthians). According to Acts, communications between Jerusalem and Antioch were particularly close. The church in Jerusalem included both Palestinian-Jewish members and Hellenistic-Jewish ones. The church in Antioch was the first to accept Gentiles as members. The letters of Paul presuppose a thorough knowledge of the Jewish scriptures. Those scriptures supply the proof texts that form the starting point of Paul's explanation or clinch his argument. The many Gentile Christians in the congregations that received these letters were evidently expected to understand Paul's language and to accept his way of arguing. Now not all Christians of Gentile descent in Rome, for instance, could have grasped the meaning of Romans, chapters 9–11, with its profusion of passages from scripture illustrating God's relation with Israel in the past, the present, and the future. But it is clear that Paul regarded his conclusions as convincing and binding for *all* Christians. Very likely many of the Gentile Christians were recruited from the ranks of "God-fearers," regular visitors of the synagogue and sympathizers with Jewish beliefs, who nevertheless did not embrace Judaism as proselytes. It would seem probable that they explained the Old Testament citations to their fellow Christians.

Recently M. Hengel[7] has rightly emphasized the role of Hellenistic-Jewish Christians in and outside Jerusalem in maintaining communications between the earliest Christian communities. He has also argued that the great variety of Christological conceptions already present in the earlier letters of Paul proves that these early Christian communities must have been very creative Christologically. They were scattered over a geographically restricted area (Palestine and Syria), and it all happened in the less than twenty years between Jesus' death and Paul's visit to Corinth in A.D. 50, the year he wrote 1 Thessalonians. This explosive growth throws doubt upon any clear distinction between different types and stages of Christological thinking connected with different types of churches. At least this seems true during the early period. Already in our oldest written sources there is a great diversity of conceptions, some of which must have originated in the short period indicated by Hengel. Early Christology must have been complex from the beginning. Modern interpreters should beware of giving a simple picture of growth and development along distinct lines in different types of Christian communities.[8]

But any survey of the early Christian response to Jesus should start with at least a brief outline of what Jesus thought and told about himself. How did he understand his relation to God and his role in God's dealings with Israel and humanity? The problem here is that we know Jesus only through the testimonies of his followers as those testimonies were incorporated into the documents of a later period. They describe what he did, how he suffered and died; they report how he appeared to a number of his disciples and commissioned them to go out and preach the gospel. They also record his teaching, including that about himself. But they do so in the context of their proclamation of the gospel concerning (Jesus) Christ, and in the context of their teaching to insiders and outsiders about this person who had become their Lord.

This is not the place to describe the history of the so-called *Leben-*

Jesu-Forschung; that is, the investigation into the life and teaching of the "historical Jesus."[9] Reconstruction of Jesus' own Christology is extremely difficult, because of the variety of responses to Jesus in the earliest sources and the complex problems we encounter when we try to pursue certain lines backward in time. Moreover, the pursuit is bound to be somewhat subjective. Yet we may be sure that response to Jesus has always been part of a two-way process. Of course the earliest believers looked to Jesus with their own eyes. They were influenced by their personal, social, and cultural situations. They thought in terms of their environment. They continued to read the Jewish scriptures, trying to interpret them meaningfully in the light of what they had experienced and of their own plight at the time. But it was *Jesus* they spoke about, and to *him* they assigned a central role in God's dealings with humanity. Therefore we have to take into account what he said and did, what happened to him, and how he called people to follow him and to regard him as a unique agent between God and people.

Jesus is at the center of all early (and later) Christology. This presupposes some degree of continuity between what he said and did and people's reactions. It also presupposes some continuity between the situation of his followers before Jesus' cross and resurrection[10] and their situation after those events. The gospel of Christ *(euaggelion tou Christou)* that is proclaimed centers around the life, cross, and resurrection of *Jesus.* That is why in this book the last chapter is devoted to the life and teaching of the man Jesus, with whom it all began.

Methods to Be Employed

Interpreters of early Christian literature have an impressive array of exegetical tools at their disposal for the analysis of texts. In support of my investigation I shall try to explain what literary criticism, form and tradition criticism, and the comparative study of religious concepts or ideas may contribute to our knowledge of early Christology.

Traditionally, New Testament *literary criticism*[11] has concentrated on the identification of sources and later additions or redactions of particular writings. In the case of the Gospels and Acts its aim was to sort out the earliest evidence to be used in a historical reconstruction of the life and teaching of Jesus and of the community of his disciples. Or, in the case of the epistles, it tried to determine what the author had actually written and where later believers, in handing down the texts, had altered them for a variety of reasons. Literary and historical criticism together have reached impressive results, as books on "Introduction to the New Testament" show. We shall have to take these results seriously.

Yet we shall have to proceed with great caution where comparison between three (or more) documents is impossible. Already in the case of Q, the common source of Matthew and Luke, where two Gospels may be compared, it is often not possible to decide whether or not a particular saying of Jesus belonged to Q; or, if it did, to determine its wording and reading in the context of this reconstructed document. Or, to mention another example, it is plausible that Mark was not the first to compose a narrative of the passion and crucifixion of Jesus. Indeed, to the earliest followers of Jesus it must have been of the highest importance to know what led to Jesus' ignominious death. They had to explain this both among themselves and to their opponents, Jews and non-Jews alike. An early pre-Markan passion narrative would be an extremely valuable source for the description of the earliest Christian response to Jesus. It is very likely that such a narrative existed in one form or another. It is, however, extremely difficult to reconstruct such a document, and consequently there is by no means unanimity among scholars with regard to its content.[12] Whatever an earlier passion narrative may have contained, what we have is its Markan redaction. This is not to say that Mark may not have preserved many, even essential, points of the narrative (or narratives) he used. It would have helped him considerably in shaping the picture of Jesus he wanted to present to his readers. But for lack of evidence outside the Gospel we are not able to distinguish with any certainty between Markan and pre-Markan elements and wording.

Literary critics have always made use of unevenness, reduplications, sudden changes in form and content, and further signs of inconsistency in their attempts to identify sources. But are modern methods of scientific analysis and modern standards of consistency always applicable? What seems inconsistent or illogical to a critic of the nineteenth or twentieth century may have made good sense to the person who wrote it and to the people for whom he wrote. Literary critics are right in drawing attention to unevenness, sudden transitions, changes in vocabulary or argumentation, or use of different literary genres. But they should first of all try to explain those as parts of the fabric of the text, as means of expression fitting the author's overall strategy. The application of these wider criteria may help us to spot the places in the text where the author uses oral or written material shaped before him, and/or vocabulary coined by others but taken over as meaningful. Any author communicating with an audience will express the message in his or her own words as well as in words that are common property. One cannot get something new across if one does not combine the personal and the traditional, the new and the old. It is important to attempt to define the interplay between these two sets of elements as exactly as possible—but only rarely will one be able to establish written sources with any degree of certainty, or feel compelled to assume later additions or redactions.

The discipline commonly called *form criticism*[13] concentrates on the period of oral transmission of "text units" embedded in the early Christian writings we have been discussing. Form criticism occupied itself mostly with the material incorporated in the Synoptic Gospels, but it has also been applied to the letters and to the apocalyptic material in Revelation. It has tried to define and classify certain standardized "forms," ranging from individual sentences to longer stories, and to connect them with specific typical situations in the life of the early communities. These typical situations are called *Sitze im Leben.* In New Testament scholarship they have been related specifically to the activities within and around the communities: missionary activity, apologetics and polemics, instruction of converts, teaching and preaching to members, celebration of baptism and the community meal ("table of the Lord"), the activity of prophets in the congregation, and the like.

The form-critical approach has led to results which are relevant for the present investigation. In the following chapters we shall deal with liturgical material, the "forms" connected with the community meal and baptism, hymns, prayers, confessional formulas, doxologies (liturgical formulas of praise), acclamations, and others. Among the very rich material used in teaching and preaching we may mention different types of short stories, which find their climax in, or center around, a pronouncement or a healing of Jesus, or his instruction to disciples, or his polemic against his adversaries. There are numerous stories about Jesus (incidentally, also about John the Baptist), all intended to show who he was, what he did, and what he said, all emphasizing his unique insight, power, and authority. Many of Jesus' pronouncements were handed down individually or in groups, and they again illustrate his authority as a prophet, as a seer, as a lawgiver or a wise man. This list is by no means complete. But the examples given may show that the search for standardized "forms" in our written Gospels may help us to trace the prehistory of the texts concerned. Also, they may help us to understand the activities of the Gospel writers as collectors and redactors on behalf of the groups of Christians whom they represented and wanted to guide. Finally, they remind us that the form, function, and content of the unit concerned are interrelated.

Yet again, a caution is in order. We have these text units before us in a written form, as part of a written text, and we attempt to work back to an earlier stage: that of oral transmission. But we cannot be sure that oral tradition immediately preceded the composition of the Gospel. Orally and in writing, there may have been intermediate stages in the collection of stories or in the forming of strings of sayings. Oral transmission was not a simple process, either from complex to simple or from simple to complex. We may not assume, for instance, that stories with a single point are necessarily earlier than those which combine several elements, and that the latter are therefore less pure. We must be very careful when we attempt to sketch a history of transmission from the supposed original form of a saying to its form and function in the Gospel of Mark.

Further, oral transmission may have led to standardization, but not necessarily to uniformity. When we look at statements expressing the central elements of the faith (confessional formulas) in the Pauline letters, for instance, we find all sorts of little variations. This is partly because of the context in which they appear but also, very probably, because of the lack of a fixed set of creedal formulas to be repeated verbally in all communities to which Paul was writing. The story of Jesus' instruction to celebrate "the table of the Lord" clearly got a standard form very early. It is transmitted to us by Mark in 14:22–25 and by Paul in 1 Cor. 11:23–26. The account is the same, but there are numerous differences even in the words spoken over the bread and the cup, which were no doubt intended to be repeated in liturgy.

We shall also have to be cautious in connecting a particular form too closely and too one-sidedly with a particular *Sitz im Leben*. In Phil. 2:5–11, for instance, Paul quotes a hymn about Christ in support of his exhortations ("have this mind among yourselves, which is yours in Christ Jesus, who . . ."). Comparable switches from one aspect of Christian community life to another, from liturgy (including hymn singing) to exhortation, also took place in the oral stage of transmission. Hymns were sung, with all sorts of variation fitting the occasion, but they may also have been quoted and commented upon in teaching and preaching. "Confessional formulas" were pronounced in entering the community and at baptism, but they also were explained in catechetical teaching or in missionary activity. Once standard forms were there, they were applied in a variety of ways.

Finally, form-critical argumentation has been used too easily in questions of historicity. We shall have to take seriously that oral transmission shapes and transforms. We must also consider that all material was transmitted because it answered the questions and the needs of the early groups of believers after the resurrection. A considerable number of scholars have become reluctant, therefore, to go further back than the *Sitz im Leben* in the earlier communities. Form criticism has undoubtedly complicated the search for the historical Jesus (see part IV), but there is no reason for despair. One may argue that the conditions of discipleship in Jesus' lifetime had a number of elements in common with community life and missionary preaching after his death and resurrection. Moreover, a number of Jesus' personal followers were certainly there when communities after Easter assembled and expanded. There is no doubt that the tradition material was shaped and reshaped during the period of oral transmission—as it was reshaped in a great number of cases when Matthew and Luke took it over from Mark—but it did not necessarily originate during that period.

At this point it is useful to mention a number of criteria which may be applied in discovering earlier traditional units and to illustrate the procedure which may be followed in distinguishing them in one particular instance, that of the confessional formula transmitted by Paul in 1 Cor. 15:3–5.[14] Here we find, first, introductory remarks pointing to the use of traditional material ("I delivered to you . . . what I also received," v. 3). In other cases the introduction is much simpler ("if we believe . . ."; "we confess . . ."; "knowing that . . . ," etc.). There are also other indications that the author appeals to something he has in common with his readers. Next, there is a clear beginning in Christological formulas; here, as often, "that" (v. 3, Greek *hoti*), in others a relative pronoun *(hos)*. Third, the text unit will often have a fixed, strophic form, as here:

> that Christ died for our sins in accordance with the scriptures,
> that he was buried,
> that he was raised on the third day in accordance with the scriptures
> and that he appeared to Cephas, then to the twelve.

Fourth, a detailed analysis of the vocabulary and syntax shows, here and in many other cases, that they are not those regularly used by Paul. Fifth, we often find that an author cites more of a certain unit than he needs for his argument. In 1 Cor. 15 Paul aimed to refute the opinion of certain Corinthians that there is no resurrection of the dead (v. 12). He starts off with a formula speaking about Christ's death and resurrection. Then he expands the formula by adding a list of further appearances of Christ (including one to himself), thereby highlighting Christ's resurrection; but he mentions Christ's death first because it was connected with the resurrection in the received formula. Sixth, we shall often find the traditional text unit, or significant parts of it, employed in other contexts also by different authors. In the case of 1 Cor. 15:3–5 we may point to other "double formulas" dealing with Christ's death and resurrection, or to the expression "Christ died for our sins" (see below).

Not all traditional material has been handed down, orally and in writing, as part of or in the shape of the "forms" distinguished in form criticism. There are also fixed combinations of words and concepts, often-used phrases and expressions, complexes of ideas that clearly represent ways of thinking and speaking current in certain circles. *Tradition criticism* attempts to list and analyze these common elements and to study the way they are used, in the text under consideration *and* in other contexts. Careful study shows that certain words often occur together with other ones, that particular phrases often serve to denote certain human activities (or actions of God) or to describe certain situations.

These traditional expressions represent the element of continuity in the communication process. They help us, once again, to get a clearer view of the interaction between the traditional and the personal in a particular document. One should realize, of course, that their forms may show variations and that they are adaptable to new situations and new contexts. Continuity does not imply rigidity in form and content, but, rather, flexibility. Surveys of the use of a traditional expression in a number of writings over a period of time will not reveal a straight line, but one undulating within certain boundaries, and perhaps even dividing itself in different directions.

It is also important to note that traditions of this type are often not confined to one religious or social group. Of course the early Christians used the language of Hellenistic culture in the Roman Empire. In particular they shared Jewish views about God, Israel, and humanity and used the vocabulary and the complexes of ideas current in Judaism. They used these, no matter how many changes were needed as the result of their response, in life and thought and words, to Jesus, whom they had come to regard as their master. Extending the study of traditional expressions and complexes of ideas beyond the limits of early Christianity will reveal continuity, as described in the preceding paragraph, but it will also reveal distinct points where one should speak of discontinuity. Again, attempts to analyze the elements of continuity and discontinuity together will help us define more clearly the essentials of the response to Jesus, in early Christianity in general and in some early Christian groups in particular.

Tradition criticism, if applied to traditional expressions and complexes of ideas shared by different religious groups, borders on and partly overlaps with *comparative study of religious concepts and ideas.* In the case of early Christology much attention has been paid to Hellenistic and Jewish ideas about salvation and savior figures, particularly those expected in the future (hence the special interest in the Jewish and Hellenistic background of the "Christological titles").

Also eschatology—in the sense of the whole of expectations concerning God's decisive intervention in the course of events on earth in the (near) future—has been given much attention. In order to understand properly Jesus' activity as prophet, teacher, exorcist, wise man, and the like, it is necessary to study contemporary ideas about prophecy, teaching, exorcism, and wisdom. If the salvation and redemption brought about by Jesus Christ are expressed in a number of technical terms replete with meaning at the time, it is important to determine that meaning by comparison with contemporary non-Christian texts. This subject will receive due attention in part III. In this introduction, however, I want to restrict myself to a number of remarks—again cautionary—concerning the possibilities and limitations of such an approach.

First, Jesus was a Jew and his followers were Jews; for a long time Jewish modes of thought prevailed in the church. But Judaism around the beginning of the Christian era was a conglomerate of many different trends and groups, all interpreting and obeying the law of Moses and adhering to the traditions of past generations, but arriving at very different results in theory and practice. The Pharisees did not agree on important issues with the Sadducees and founded their own fraternities fostering their own practice; the Qumran sect felt obliged to separate from the rest of Judaism and to obey strict rules in their center near the Dead Sea. Jews in the Egyptian city of Alexandria, among them Philo, tried to develop their own method of interpretation to discover the implications of Moses' instructions for their life in Egypt. Judaism was in no way a secluded island in a sea of Hellenism. As M. Hengel[15] and others have reminded us lately, all groups in Judaism had, in one way or another, to come to terms with the all-pervasive Hellenistic culture in which they lived and the Roman Empire which formed the dominant stabilizing political force in the eastern (and western) Mediterranean. And all these groups, reactionary and receptive, were in some way influenced by the ideas prevailing in a culture in which Jews had had to live since Alexander the Great.

Consequently it is not really possible to distinguish between what is typically Jewish and typically Hellenistic, or to emphasize differences between Jews in the dispersion and those in the land of Israel. We shall have to compare the ideas and concepts of specific sources emanating from specific groups: Jewish and Hellenistic as well as Christian. We shall have to pay full attention to their particularities. The same applies to the methods used in interpreting the scriptures among Jews and Christians.

Given this variety, the comparison of concepts and ideas, including the Christological titles, is extremely complicated. Analysis of the use of the term "the Anointed One" in Judaism, for instance, reveals variety already in the Old Testament. This term was used in the Psalms in connection with historical kings and in idealized pictures of the king in his relation to God. It was never so used in the prophets, not even in passages describing a future royal son of David. A number of times the term was also used for the high priest (and other priests), and once or twice in connection with prophets. Also in the Judaism of the period 200 B.C.–A.D. 200 the term occurred surprisingly seldom; it was used for the high priest (Qumran), an eschatological prophet, and the historical prophets (again Qumran), and for the future king of the house of David. The expectation of a future son of David seems to have been the prevailing and most widely accepted one, yet his status as "anointed" was seldom mentioned. Consequently, the study of the background of the title *christos* in early Christianity[16] cannot restrict itself to the occurrence of the term but will have to analyze various combinations of traditional concepts derived from, or at least connected with, different texts of scripture. These groups of concepts were used in and adapted to specific contexts and served to address specific situations in which believers found themselves.

There is yet another important point. People who use traditional language, and go back to various texts in the scriptures, tend to be inclusive rather than exclusive. Early Christological thinking was inclusive and complementary. All concepts and ideas served to express certain convictions about Jesus, highlighting various aspects of his teaching, his actions, his death and resurrection, and the salvation brought about by him. In speaking about Jesus there was little room for either/or. There was so much to be expressed, because so much had been discovered, that one could say, "He is also this or thus." Or, "Also this passage from scripture refers to him," and so on. The development of Christian faith and practice led perpetually to new terminology and to new interpretations of Jesus' person and work, of the circumstances in which one lived, and of scripture. As we can see in the writings of the New Testament, a great number of approaches to Jesus were tried out and found expression in "forms," traditional expressions and complexes adapted to the new circumstances. Concepts and ideas current in the environment were applied to this particular man, and to the hopes and expectations he had aroused. Entirely unexpected new clusters of expressions grew around him. Some had a future and were taken over by many believers; others proved inadequate and were abandoned. In the beginning there was no orthodoxy and heresy. There were only parallel attempts to come to grips with the rich reality of salvation through Jesus Christ. It is therefore wrong to attach to certain Christological conceptions of this period labels current in the Christological conflicts of the following centuries.

This variety in Christological approaches was found not only in Christianity as a whole but, no doubt, also in various local and regional groups of Christians; we shall do well not to connect certain types of Christology too closely with certain types of congregations, though there were congregations that tended to prefer one approach to the other. And already in Paul's Corinthian correspondence we find that he combated Christological deviations and one-sided soteriological and ethical conclusions connected with them.

Comparative study of religious concepts and ideas in the world in which early Christianity originated, however difficult it may be, is certainly needed to get a fuller picture, in depth, of the Christological convictions of the first congregations and the ways these convictions found expression.

The Outline of This Book

The considerations laid down in the three preceding sections lead to the following outline of this book. Part I deals with the earliest material. Chapter 1 assembles the not specifically Pauline material in the letters of Paul and analyzes how Paul used it in his own argumentation. (A more coherent picture of the main points of Paul's own Christology is given in chapter 6.) Chapter 2 deals with the Gospel of Mark and the pre-Markan material contained therein. In this case a clear distinction between tradition and redaction is much more difficult than in Paul. Therefore Mark's own Christology will be analyzed too. In chapter 3 the same treatment is given to Q, the common source of Matthew and Luke, and the traditional material that was transmitted in it.

After a short survey of the ancient material common to Mark, Q, and Paul, part II, "Continued Response to Jesus," analyzes the views on Jesus Christ found in other early Christian writings incorporated in the New Testament. It pays special attention to continuation and development. Did statements, patterns, and concepts belonging to the earliest stages of Christological thinking continue to be used? Were they developed or combined with other concepts? Did new responses to Jesus in different situations give rise to different approaches? Here we find chapters on the Gospel of Matthew (with an appendix on the letter of James), on Luke-Acts, on Paul, on the Pauline school, and on Hebrews, 1 Peter (with an appendix on Jude and 2 Peter), and Revelation, and, finally, on the Gospel and the letters of John.

Part III deals with the conceptions and ways of thinking applied by Christians in their response to Jesus. In view of the very great variety in this response it concentrates on the earliest stages of Christology. It discusses material relevant to a better understanding of the concept of Jesus as the herald of a New Age (chapter 10); of the interpretations of Jesus' death, resurrection, and exaltation (chapter 11); and, finally, of the relation between Jesus Christ and God before Jesus' mission on earth (chapter 12). Some remarks on the so-called Christological titles (especially Messiah, Son of God, Son of man, and Lord) and on the early interpretation of Ps. 110:1 are added.

The last part of the book returns to "the One with whom it all began" and his own interpretation of his task and destiny. Particular attention is paid to his preaching of the kingdom of God and the conflict with the Jewish authorities and the Romans, leading up to his death. Did Jesus ever apply to himself any of the Christological titles that are so important to his followers?

Finally, an epilogue looks back briefly on the very rich and complex Christology found already at the earliest stages and considers the call to a continued response to Jesus.

PART I
The Earliest Material

1
Early Christology in the Letters of Paul

Paul writes with authority, as an apostle of Jesus Christ. He is convinced that he has been called to preach the gospel among the Gentiles, the non-Jews (Gal. 1:16). He finds himself faced with the task of spelling out the meaning of the gospel for non-Jews, both in theoretical and in practical terms. This has immediate consequences for the relationship between Jews and non-Jews in the Christian communities (see, e.g., Gal. 2:11–14). Paul's task affects also the Jewish-Christian understanding of the gospel (Gal. 2:15–21).

Paul's letters are directed to concrete situations in early Christian groups and try to clarify important issues. They represent Paul's point of view developed in response to various questions, objections, and misunderstandings. Yet Paul does not bring a new message, but tries to show the implications of the gospel that he shares with his readers. To convince them he refers to the essentials of the faith they have in common with him.

To these essential elements belong various statements about Jesus. This chapter has two goals. One is to detect some of the traditional statements that Paul quotes or alludes to; the other is to see how they were used, by Paul in his letters and in other typical settings in the life of the early church. We begin in each case by analyzing Paul's argument. The examples are taken from 1 Thessalonians, Galatians, and 1 Corinthians. The fourth section discusses one further case, Rom. 1:3–4, and a short final section formulates some concluding observations.

References to Early Christological Statements in 1 Thessalonians

The first epistle to the Thessalonians is one of the earliest, if not the earliest, of Paul's letters. It was written around A.D. 50 on Paul's journey through Greece. He wrote it in Corinth, not very long after his activity in Thessalonica (see 1 Thess. 2:17–3:13 and Acts

17:1–18:11). In this letter Paul addresses a young congregation of non-Jewish descent which is very dear to him.

In 1 Thess. 1:4–2:16 Paul looks back on his first contacts with this group of believers. Everywhere in Macedonia and Achaia people tell about the Thessalonians' "faith in God" (1:8). Paul writes: "All these people speak about you, how you received us when we visited you" (1:9a, TEV), and then proceeds to elaborate on the effects of his initial mission before returning to the fact of the visit in 2:1, "Our brothers, you yourselves know that our visit to you was not a failure" (TEV). Verses 9b–10 (below, RSV alt.) form a clearly significant excursus reminding the reader of the essentials of "faith in God":

1 You turned away from idols to God,
2   to serve a living and true God,
3 and to wait for his Son to come from heaven,
4   whom he raised from the dead,
5   Jesus who rescues us
6   from God's anger that is coming.

Faith in God consists in serving the one God of Israel, whom the Old Testament and Jewish literature call the "living" and the "true" God over against dead "idols"—false gods (and their images). Paul, and indeed all Christians, profess the God of Israel. Jewish-Christian preaching to the Gentiles starts with this essential point, but immediately Jesus as God's Son is mentioned also. The emphasis is on his *parousia,* his (future) coming from heaven, at the last judgment ("God's anger that is coming"; RSV alt.). To wait for him implies trust in his ability to rescue us, now and forever, from being condemned and punished at that judgment. This trust is based on the conviction that God raised Jesus from the dead (a formulaic expression found elsewhere; see below on 4:14). Paul formulates very succinctly, clearly reminding his readers of these essentials in a form already familiar to them. The statement is arranged in strophes, rhythmic, connected lines: clauses 1–2–3 (past-present-future) are followed by 4–5–6 (again, past-present-future) in such a way that 4–5–6 provide the grounds for clause 3. Precise analysis shows that the vocabulary is not specifically Pauline; and we find similar formulations of preaching to Gentiles, also outside Paul's letters, in Acts 14:15–17; 17:24–31; and Heb. 6:1–2.[1]

Next we turn to 1 Thess. 2:14–16, where Paul refers to the sufferings his readers had to endure from their own fellow countrymen. In this they are "imitators of the churches of God in Christ Jesus which are in Judea"; those were persecuted by their fellow Jews (2:14). Paul then continues by accusing the Jews of obstruction all along: ". . . who killed both the Lord Jesus and the prophets, and drove us out, and displease God and oppose all men by hindering us from speaking to the Gentiles that they may be saved—so as always to fill up the measure of their sins. But God's wrath has come upon them for ever" (2:15–16, RSV margin). Paul criticizes the Jews for their persecution, and particularly for their efforts to prevent him and his companions from preaching to the Gentiles (Acts 17:5–9, 13). In this they go against the will of God, who expressly commanded Paul to preach the gospel to the Gentiles "that they may be saved." From this it is clear that they are "opposed to everyone"; here Paul repeats a common ancient characterization of the Jews.[2] At the same time he links the persecution of the apostles with the killing of Jesus and the prophets. Jesus is mentioned first, and to emphasize the seriousness of the transgression of the Jews he is called "the Lord." Then God's messengers before *and* after Jesus are mentioned. All along it has been the same story. An identical view of the opposition of the Jews to the prophets, culminating in the killing of Jesus, is found in Mark 12:1–9 (and par.) and Acts 7:52. The persecution of Christians in general, or of messengers of Jesus Christ in particular, is connected with Israel's hostility toward the prophets in Matt. 5:11f. (par. Luke 6:22f.); Matt. 23:29–36 (par. Luke 11:47–51); and Matt. 23:37–39 (par. Luke 13:34–45)—all passages that go back to Q, the common source of Matthew and Luke. Parallel to 1 Thess. 2:16[3] we find references to God's judgment in Mark 12:9; Matt. 23:33; Matt. 23:34–36 (par. Luke 11:49–51); and Matt. 23:38 (par. Luke 13:35).

Thus we discover that Jesus' death is attributed to the hostility of the Jews, not only in 1 Thess. 2:14 but also in other strands of the Christian tradition, including a number of words attributed to Jesus which are directed against the Jews. The passages under discussion fit into a long series of passages in the Old Testament and ancient Jewish literature that speak of Israel's negative response to the prophets who attempt to bring it back to a life of obedience to God. A particularly vivid example is Ezra's critical survey of Israel's history in Neh. 9:6–38, especially verse 26 (which speaks about the time after the settling in Canaan): "Nevertheless they were disobedient and rebelled against thee and cast thy law behind their back and killed thy prophets, who had warned them in order to turn them back to thee."[4]

We should note that this interpretation of Jesus' death views him as one sent by God as his final envoy in a long succession of prophets at a crucial moment in Israel's history. This Christology is anything but a theoretical construction. It arose out of the very concrete experience of followers of Jesus who were persecuted by their fellow Jews and gave meaning to their fate by connecting it with that of their master.

From 1 Thess. 4:13–18 it is clear that the new Christians in Thessalonica eagerly expected the return of Jesus Christ and the final judgment. After 1:10 and 2:16 (cf. 3:11–13) this does not come as a surprise. A number of Christians have died before Jesus' return, and there is uncertainty about their fate. Paul reassures his Thessalonian brothers and sisters. Those who have died "in Christ" (that is: believing in Christ, in communion with him) will rise to life before they are joined by the believers who are alive at that supreme moment (Paul among them!) in order to meet the Lord and to be always with the Lord (= Jesus Christ).

In his explanation Paul makes use of a creedal formula in 1 Thess. 4:14: "Since we believe that Jesus died and rose again," and of a "word of the Lord" (4:15). In the case of the latter it is not quite clear what this word may have contained; Paul obviously paraphrases rather than quotes.[5] The most likely explanation appears to be that he had a word in mind like that found in Matt. 24:30f. (par. Mark 13:26f.). We may note that also in 1 Corinthians Paul mentions "words of the Lord" he expects to be accepted as authoritative (hence the use of the term "the Lord" for Jesus); see 7:10, 12, 25; 9:14; 11:23; and 14:37 (cf. Acts 20:35). He obviously has recourse to a collection of words of Jesus intended and accepted as directions for life in the Christian communities.

The formula "Jesus died and rose again" is one of relatively many found, with some variations, in Paul's letters and elsewhere. It is a "double formula," in contrast to single formulas speaking only about the resurrection or only about Jesus' death. We have already come across a resurrection formula in 1 Thess. 1:10; a formula about Jesus' death is found in 5:9–10, in a context resembling that of 1:10 and 4:13–18: "God did not choose us to suffer his anger, but to possess salvation through our Lord Jesus Christ, who died for us in order that we might live together with him, whether we are alive or dead when he comes" (RSV alt.). Clearly Jesus' death "for us" and his resurrection are of utmost importance for the expected salvation, which already determines the Christian life in faith, hope, and love (5:8). We shall do well to take a somewhat closer look at the two single formulas as well as at the formulas speaking about Jesus' death and resurrection together.[6]

In 1 Thess. 5:9–10 Paul has come to the conclusion of his argumentation and exhortations, and for that reason he prefers the solemn "our Lord Jesus Christ" before mentioning his death "for us" explicitly and his resurrection implicitly. In other passages the title

"Christ" is used. "Christ died for . . ." is found in many different contexts as a basic statement with consequences for the faith and the communal life of Christians. We may mention here Rom. 14:15 (also 1 Cor. 8:11, where a different Greek preposition is used[7]) and 2 Cor. 5:14–15. To Paul's question in 1 Cor. 1:13 "Was Paul crucified for you?" the answer should be: "No, Christ was."[8] Similarly, Paul's conclusion in Gal. 2:21, "if justification were through the law, then Christ died to no purpose," presupposes the formula under discussion, just as in Gal. 3:13, where Paul, for the sake of his very special Pauline argumentation (see p. 113), varies it to "Christ . . . , having become a curse for us."

We find a related formula, "Christ suffered for you," in 1 Peter 2:21, and "For Christ also suffered for sins once for all, the righteous for the unrighteous," in 1 Peter 3:18 (RSV margin). In both cases the formula is related to a larger traditional complex: in 1 Peter 2:22–25 a hymn about Christ modeled upon Isa. 53 follows, and in 1 Peter 3:18–22 the formula is part of a larger Christological section that may go back to another Christological hymn. Two things may be noted in connection with the formulas in 1 Peter. First, "suffered" clearly includes death (as, e.g., in Luke 24:26, 46; Acts 3:18; 17:3, cf. 26:23[9]). Second, the expression "suffered for sins" in 1 Peter 3:18 (a different Greek preposition is used[10]) resembles "Christ died for our sins in accordance with the scriptures" in 1 Cor. 15:3, an expression that forms part of a double formula. We may also point to another traditional formula used in Gal. 1:4 and elsewhere, to be discussed below.

The single formulas speaking about Jesus' resurrection introduce God, explicitly or implicitly, as the one who has raised Jesus; there is no connection with a particular title. We have already mentioned 1 Thess. 1:10, and may add Gal. 1:1: ". . . Jesus Christ and God the Father, who raised him from the dead." Next, there are Rom. 8:11 (twice); 10:9; 1 Cor. 6:14; 15:15; 2 Cor. 4:14; compare the deutero-Pauline Eph. 1:20 and, outside the letters of Paul, 1 Peter 1:21. Romans 4:24 speaks about "us who believe in him that raised from the dead Jesus our Lord," after emphasizing that the Christians share the faith of Abraham who believed in the God "who gives life to the dead and calls into existence the things that do not exist" (Rom. 4:16–17; cf. 2 Cor. 1:9 and Heb. 11:19). In these passages Paul expresses the belief of the (Pharisaic) Jews in the living God, "who quickenest the dead," as it is formulated in the second of the so-called Eighteen Benedictions, one of the central Jewish prayers until the present day. The form of the Jewish benediction may have influenced that of the Christian formula. In any case it is interesting to note that Paul employs the formula often where he wants to emphasize that God, who raised Jesus from the dead, will also grant resurrection and life to those who are "in Christ." (See Rom. 8:11; 2 Cor. 4:14; and the elaborate exposition in 1 Cor. 15.) The same emphasis is made when he uses the double formulas, to which we now turn.

In most of the double formulas we find "Christ" and "died" in the first clause, and a passive form of the verb *egeirein* = to raise (used in the active mood in the single resurrection formulas) in the second clause, but neither the title nor the verb is used exclusively. In 1 Thess. 4:14 we find an exception: here "Jesus" is the subject, and a different Greek verb is used. On the other hand, the use of the formula is typical of Paul insofar as he here connects the future resurrection and eternal life of the Christians with that of Jesus who died and rose again. We may compare Rom. 14:9 ("Christ died and lived again") and, in a comparable context, Rom. 8:34 ("Christ Jesus, who died, yes, who was raised from the dead"). Second Corinthians 5:14–15 is interesting because it brings out very clearly the ethical implications of living with Christ (cf. Rom. 14), *and* because it introduces the "for them" in the double formula: "For the love of Christ controls us, because we are convinced that one has died for all; therefore all have died. And he died for all, that those who live might live no longer for themselves but for him who for their sake died and was raised." The link with the well-known, very full double formula 1 Cor. 15:3–5 (discussed on p. 25) is obvious. There we find "Christ died for our sins" and, at the same time, the strong connection between the resurrection of Christ and that of the Christians in the entire chapter.[11]

We should add that in Rom. 6:1–11 Paul speaks about dying and rising with Christ (with all its implications) in the context of baptism (compare Col. 2:12–13; 3:1–4). The instances mentioned in the previous pages show how important the various formulas speaking about Jesus' death and resurrection are for Paul's Christology *and* for his thinking about the salvation of the Christians as people closely connected with Christ. Scholars rightly speak here of Paul's "corporate thinking," of which we shall find more examples below, particularly in liturgical texts. We shall then have occasion to ask whether this type of Christological thinking, which figured so prominently in Paul, does not go back to earlier expressions arising from ritual experiences.

Another characteristic point is that Paul's corporate thinking can be linked very easily with the notion that "Christ died for us (you, etc.)," which also presupposes a direct solidarity between individual and group, between Jesus Christ and those who believe in him. We shall meet with this important expression also in other contexts in the following sections; later, in chapter 11, we shall examine its background and attempt to determine its meaning more precisely.

References to Early Christological Statements in Galatians

In Galatians the distinctive features of Paul's theology come out very clearly. The apostle defends himself and his mission to the Gentiles against Judaizing Christians who have tried to introduce what Paul calls a different gospel, even a perverted gospel of Christ (Gal. 1:6f.) in the Galatian communities. There is no other gospel than the one Paul has preached to them (1:8–9). Paul was called by God himself to preach the gospel to the Gentiles (1:16) and did so in relative independence of the leaders in Jerusalem (1:16–22), who, however, recognized his calling at a later time (2:1–10). Paul says they saw "that I had been entrusted with the gospel to the uncircumcised, just as Peter had been entrusted with the gospel to the circumcised" (2:7).

Somewhat later, during a visit of Peter to Antioch, a mixed congregation of Jews and Gentiles (Acts 11:19–26), Paul and Peter (Cephas), followed by other Jewish Christians, had a conflict about the practical consequences of living together as Jews and Gentiles in one community. After the arrival of people from Jerusalem, Peter and other Jews who had common meals—no doubt including the Lord's Supper—with Gentile Christians, felt obliged to withdraw. In this way the unity of Christ was violated. Paul, who recounts this incident in Gal. 2:11–14, takes this as a typical instance necessitating a thorough exposition of the implications of preaching the gospel to the Gentiles and admitting these Gentiles into the one community of Christ, on the basis of their faith and their baptism into Christ (see 1:15–3:11). If faith in Christ and union with Christ are the primary requirements for membership in the church, no one can maintain any longer that the right relation between human beings and God depends on the strict obedience to the rules laid down in the law of Moses, among which are the rules concerning clean and unclean food. Galatians very much presents Paul's own theology; yet there are surprisingly many references to earlier expressions of the faith shared by Paul and his opponents.

In the beginning of the letter Paul presents himself as an apostle of Christ. In other letters he calls himself "an apostle of Christ Jesus by the will of God";[12] here, he uses a more elaborate introductory formula in view of the attacks on his apostleship: "an apostle—not from men nor through man, but through Jesus Christ and God the Father, who raised him from the dead" (Gal. 1:1). We have already seen that "who raised him from the dead" is traditional. Here the expression serves to emphasize the close link between Jesus Christ and God, and to prepare for the statements of Paul's calling in 1:12, 16. In the salutation that follows, Paul again connects God and Jesus Christ: "Grace to you and peace from God the Father and our Lord Jesus Christ" (1:3); he continues with a Christological statement: "who gave himself for our sins to deliver us from the present evil age," stressing again that this was "according to the will of our God and Father" (1:4).

The expression "who gave himself for our sins" can be shown to be traditional.[13] As so often, we find variations: "for our sins" alternates with "for us" (compare the single formulas about Jesus' death discussed above). In Gal. 2:20 Paul speaks of the "Son of God, who loved me and gave himself for me" and uses this parallel to "Christ died for me/us" hinted at in the next verse. The same combination of "loved" and "gave himself" also occurs in Eph. 5:2, 25. Another variant is to be found in Rom. 4:24, where the verb is used in the passive mood in the context of a double formula: "Because of our trespasses he was handed over and he was raised (to life) for our justification" (RSV alt.). God is the implied subject here, as is clear from Rom. 8:32: "He who did not spare his own Son but gave him up for us all." Returning to texts where Jesus Christ is the subject, we find three instances where a different but related Greek verb is used:[14] Mark 10:45 (par. Matt. 20:28) speaks about the Son of man who came "to give his life as a ransom for[15] many"; 1 Tim. 2:6 mentions the man Christ Jesus "who gave himself as a ransom for all"; and Titus 2:14 explains: "who gave himself for us to redeem us from all iniquity"—language reminiscent of Gal. 1:4.

In all variants of this traditional expression, "for us" is found. The emphasis is on the (self-)sacrifice of Jesus Christ, delivering those who put their trust in him from the sins that separated them from God, thus granting them salvation now and forever.

In his vehement attack on his opponents in Galatians, Paul insists that there is only one "gospel of Christ"—the one he has preached and still preaches (1:6, 7; 2:5, 7, 14). In 1 Cor. 15:1–11 he makes clear that this gospel, received by him from others and preached by him to the Corinthians, is concerned with Christ who died for us, who was raised, and who appeared to others. In the often used expression "gospel of Christ" (see, e.g., Rom. 15:19; 1 Cor. 9:12; 2 Cor. 2:12; 9:13; 10:14; 1 Thess. 3:2), "Christ" denotes the basic Christian belief expressed in the single and double formulas in which this title occurs. (We shall have to return to this when we discuss the beginning of the Gospel of Mark in the next chapter.) The same applies to those cases where "Christ" is the object of "to preach" (for instance in 1 Cor.

15:12–16) and "to believe" or "faith" (see 1 Cor. 15:17). We cannot go into detail here, but should note Gal. 1:11, 16, 23 ("preaching the faith"); 4:13; and, in particular, the expressions "faith in Christ (Jesus)" / "believe in Christ Jesus" which are central to Paul's argument in 2:16 (cf. v. 20) and also in 3:22.

The context of the expressions in which "Christ (Jesus)" occurs is typically Pauline, but, as W. Kramer has argued,[16] there are good reasons to assume that they were used before Paul used them.

In the central passage Gal. 2:15–21, where Paul gives a very condensed exposition of his views on justification by faith, rejecting justification by works of the law, Paul does not use only faith-language; he combines it with the corporate notions that were briefly mentioned above. Verse 16 centers around faith in Christ, but verses 19 and 20a use corporate language ("I have been crucified with Christ"—5:24; 6:14; and Rom. 6:1–11) before returning to faith-language, "I live by faith in the Son of God . . . ," in verse 20b. In chapter 3 "believing" and "faith" are the central expressions, but at the end of this chapter Paul again uses corporate language in verse 26: "in Christ Jesus you are all sons of God, through faith." This is so because they were "baptized into Christ"—an expression that is used in Rom. 6:3f. in the context of dying and rising with Christ (cf. Col. 2:12f.; 3:1–4) and that, elsewhere, underlines the unity of the believers "in Christ." This is clear in Paul's argument in 1 Cor. 1:11–17, where the divided and quarrelsome Corinthians are urged to remember that they have been baptized into the name of Christ who was crucified for them. Christ is not divided; people do not belong to Paul, Apollos, or Cephas, they all belong to Christ: they are "of Christ." In Gal. 3:26–28 Paul draws the same conclusion: "you are all one in Christ Jesus" . . . "you are Christ's." The word "one" has a masculine form. Elsewhere Paul uses the metaphor of the body, e.g., in Rom. 12:5, "we, though many, are one body in Christ," and in 1 Cor. 12:4–31, with a reference to baptism in verses 12–13: "For just as the body is one and has many members, and all the members of the body, though many, are one body, so it is with Christ. For by one Spirit we were all baptized into one body—Jews and Greeks, slaves or free—and were made to drink of one Spirit."[17]

"In Christ" all believers are "one body." This leads to the consequence that all distinctions between human beings have disappeared. In Gal. 3:28 this rule is applied to Jew and Greek—very important in the context of Paul's argument in this letter; compare also 6:15— slave and free, and even male and female. In 1 Cor. 12:13, just quoted, only the first two pairs are mentioned; in Col. 3:11, another variant of the same rule, we find: "Here there cannot be Greek and Jew, circumcised and uncircumcised, barbarian, Scythian, slave, free man, but Christ is all, and in all."

The elaborations of the theme of the "corporate Christ" are probably Paul's, and the variations between Gal. 3:28; 1 Cor. 12:13; and Col. 3:11 may also come from Paul and his followers. But we must seriously consider the possibility that already before Paul baptism into Christ, i.e., the Christ who died and was raised from the dead, was celebrated as a rite of complete personal renewal and admission to a new "body" governed by Christ. And in this ritual the newly baptized may have been addressed as new beings who "have put on Christ"; belonging to Israel or to the Gentiles, or being a slave or a free man or woman no longer counts; even the distinctions between male and female have lost their significance. If we read Gal. 3:27–28 against the background of the baptismal ritual (as we can reconstruct it from various sources), we are able to understand that the "performative language" inherent in the ritual has constituted a new reality of life as children of God in communion with Christ. Paul forcefully reminds his readers of this new reality in his controversy with his Judaizing opponents.[18]

In Gal. 3:29 Paul draws the conclusions from verses 26–28 for his demonstration in the earlier part of the chapter (vs. 3–14 and 15–25); the transition is via the clause "if you are Christ's [and you are indeed], then . . . ." "To be Christ's" is a clearly traditional phrase that is also used elsewhere to characterize the followers of Jesus. We may mention here also Gal. 5:24; 1 Cor. 1:12; 3:23; 15:23; 2 Cor. 10:7; *and* Mark 9:41.[19]

In Gal. 4:1–11 Paul continues his exposition, in the course of which he argues that in the time before Jesus Christ people were only children, minors, kept in custody under the law as far as they were Jews (3:23–25), and, in fact, all enslaved under "the elemental spirits of the universe."[20] When Jesus Christ came, however, they could really and fully live as children of God. Paul says: "When the time had fully come, God sent forth his Son, born of woman, born under the law, to redeem those who were under the law, so that we might receive adoption as sons. And because you are sons, God has sent the Spirit of his Son into our hearts, crying 'Abba! Father!' " (4:4–6).[21] Because of this divine initiative the believers are no longer minors, enslaved, but truly sons and heirs (4:7). The emphasis is clearly on "the redemption from the law" (cf. 3:19–25), essential for Jewish Christians; at the same time, it is on the "adoption as sons," which is essential for Jewish as well as Gentile Christians (the latter having been subjected to other, cosmic powers). Their status as sons is clear from the possession of the Spirit, which is the Spirit of the Son, likewise sent by the Father. This Spirit enables them to pray "Abba," the ancient Aramaic term for "Father," no doubt used in the early Christian congregations. Because of the link with 3:28, we may conjecture that newly baptized persons shouted out "Abba" in virtue of their being adopted as "children of God." There is a clear parallel here with Rom. 8:15–17, which speaks of the spirit of sonship (literally: adoption) enabling people to cry: "Abba! Father!"[22]

To effect this redemption and this full life as sons of God, it was necessary that God sent his Son "when the time had fully come." The expression used belongs to the Jewish eschatological language used in early Christianity. So the first word spoken by Jesus in the Gospel of Mark is: "The time is fulfilled, and the kingdom of God is at hand" (1:15). A striking parallel is found in Mark 12:1–9, where the owner of the vineyard, after sending several messengers, sent his son and heir. "He had still one other, a beloved son; *finally* he sent him to them . . ." (v. 6). The owner of the vineyard in this parable clearly stands for God, and the son for Jesus Christ as God's Son. The basic pattern of sending is the same as in Gal. 4:4, but here God's sending of the Son is part of a whole series of commissions of messengers to a disobedient Israel (see the first section, above). The expression "God sent his Son in order that" is used by Paul also in Rom. 8:3f., in the course of another complicated argument concerning the validity of the law, again to make clear how Christ made people free from the burden of the law, and also in connection with the granting of a new possibility of life in the Spirit. In John 3:16f. we find "God . . . gave his only Son, that" and "God sent the Son into the world, . . . that" embedded in the context of a typical Johannine view on God, Jesus, and the world, in which the concept of sending plays an important role (see chapter 9). A parallel to John 3:16f. is found in 1 John 4:9.

"God sent his Son in order that . . ." seems to have been a useful pattern of thought in early Christianity. It was used to express the special authority of Jesus as the result of his unique commission by God. At the turn of the times, he brought about a fundamental change for those who entrusted their life to him. Paul and John use their own terminology to describe the new life Christians have received; the parable in Mark describes the negative reaction of Israel. The way Paul and John use the pattern implies that for them the Son was already with the Father before being sent. However, the pattern itself does not emphasize preexistence, and there is no evidence that those who used it had begun to work out a doctrine of preexistence, as the later church would have to do.[23] In Mark 12:1–9 the sending of the son/heir is unique and final; it is clear that the parable emphasizes the eschatological character of Jesus' mission and his personal relationship with his Father. However, this does not necessarily imply preexistence.

References to Early Christological Statements in 1 Corinthians

Paul's first letter to the Corinthians was written around A.D. 55 in Ephesus, to a congregation founded by him a few years before, when, according to Acts 18:1–18, he worked in Corinth for a year and a half. Corinth was a relatively new city, refounded as a Roman colony about a century earlier, in the days of Julius Caesar. It was a center of trade, with two harbors, and a center of administration as the seat of the Roman proconsul of the province of Achaia.

Paul wrote the letter after the arrival in Ephesus of a delegation from the Corinthian church (1 Cor. 16:15–18) with a letter to which he replies in chapters 7–15 (see, e.g., 7:1; 8:1; 12:1). At the same time he addresses a number of other situations in Corinth, reported to him by the official delegates and by others such as "Chloe's people" mentioned in 1:11. It is evident that there are factions in the church of Corinth, and different opinions as to the consequences for faith and conduct of living in such a modern Hellenistic city. Paul takes great care in giving responsible answers to the questions put to him, and reacts forcefully to abuses brought to his notice. This letter is only one in a series (1 Cor. 5:9; 2 Cor. 2:2–4; 2 Cor. 1:1). Paul's relations with the Corinthians were already strained before his writing 1 Corinthians, and clearly became even more so afterward. The result is a lively letter that allows us many glimpses into the concrete circumstances in which the (mainly non-Jewish) Christians lived.[24] Paul's instructions and advice are, again, those of a man of great faith and insight, who speaks with authority. But in this letter, too, he is at pains to convince and persuade his readers, referring continually to what they already know and believe.

Here I shall pass over Paul's references to "Christ who died for us" and to "baptism into Christ" in his first section criticizing the divisions and quarrels in Corinth (1 Cor. 1:10–17), because we have already mentioned them in the preceding pages. There we have also discussed Paul's insistence on unity in Christ in 1 Cor. 12, and his use of the death-and-resurrection formula in 1 Cor. 15.

Two passages dealing with the Lord's Supper are important. The first, already briefly mentioned in note 17 to this chapter, is 1 Cor. 10:14–22, which sharply condemns the worship of idols. Christians have to choose between the Lord (= Jesus) and demons. Christians participate in the blood of Christ and in the body of Christ; therefore they form "one body in Christ." This participation/partnership excludes partnership with demons. Christians may have their doubts as to whether idols really exist (see 1 Cor. 8:4–6, to be discussed presently), yet it is very clear that pagan sacrifices are offered to demons and not to God.

The necessity of unity in Christ within the congregation is argued differently in 1 Cor. 11:17–34. The Corinthians should realize that they eat the Lord's Supper (11:20).[25] It was the Lord Jesus who—according to the tradition received by Paul from the Lord—broke the bread and distributed the cup on the night he was betrayed. He said to his disciples, "This is my body which is for you," and "This cup is the new covenant in my blood." He also commanded them to repeat his actions and his words in remembrance of him; in doing so they proclaim "the Lord's death until he comes" (11:23–26).

A few things are worth noting: (a) In order to remind his readers of the essentials of the Lord's Supper, Paul quotes a tradition that he believes goes back to the Lord himself. (b) He in fact refers to an account of the last supper of Jesus with his disciples that we find in a slightly different form in the passion story in the Synoptic Gospels (Mark 14:22–25 and Matt. 26:26–28; Luke's version in 22:19–20 is closest to Paul's). Clearly, this account early received a more or less standardized form, because it was the point of reference for the cultic commemoration. (c) Paul speaks about Jesus as *the Lord,* and stresses that the commemoration concerns the Lord's death (1 Cor. 11:26). The formula "for you" reappears (v. 24), Jesus' death is said to constitute a new covenant (v. 25, combining ideas from Jer. 31:31 and Ex. 24:8). (d) Finally, the emphasis on the (second) coming of the Lord is to be noted (v. 26, end; cf. Mark 14:25; Matt. 26:29; Luke 22:18).

Paul cites these traditional words to urge his readers to mend their ways and to restore the unity of the congregation in all aspects of community life, not only when eating their common meals. It is important to note that he refers to a tradition concerning a central ritual that constitutes communion with the Lord and with one another. This rite centers around the commemoration of Jesus' death "for us." Of course the Lord is regarded as living, and the believers look forward to his return, but the bread that is broken and the cup that is shared symbolize his death for others, seen as a sacrifice inaugurating a new covenant (just as the blood of oxen inaugurated the [now old] covenant at Sinai, Ex. 24:1–8).

At the celebration of the Lord's Supper the participants are reminded of the central content of the initiatory rite of baptism. "Both rituals keep in the minds of the believers the fundamental story of the Lord's death."[26]

In the texts about the Lord's Supper just mentioned, Jesus is called "the Lord." The meaning of this title and its connotations will occupy us later (see chapter 11). Here, we need to add that 1 Corinthians contains a few more examples of this term in ancient formulas.

In 1 Cor. 12–14 Paul discusses the many "spiritual gifts" granted
to the church, and he evidently tries to counteract overvaluation of
some of them. There is only one Spirit, one Lord, one God, and all
manifestations of the Spirit must be for the common good (12:4–7).
Wherever the Spirit operates, people will confess: Jesus is Lord. This
confession unites the Christians and separates them from the Gentiles who worship idols—a group to which many of the Corinthians
once belonged (12:2–3).[27] "Jesus is Lord" was undoubtedly repeated
many times at different occasions when Christians assembled. Those
who confess accept Jesus' authority and proclaim themselves as his
servants.[28] Not only do they accept his leadership, they also expect
his help. In Rom. 10:9 Paul combines "if you confess with your lips
that Jesus is Lord" with "and believe in your heart that God raised
him from the dead." He assures his readers that this confession and
this faith will save them. There is no distinction between Jew and
Greek; "the same Lord is Lord of all and bestows his riches upon
all who call upon him" (vs. 9–12). This is proved by quoting Joel 2:32
in verse 13, "for every one who calls upon the name of the LORD will
be saved"—a scriptural text also used or hinted at elsewhere in the
writings of the New Testament, e.g., in Acts 2:21; 9:14, 21; and in
1 Cor. 1:2, where the Corinthians are joined with "all those who in
every place call on the name of our Lord Jesus Christ." Romans 10:9,
as well as Acts 22:16, suggests a particular connection between confessing Jesus as Lord and baptism. So also 1 Cor. 6:11 may remind
the Corinthians of their baptism with the words: "But you were
washed, you were sanctified, you were justified in the name of the
Lord Jesus Christ and in the Spirit of our God" (cf. Acts 8:16; 19:5).[29]
But "in the name of the Lord Jesus" is certainly not confined to
baptism only. In 1 Cor. 5:4 the congregation meets "in the name of
the Lord Jesus" to make important decisions, and in Col. 3:16–17
an admonition to let the word of Christ dwell richly in the congregation, in teaching and singing, is concluded with the words "do everything in the name of the Lord Jesus, giving thanks to God the Father
through him."

This leads us to the famous hymn inserted by Paul in his exhortations to the Philippians in Phil. 2:6–11. The hymn is quoted here
because of its first half, which speaks about the humility of Christ
Jesus, but continues to speak about his exaltation (vs. 9–11).

> Therefore God has highly exalted him
>   and bestowed on him the name
>   which is above every name,
>   that at the name of Jesus
>   every knee should bow,
>   in heaven and on earth and under the earth,

and every tongue confess that
Jesus Christ is Lord,
to the glory of God the Father.

We can imagine how this hymn was sung in a congregation of Christians; perhaps they bent their own knees, together with all earthly and heavenly beings, stretching their hands to heaven and confessing Jesus as their Lord,[30] the Lord of the church as well as the Lord of creation. There is a clear reference here to Isa. 45:23; without any hesitation early Christians used texts speaking about YHWH the God of Israel to refer to Jesus Christ (Joel 2:32, quoted above, is another example). Yet, as the final clause shows, they did not regard this as an infringement of God's supreme sovereignty. The formula quoted by Paul in 1 Cor. 8:6 is especially significant:

Yet for us there is one God, the Father,
from whom are all things and for whom we exist,
and one Lord, Jesus Christ,
through whom are all things and through whom we exist.

In the context of this formula Paul discusses the problem of eating food offered to idols, a burning question in Corinth, answered differently by different members of the congregation. We cannot go into detail here;[31] it is sufficient to bear in mind that poor people ate meat seldom, perhaps only at special public festivals. The more affluent, however, not only could afford to eat it regularly at home, but also received invitations for dinners at pagan homes or even in temples. These dinners were social rather than religious occasions. Paul's attitude is at the same time ambivalent and consistent. In 1 Cor. 8 and 10 he posits: Eating or not eating in themselves do not bring us nearer to God (8:8); one may eat freely what is sold at the meat market (10:25–26); one may accept an invitation for dinner unless it is expressly designated as a cultic occasion (10:27–28). But, above all, one should give up one's own freedom in behalf of a "weak" fellow Christian for whom eating such meat is still closely associated with pagan worship (8:7–13; 10:24, 28–33).

In 1 Cor. 8:4 (as in 10:19) Paul states firmly: an idol has no real existence, there is only one God. As in 1 Thess. 1:9–10 (quoted early in this chapter), this statement is in agreement with the standard preaching of Jews to non-Jews (see the *Shema' Yisrael* in Deut. 6:4; and Isa. 44:8; 45:5, etc.),[32] and followed by Jewish Christians in their approach to interested Gentiles (cf. Gal. 3:20; Rom. 3:30; James 2:19; 4:12). Yet, Paul continues, there are many so-called gods in heaven and on earth; we cannot deny that there are many gods and many lords for people who take them seriously and worship them. In this context he quotes what is clearly a formula with which his readers should be familiar. "For us there is one God . . . and one Lord" (1 Cor. 8:6). God is called the Father (of Jesus, the Son, and of the believers as children of God), and he is the Creator. There is one Lord, Jesus Christ, the agent of creation *and* the agent of redemption. We should note that in Rom. 11:36 (cf. Col. 1:15–18; John 1:3; and Acts 17:28 [after v. 24]; Heb. 2:10) Paul exalts God with the words "from him and through him and to him are all things," and that his terminology is certainly influenced by pantheistic formulas current in Stoic circles.[33] Jesus Christ, the Lord, is mentioned directly beside God, the creator. He is the agent, the mediator of creation, not the creator himself, and at the same time he is the agent of redemption. His activity at the creation implies preexistence, but this aspect is not prominent; Paul's emphasis is on the functional identity of the one God and the one Lord vis-à-vis those who profess their loyalty toward them (cf. 1 Cor. 12:4–6; Eph. 4:5–6; 1 Tim. 2:5–6).

Finally, we note 1 Cor. 16:22, part of Paul's personal greetings at the end of this difficult letter: "If any one has no love for the Lord, let him be accursed. Maranatha!" (RSV margin). The criterion for belonging to the Lord does not consist in agreeing with Paul's or anyone else's opinion about matters of faith or conduct, but in loving Jesus the Lord (cf. 1 Cor. 12:3, discussed above). Whoever does not really love the Lord has no place in the community and no share in the salvation accomplished by the Lord, now and in the future. Paul's "anathema" is underscored by "Maranatha"—an Aramaic expression that may be translated "Our Lord has come," but most likely means "Our Lord, come!" (cf. Rev. 22:20). The expression is also found at the end of a thanksgiving prayer prescribed for the communal meal in chapter 10 of the *Didache.* Here the congregation prays for the coming of the Lord that he may bring together the church and bring it together into his kingdom. Then those who are holy may come, and those who are not must repent! Paul probably took the traditional archaic term from the liturgy of the Lord's Supper as he knew it, in order to make clear that the (second) coming of the Lord would reveal who really belonged to him and who did not (cf. 1 Cor. 1:7–8; 4:5; 5:5). After all, the meal was celebrated in order to proclaim the Lord's death "until he comes."[34] The use of the title "the Lord" in connection with the *parousia* in Paul's letters is probably influenced by this *maranatha.*[35]

One Further Case: Romans 1:3–4

This chapter does not pretend to be exhaustive; but one passage from the letter to the Romans still deserves closer scrutiny. Because

Romans was written by Paul in preparation for a planned visit to a congregation hè had not founded himself, it is especially useful as a source for traditions widely shared in early Christianity.

In Rom. 1:1–7 he introduces himself, very carefully, as an apostle: he is "a servant of Jesus Christ," "an apostle, set apart for the gospel of God" (cf. Gal. 1:15–16). This gospel is presented as "promised beforehand through his prophets in the holy scriptures" (cf. "in accordance with the scriptures" in 1 Cor. 15:3–4). It is "the gospel concerning his Son"—an expression which, together with the full formula "Jesus Christ our Lord" at the end of verse 4, seems to form Paul's frame for the double formula in between:

> who was descended from David according to the flesh
> and designated Son of God in power according to the Spirit
> of holiness by his resurrection from the dead.

Thus Paul stresses that it was Jesus Christ who entrusted him with his apostleship to the Gentiles—to whom the Roman Christians also belong; they, too, have been called by Jesus Christ (vs. 5–7).

The double formula quoted by Paul is concerned with two stages in the life of Jesus Christ that succeed one another; the second stage is clearly the more important one. On the human level Jesus was a descendant of David, a point that was not usually stressed by Paul (see, however, Rom. 9:5), but was no doubt traditional—as the use of "son of David" in the Gospels shows (see pp. 60–61, 94). As a descendant of David, Jesus was qualified to be a royal son of God (cf. 2 Sam. 7:14; Pss. 2:7; 89:27–28). In fact, he proved to be more: he was appointed "Son of God in power," as became evident at his resurrection, according to the "Spirit of sanctification" (an expression used only here in the New Testament).

We may differ as to the exact delimitation of the ancient formula and possible Pauline additions ("in power," even "according to the flesh"—"according to the Spirit of holiness"), but the structure is clear. Compare 2 Tim. 2:8: "Remember Jesus Christ, risen from the dead, descended from David, as preached in my gospel," and Mark 12:35–37 (to be discussed in the next chapter). Jesus is introduced as a descendant of David, but the emphasis is on his designation as Son of God, at the resurrection (cf. Acts 2:22–36; 13:32–41). For Paul this was no doubt a one-sided view on Jesus' divine sonship (see Rom. 8:3, 4; Gal. 4:4–5). He therefore introduced the formula with the word "concerning his Son" and stressed (or even added) the words "in power."[36]

Some Concluding Observations

In the preceding sections we have reviewed the traditional Christological material as we saw it in Paul's letters and elsewhere within
and outside the Pauline corpus. In the next chapters we shall make
a similar review of the Christological traditions contained in Mark
and the common source behind Matthew and Luke. Only after that
can we assess the combined findings properly. It is appropriate,
however, to make some brief observations about what we have found
so far.

First, it has become clear that it is difficult if not impossible to
determine the exact wording of the ancient traditional expressions.
Not only have we found many small variations in the use made of
them by Paul and others; we have also observed that these variations
must have existed before Paul. This is what could be expected. Given
the diversity of the small Christian groups and their scattered situation around the eastern part of the Mediterranean, *and* the short
time between the founding of these congregations and Paul's letters,
there could scarcely have been more uniformity in creedal formulas,
liturgical orders, etc. Paul does all he can to keep his congregations
together and on the right track. He traveled much himself, he sent
his deputies to various places, and on various occasions he decided
to write letters. He continually reminded his fellow Christians of
what all Christians should affirm as their common heritage. But he
and his fellow Christians were clearly not so much interested in the
verbal repetition of formulas as in adherence to the essentials of the
faith by means of them.

Second, we have noted a very great diversity in the formulas
employed. Right from the beginning different terms, concepts, and
patterns of thought must have seemed appropriate to express the
essence and the importance of Jesus' saving activity in behalf of those
who believed in him as one sent by God. Yet the Christological
traditions preserved and applied by Paul concentrate mainly on the
meaning of Jesus' death and his resurrection for the present life of
the believers in expectancy of his *parousia,* which will bring the
definitive revelation and realization of God's salvation and judgment.
Jesus is sent by God and refused by Israel. He is sent as the Son, to
give life to those who thereby may become children of God. Both 1
Cor. 8:4–6 and Phil. 2:6–11 hint at the preexistence of him who is
worshiped as Lord. Romans 1:3–4 mentions that he is a descendant
of David. About his preaching and teaching, however, we hear next
to nothing; in only a few cases Paul refers to an authoritative "word
of the Lord." For Christological statements connected with and
based upon Jesus' preaching we have to look elsewhere.

Third, we have found that many of the Christological statements and formulas used by Paul have their *Sitz im Leben* in the assemblies of the early Christians. We have noted connections with the ritual of baptism and the communal meals with their commemoration of the last supper. Here in particular Jesus' death for us leading to his resurrection was remembered and symbolically communicated as a source of a new life for those who belonged to him—as a community, as well as individually. In 1 Cor. 14 Paul gives a lively picture of what could happen when Christians assembled. In prayers, short speeches, hymns, exclamations, etc., they reminded one another of Jesus Christ their Lord, in whose name they were gathered; time and again the essential statements were repeated, applied, and interpreted.

It is, perhaps, remarkable that we have found only one hymn (Phil. 2:6–11) in Paul's letters; there are indeed other hymns in the New Testament, but mainly in later writings. We have already had occasion to mention Col. 1:15–20 in connection with 1 Cor. 8:6, and may add now the following (fragments of) hymns: Eph. 5:14; 1 Tim. 3:16; Heb. 1:2–3, followed by a number of fragments of psalms; 1 Peter 2:21–25; 3:18 plus 22; Rev. 5:9–10. But it is difficult to determine their age and their original form. The authors who refer to them could not copy a fragment from a hymnbook and incorporate it in their own discourse. In 1 Cor. 14:26; Col. 3:16–17; and Eph. 5:19–20 we see that hymns were sung spontaneously, inspired by the Spirit to glorify God and Jesus Christ, and to edify, teach, and admonish the congregation. In singing them, people would have followed common patterns and stereotyped turns of phrase, including lines from scripture and Christian formulas.[37]

On the basis of Phil. 2:6–11; 1 Tim. 3:16; Heb. 1:3; and 1 Peter 3:18, 22 (cf. Eph. 1:20–22 and Rom. 8:34b), M. Hengel[38] has tried to reconstruct a basic scheme for a hymn to Christ. He also points to the description of heavenly worship in Rev. 4–5 (see especially 5:9–10, 13), which may be assumed to reflect the liturgical usage of the seer's own community. In his analysis he mentions three main points: (a) Jesus' sacrificial death as the basis for his exaltation; (b) the crowning with glory, enthronement at the right hand of God; (c) subjection of the whole creation and homage by all creatures. These hymns would have been influenced by elements in the psalms that we know otherwise to have been important for early Christian thinking (e.g., Pss. 2, 8, 110). These psalms, too, may have been sung regularly in the assemblies of the early Christians. Later on, other elements such as Christ being "the first-born of all creation" (Col. 1:15) may have been added.[39]

A final remark is in order. In the review given in this chapter the term "pre-Pauline" has been avoided. In some cases Paul himself tells his readers that he received his knowledge from others before him. In 1 Cor. 11:23–26 and 1 Cor. 15:1–11 there is clearly contained a pre-Pauline liturgical account and a pre-Pauline confessional formula. In a number of other cases we have found that traditional expressions are also used outside the Pauline letters, e.g., in Acts, Colossians, Ephesians, the Pastorals, 1 Peter, James, or Mark. This primarily points to the continuity and viability of particular traditional forms; it is difficult to prove beyond doubt that they were transmitted by different channels, independently. We can go no further than establishing that Paul refers to this traditional material because it represents the essentials of the Christian faith which he and his readers have—or ought to have—in common. What we have gathered is not peculiarly or exclusively Pauline; it was accepted and acknowledged by those who did not share (or who even opposed) Paul's very personal opinion.

2
The Gospel Material in Mark

In all likelihood Mark was the first to give an account of Jesus' activity in Galilee and Judea, which culminated in his crucifixion in Jerusalem. Mark wants not only to tell a story but also to convey a message to his readers, and in fact his story and his message are intertwined. This becomes clear in the introduction to his work (Mark 1:1–15), which will occupy us presently, and at the end, when the young man in a white robe tells the women who come to anoint Jesus' body: "Do not be amazed; you seek Jesus of Nazareth, who was crucified. He has been raised,[1] he is not here" (16:6, RSV alt.). The women are told to announce to the disciples and to Peter that the risen Jesus will reassemble his small flock in Galilee; there they will see him—and, no doubt, be sent out to preach the gospel (cf. 1 Cor. 15:3–5). Mark's own view of Jesus predominates in the story; yet he had to rely on earlier reports of events in Jesus' life and words spoken by him (see pp. 23–24). He knew traditional formulas expressing the meaning and purpose of Jesus' mission. In our analysis we shall have to pay attention to both elements: Mark's own Christology and the views of Jesus that are present (explicitly or implicitly) in what Mark both took over and handed on.

The Beginning of the Gospel of Mark

In Mark 1:1–15 we can distinguish five elements:

a. verse 1;
b. verses 2–8: the description of John the Baptist, to be subdivided as follows: 2–3, Isaiah's announcement, 4–6, John's ministry in general, and 7–8, John's prediction of one greater than himself;
c. verses 9–11: Jesus' baptism and God's solemn declaration to Jesus;

d. verses 12–13: the temptation by Satan;
e. verses 14–15: a characterization of Jesus' preaching.

Each of these elements deserves a short discussion. Together they set the tone for Mark's narrative.

The opening sentence in Mark 1:1, "the beginning of the gospel *(euaggelion)* of Jesus Christ, the Son of God," presents a number of difficulties. First, there is the question whether "the Son of God" was present in the original text or was added later. The various editions of the Greek text, and the translations dependent upon them, differ on this point.[2] We may say, however, that if "the Son of God" was added later, it was in keeping with Mark's own Christology. For Mark, "Son of God" is the central Christological title (see below).

Second, "the gospel of Jesus Christ" undoubtedly means "the gospel *about* Jesus Christ," in accordance with the use of the term in Paul—which goes back to earlier usage, as we have seen. As in Paul's letters, "Jesus Christ" has become a double name; "Christ" is no longer clearly felt as a title or a designation of office (see chapter 6).

Next, for Mark the good news concerning Jesus Christ clearly includes the story of his activities in Galilee and Jerusalem. Mark extends the term *euaggelion* to designate the narrative of Jesus' ministry that begins with the Baptist's appearance and ends with Jesus' death and resurrection in Jerusalem. In 8:35 and 10:29 Jesus' followers are urged to give up everything, even their lives, "for my sake and for the gospel"; 13:10 assures that "the gospel must first be preached to all nations," before the end will come. In 14:3–9 it becomes clear that the story about Jesus forms an integral part of the message concerning him; the story of the woman who anointed Jesus ends with Jesus' announcement: "Wherever the gospel is preached in the whole world, what she has done will be told in memory of her."[3]

The word *euaggelion* returns in Mark 1:14–15, where Jesus' public appearance, after the arrest of John the Baptist is characterized as "preaching the gospel of God." "The gospel of God" is the gospel proceeding from God, the message that God wants his messengers to preach. Paul uses the expression in 1 Thess. 2:2–13 and in Rom. 1:1; 15:16; 2 Cor. 11:7 (cf. 1 Peter 4:17). It may have been a technical term before Paul. In 1 Thess. 2:2–13 he uses it directly after quoting 1:9–10, and in Rom. 1:1 before the ancient formula in 1:3–4 (both discussed in the previous chapter). Here in Mark 1:14–15 Jesus himself is the messenger, indeed the herald of the approaching kingdom of God. "The time is fulfilled, and the kingdom of God is at hand; repent, and believe in the gospel." We are reminded of Isa.

52:7, "How beautiful upon the mountains are the feet of him who brings good tidings, who publishes peace, . . . who says to Zion, 'Your God reigns.' " The verb "to bring good tidings" (Greek *euaggelizesthai*) in Isa. 40–66 (see also Isa. 40:9; 60:6; 61:1) has clearly influenced the use of the same verb and the noun *euaggelion* in early Christianity (cf. also Matt. 11:2–6 [par. Luke 7:18–23], to be discussed in the next chapter).[4] The expression "kingdom of God" occupies a prominent place in Jesus' preaching, both in Mark and elsewhere in the New Testament. Jesus calls people to believe in the good news about God's sovereign rule that is about to become reality (Mark 4:26–29; 9:1; 14:25), and to repent. One has to accept it as a child and should be ready to sacrifice everything to enter into the kingdom (10:14, 15, 23, 24, 25; cf. 12:34 and 15:43). The kingdom of God is at hand, and in a way it has already begun with Jesus' activity on earth,[5] yet all emphasis is on its full realization and the readiness of people, including Jesus' disciples, to direct their lives toward it.

An integral part of "the gospel about Jesus Christ" is Jesus' own message about the arrival of God's kingdom.[6] Mark's picture of Jesus as a messenger at the turn of the times announcing the dawn of a radically new period in the history of God's dealings with Israel and humanity is no doubt traditional; so is his use of the phrase "preaching the good news" to characterize Jesus' proclamation of the kingdom of God (see further the next chapter).

It is significant that Mark begins with a reference to the scriptures introduced by "as it is written in Isaiah the prophet" (although, strictly speaking, only verse 3 is a slightly adapted quotation from Isa. 40:3). We are immediately reminded of the traditional phrase "in accordance with the scriptures" (1 Cor. 15:3–5) and of Paul's "the gospel of God which he promised beforehand through his prophets in the holy scriptures," in Rom. 1:1–2. Mark shares the conviction of those before him that the true meaning and significance of the Jesus story can only be understood in the light of the holy scriptures. The fulfillment of time brings the fulfillment of what was announced by the prophets. We should note that Mark selects a passage from Isa. 40–66. The voice of one crying in the wilderness is John. The one announced by him ("the Lord") is Jesus.

John the Baptist is depicted as a preacher of the coming judgment of God, of an eschatological baptism as a sign of repentance and divine remission of sins, and as a herald of Jesus, the greater one who will baptize with the Holy Spirit. For Mark, John's activity belongs to "the beginning of the gospel concerning Jesus Christ" (RSV alt.). Also in Mark 1:14; 6:14–16; 8:27–30; 9:11–13; 11:27–33, John and Jesus are mentioned together. We are told that people called Jesus a second John the Baptist (6:14–16; 8:27–30), and indeed the two have much in common as preachers of the approaching direct intervention by God. Yet John, according to Mark, is the forerunner, to be compared with Elijah (9:11–13); Jesus is the greater one, the Messiah (8:27–30).

In Mark 1:9–11 Mark reveals the true secret of Jesus to his readers by introducing God himself into the story. After Jesus was baptized by John and came up out of the water, a voice came from heaven, audible to Jesus only (or perhaps to Jesus and John), saying, "Thou art my beloved Son; with thee I am well pleased." Exegetes have pointed here to Isa. 42:1 (particularly in the form found in Matt. 12:18); Ps. 2:7; Ex. 4:22f.; and Gen. 22:2, 12, 16, but it seems unlikely that Mark intends to refer to one of these passages in particular. He wants to stress that Jesus, the Son of God, stands in a unique relation to God.

This conviction constitutes the very heart of Mark's Christology. The people in Galilee who listen to Jesus will not be able to penetrate into this secret. The three most intimate disciples of Jesus will hear the same voice making nearly the same declaration at Jesus' transfiguration: "This is my beloved Son; listen to him" (Mark 9:7). The beloved son is the final envoy sent by the owner of the vineyard to the wicked husbandmen (12:1–11). What is said here in parables is revealed openly at the trial before the Sanhedrin (14:61–62) and confessed by the Roman centurion after he has seen Jesus die: "Truly this man was the Son of God!" (15:39).

This beloved and unique Son of God receives the Spirit of God, the true source of his preaching with authority and his exorcistic activity which makes demons and evil spirits tremble (see below). It is this Spirit that makes him withstand Satan once and for all (1:12–13).

Was Mark the first to incorporate significant elements of the Jesus story in the "gospel about Jesus Christ"? He certainly was the first to write a "gospel" in the later sense of the word; in fact, because he introduced his book with the words found in 1:1, later authors spoke of the Gospel according to Mark (Matthew, Luke, or John). Thus the word denoting "the good news (about Jesus Christ)" became the technical term for a literary genre.[7] But were biographical elements perhaps subsumed under the heading *euaggelion* already before Mark? Here scholars often point to Peter's sermon to Cornelius, his household, and his friends in Acts 10:34–43.[8]

We have to be very careful in using the picture of early Christianity in Acts as evidence for the real state of affairs in the early years of the church. There is no doubt that Luke gives an idealized picture from a later perspective on the basis of the often fragmentary historical material at his disposal. The speeches in Acts, in particular, bear signs of Luke's redactional activity. In Acts 10:34–43, for instance, the phrase "God *anointed* Jesus of Nazareth with the Holy Spirit and with power" in verse 38 seems Lukan (note the prominent place of the quotation of Isa. 61:1 in Luke 4:18; see also pp. 99–100, 104–105); and the contrast "they put him to death . . . God raised him" in Acts 10:39–40 is typical of Acts (see pp. 108–109). Nevertheless, there are a number of elements in this short sermon that agree with what we find in Mark. The God who sent his word to the sons of Israel (Ps. 107:20) is characterized as "preaching good news *(euaggelizomenos)* of peace by Jesus Christ" (Acts 10:36; Isa. 52:7; Nahum 2:1; Mark 1:14–15). "Beginning from Galilee after the baptism which John preached" (Acts 10:37, as Mark; Luke, like Matthew, begins with the infancy narratives). Jesus' activity after receiving the Spirit is particularly concerned with "doing good and healing all that were oppressed by the devil" (Acts 10:38b; cf. Mark 3:20–29). The story in Peter's sermon culminates in Jesus' death and resurrection, described in terms found elsewhere in Acts but also with knowledge of the tradition in 1 Cor. 15:3–5 ("on the third day," "made him manifest to . . . ," Acts 10:40–41). It is difficult to speak here with certainty, but it is possible that this speech by Peter in Acts preserves traditional material parallel to that behind Mark, and that this described Jesus' preaching, healing, and exorcisms under the heading "God's good news by Jesus Christ."[9]

Jesus the Messiah and the Son of God in Mark

The actual body of the Gospel of Mark may be divided into three parts: Jesus' ministry in Galilee (1:16–8:26); Jesus and his disciples (8:27–10:52); Jesus in Jerusalem, his death and the message of his resurrection (11:1–16:8). Before turning to 1:16–8:26, we shall first analyze the main points of 8:27–10:52 and 11:1–16:8, where the characteristic features of Mark's own Christology come out clearly.[10]

In the second part of the Gospel the section 8:27–9:1 requires our special attention. Jesus, alone with his disciples, asks them: "Who do the people say that I am?" (8:27c, RSV alt.). The answer is that they see him as a revived John the Baptist, as Elijah come back, or as one of the prophets (8:27–28; cf. 6:14–16). The people regard Jesus as a prophet, a herald of God's definitive intervention in human affairs, like John. For Mark these reactions must have been important, and also intelligible in view of his picture of Jesus in 1:14–15 and the following chapters. Peter, however, declares solemnly on behalf of the disciples: "You are the Christ [= the Messiah]" (8:29). This is the right confession, the familiar one for Mark and his readers, and interestingly Mark makes Peter declare this after all that the disciples had heard and seen while they accompanied Jesus through Galilee. Yet, calling Jesus "the Christ" did not necessarily imply a right understanding of him. This becomes clear in a conversation between Jesus and his disciples that follows on Jesus' command to keep this confession secret (Mark 8:30). Jesus predicts his suffering, death, and resurrection (8:31), and this prediction is repeated twice (9:31; 10: 33–34), obviously because it is very important. In fact these predictions are modeled upon the double formula about Jesus' death and resurrection that we find in Paul's letters. The emphasis is on (1) the hostility of men, especially that of the Jewish leaders, and (2) his resurrection after three days. Twice (in 9:31; 10:33–34) it is said that Jesus will be "delivered" to his enemies.[11] The verb used here is also found in a similar context in 1 Cor. 11:23–25 ("on the night when he was betrayed"). Moreover, it is sometimes used in the formulas discussed on p. 40. It does not come as a surprise, then, that in Mark 10:45 we find a variant of this type of formula: "For the Son of man also came not to be served but to serve, and to give his life as a ransom for many." Mark does not mention the "for us/for you" in Jesus' references to his death and resurrection,[12] but he does take it up in Mark 10:45 and in his version of the tradition of the Last Supper (14:24).

People who confess Jesus as the Christ should keep in mind that Jesus had to suffer and was killed before he rose again. They should also realize that followers of Jesus should be prepared to go the same way. This is expressed very forcefully in Mark 8:34–9:1. Only those who are willing to lose their lives for Jesus' and the gospel's sake will save them. Those who remain faithful will share in the glory of the Son of man when he comes in the glory of his Father with the holy angels. This will take place soon. Jesus declares solemnly: "There are some standing here who will not taste death before they see that the kingdom of God has come with power" (9:1). This same theme recurs in the following pericopes, particularly in 10:13–16; in 10: 17–31 (the story of the rich man, on the obstacles to entering the kingdom of God); and in 10:35–45 (ending with 10:45 just mentioned, about the request by James and John who want to receive special honors when Jesus returns in glory).

Those who confess Jesus as the Christ should know the whole story and be prepared to go the whole way. This is the message that Mark, making use of traditional Christological material, wants to bring home to his readers.

In conveying this message he does not take up Peter's "Christ/ Messiah" but replaces it with "Son of man" which he, like other writers of the New Testament, uses only as a self-designation of

Jesus.[13] It is found in Mark 8:31 (as well as in 9:31 and 10:33) in connection with Jesus' death and resurrection, and in 8:38 in connection with his *parousia.* If we look at the other instances in the Gospel, we find two cases where the term Son of man is connected with the authority of Jesus on earth (2:10, 28[14]). Later, in the conversation between Jesus and the disciples after the transfiguration, the term is used in connection with his resurrection (9:9) and his suffering (9:12). In the stories of the last supper and of Gethsemane it is connected with Jesus' approaching death (14:21, 41). Finally, there are two instances in which the Son of man is said to appear in or with the clouds of heaven (13:26; 14:62). The expression "Son of man" is Semitic, and strange in Greek. In view of the consistency in the use of this strange expression as a self-designation of Jesus, it is likely that Mark took it over from the tradition before him. We shall have to discuss later (see chapter 10, last section) what it meant originally, but should now note that for Mark it has titular force; in the texts dealing with the parousia there is a link with the "one like a son of man" mentioned in Dan. 7:13f. In general, the term seems to emphasize Jesus' special authority (the *parousia* texts *and* 2:10, 28) but although this leads to conflicts with the Jewish leaders, it is never taken up by his adversaries. Also it is never used in confessions by his disciples, so that we must conclude that, at least for Mark, the term does not really disclose the secret of Jesus' identity.[15]

In Mark 8:38 Jesus refers implicitly to his being "Son of God" when he speaks of the coming of the Son of man "in the glory of his Father" (cf. 10:35–40). This is confirmed in the story of Jesus' transfiguration (9:2–8), where God intervenes directly for the second time. The voice from heaven declares: "This is my beloved Son; listen to him." The three disciples who are with Jesus are told to keep what they have seen a secret until after his resurrection (9:9–13). The repetition and, in fact, explanation of the earlier command of secrecy in 8:30 underscores that Jesus' disciples will not be able to understand completely who he is until after his crucifixion and resurrection. Only after the terrifying events in Jerusalem and a new meeting with the resurrected Jesus in Galilee will they be able to proclaim the gospel concerning Jesus Christ to all the nations (see 16:1–8; 14:27–28; 13:10).

In Mark's third section, 11:1–16:8, many points deserve our attention. We shall not try to make a distinction between an earlier passion narrative and Mark's final redaction of it (see p. 22). Instead, we shall focus again on those elements in Mark's story that are meant to provide answers to burning questions in the communities for which he wrote, and on those elements that represent reactions to problems that were already important before Mark.

In Mark 11–12 we should first mention the discussion between the Jewish leaders and Jesus about his authority. It is situated after his action in the temple, but the question has wider implications (11:27–33). Jesus compares himself with John the Baptist, whom the people regard as a prophet with authority from God. He does not reveal the source of his own authority, but it is clear that he and John have much in common. In the parable of the wicked husbandmen (12:1–9) Jesus identifies himself, as we have seen earlier, with the beloved Son, the final envoy of God in a succession of divine messengers, the prophets. A reference to Ps. 118:22–23, added to the actual parable (12:10–11), gives an implicit allusion to his death and resurrection. Here Mark uses an earlier parable, applying traditional patterns (see our discussions of 1 Thess. 2:14–16 and Gal. 4:4 in the previous chapter) to bring home his special point: Jesus is the unique Son of God. Mark adds that his adversaries understood what he meant, and tried to arrest him (12:12; cf. 11:18 and 14:1; and even 3:6, much earlier in the story).

Another important pericope is 12:35–37, where Jesus, after a series of conversations with Jews representative of different groups in Jewish society, takes the initiative and asks: "How can the scribes say that the Christ is the son of David?" (12:35). He does not in so many words identify himself as "the Christ" (in fact, he never does so in Mark before 14:61f.); yet the question is obviously not a purely theoretical one about Jewish opinion. Mark wrote for readers for whom Jesus is the Christ. When the Jews speak about the Messiah, they think first of all of an ideal "Son of David." Earlier in the story, Jesus is twice addressed as "Son of David" by Bartimaeus, who hopes to be healed by him. Jesus praises his faith and Bartimaeus begins to follow Jesus (10:46–52). At Jesus' entry into Jerusalem, the disciples and other sympathizers hail Jesus as the one who comes in the name of the Lord (Ps. 118:26), and associate him with "the kingdom of our father David that is coming" (11:9–10). There is no indication that the designation "Son of David" for Jesus is wrong. Yet in 12:35–37 it is shown to be inadequate by itself. Jesus quotes Ps. 110:1, a well-known Christological proof text in the early church that will occupy us later (see chapter 11). Here it is quoted to bring out that David calls Jesus "Lord." The pericope ends with a question: "David himself calls him Lord; so how is he his son?"

Does the question imply that Jesus, whom his followers call "the Christ," cannot be regarded as "Son of David"? In view of 10:46–52 and 11:9–10 this clearly is not the case. Or is this an attempt to introduce the title "Lord"? No, for in the Gospel of Mark this title does not play any role.[16] The question only suggests that Jesus, the true Messiah, Son of David, is different from the one whom the scribes and Jews in general expect.

In fact the matter left open in Mark 12:35–37 returns in the report of Jesus' trial before the Sanhedrin in 14:55–65. It ends with a solemn declaration by Jesus. At the final question of the high priest: "Are you the Christ, the Son of the Blessed?" Jesus answers, "I am." At last he acknowledges publicly that he is the Messiah *and* that he is the "Son of God" (vs. 61–62). This declaration by Jesus clearly forms the Christological climax of Mark's Gospel. Jesus adds, however, a statement concerning his activity in the (immediate) future. With clear reference to Ps. 110:1 and Dan. 7:13f. he says: "You will see the Son of man seated at the right hand of Power, and coming with the clouds of heaven." Jesus, the Son of man, will reign as Son of David / Messiah / Son of God when God's sovereign rule is established on earth (8:38–9:1; 13:26).

In the following account of the trial before Pontius Pilate and in the narrative of Jesus' crucifixion in Mark 15, unexpectedly the designation "the King of the Jews" plays an important role. Mark has taken care to emphasize that Jesus' royal authority will only manifest itself at the time, however imminent, when the kingdom of God is fully realized on earth. Yet, Pilate—who is obviously known to the readers of the Gospel, because he receives no introduction—asks Jesus: "Are you the King of the Jews?"[17] This time Jesus answers, "You have said so," which is at the most a guarded and qualified "Yes." The term "King of the Jews" returns on the lips of Pilate in verse 12, and on the inscription attached to the cross (v. 26). It is also used by the soldiers who mock Jesus (v. 18).

"King of the Jews" is the expression used by non-Jews. When, in Mark 15:29–32, the chief priests and scribes are introduced, they use the term "the Christ, the King of Israel." They challenge Jesus to save himself so that people may believe that he is able to save others. But this Messiah does not perform miracles to convince those who do not accept him (see also 8:11–13); he does not descend from the cross. His royal status will be revealed only at the *parousia,* when the crucified Christ will be shown to be triumphant. He is, therefore, in no respect a king of Israel in the political sense, still less a rebel like Barabbas or a bandit[18] like the two with whom he is crucified. It is not denied that Jesus is the Messiah, and therefore king of Israel in the succession of David; it is clearly imperative, however, to explain what this Messiahship means and what it does not mean.

There are two indications of the direction in which this meaning must be sought. First, there is the Roman officer who declares, "Truly this man was the Son of God!" (Mark 15:39). For Mark this is the true confession—Jesus' resurrection will make it clear that the followers of Jesus (including Gentiles such as the centurion) may change the "was" to "is." Next, we note the prominent place given in the story of the crucifixion to the quotation from Ps. 22:2 (1E), "My God, my God, why hast thou forsaken me?" More elements from this psalm have been taken over in the crucifixion story (Ps. 22:19 [18E] in Mark 15:24; Ps. 22:8 [7E] in Mark 15:29), and there also seems to be influence from Ps. 69:22 (21E) in Mark 15:23, 36. Psalms 22 and 69 belong to a group of psalms in which a righteous person cries out to God for deliverance from his enemies. Both psalms end with thanksgiving and praise, because God, in his mighty compassion, has heard those who cry to him and will give help to all who are afflicted. It is possible that already before Mark wrote, Jesus' suffering, death, and resurrection were explained in terms of the suffering of righteous servants of God and their vindication by him, in the Psalms and elsewhere in the Old Testament.

We shall come back to this later (see chapter 11), but we should mention here also a possible reference to Wisd. of Sol. 2:17f. in 15:29–32 (brought out more clearly in the parallel passage Matt. 27:39–44). The righteous man in Wisd. of Sol. 2:12–20 (who is called son of God in v. 18) is condemned to a shameful death by his opponents, but vindicated by God in 5:1–7. His adversaries will see him (cf. 14:62), and will have to recognize that he is "numbered among the sons of God" and that "his lot is among the saints" (5:5). It is clear that particularly this variant of the pattern of the vindication of the suffering righteous was eminently suitable to interpret Jesus' death and resurrection.

How do we explain the emphasis on the nonpolitical nature of Jesus' Messiahship/kingship in Mark 15? Does it reflect the historical situation of Jesus' trial? Was he, indeed, falsely put to death as a political Messiah/king of the Jews? Many people have thought so, and we shall return briefly to this subject in chapter 13 when we speak about Jesus and his ambitions and conceptions. In the present context I shall restrict myself to the statement that Mark assumes his readers to be familiar with this, in his eyes, gross misinterpretation by the Jewish leaders and the Roman governor of the real aims of Jesus the Christ in whom they (his readers) believe. The true identity of Jesus the Christ must have been a burning question at the time the Gospel of Mark was written. Here we may also point to the Markan apocalypse in chapter 13, which speaks of great turmoil in Judea and persecutions of Christians, who are urged to continue preaching the gospel and who are encouraged to endure to the end. Before that end comes, with the arrival of the Son of man "in clouds with great power and glory" (13:26), people will say to the disciples: "Look, here is the Christ!" or "Look, there he is!" Do not believe them, Jesus says; false Christs/messiahs and false prophets will come and show signs and wonders to lead them astray (vs. 21–23; cf. vs. 5–6). Mark insists: our Christ is different: he has already come and was crucified, but vindicated by God; he will come again in the way he predicted (8:38; 13:26; 14:62). He is not at all like those other messiahs and prophets; he was crucified, but one would be wrong to conclude from this that he was only another religiously motivated rebel against the Romans.[19] We shall come back to this at the end of this chapter.

Jesus as Preacher, Teacher, Healer, and Exorcist

We return to the first major section in the Gospel of Mark, 1:16–8:26. Again we cannot analyze it in detail, but have to bring out a few important aspects in the picture of Jesus arising from this collection of short stereotyped stories and pronouncements.

The first story related by Mark after his characterization of Jesus' preaching in 1:14–15 is that of his calling four Galilean fishermen who leave everything and everybody behind and follow him on his way (1:16–20). In 2:13–14 he calls Levi, a tax collector, and he too follows him. It was typical of Jesus, we are told, that he called tax collectors and other sinners (= people who do not obey the law of Moses as one should, and are therefore treated as outcasts) and accepted them into table fellowship. In Mark 15:41 (cf. 15:47; 16:1; see also Luke 8:1–3) we hear of women "who, when he was in Galilee, followed him, and ministered to him," besides "many other women who came up with him to Jerusalem." In 3:13–19 Jesus chooses twelve men whom he calls the apostles, in order "to be with him, and to be sent out to preach and have authority to cast out demons." In 6:7–13 the twelve apostles are sent out: "They went out and preached that men should repent. And they cast out many demons, and anointed with oil many that were sick and healed them" (vs. 12–13). The instructions they receive are those for itinerant preachers who go from village to village. In 6:30 the apostles return and tell Jesus "all that they had done and taught."

Interestingly, in Mark 9:38–40 an incident is recorded of a man who casts out demons in Jesus' name but does not follow him. In contrast to his disciples, Jesus does not forbid him to do so. In 9:41 we hear that those who give a cup of water to drink to those who are "of Christ" (see p. 22) will receive their reward. In the story of the rich man, which dwells on the conditions for entering into the kingdom of God (see also p. 55), Peter stresses, on behalf of the disciples, that they have given up everything for Jesus and the gospel (10:17–31, especially 28–31).

Following Jesus means becoming a disciple, belonging to his fellowship. To this fellowship clearly belonged a considerable number of people who did not qualify according to stricter Jewish Pharisaic standards.[20] For some, namely the four in Mark 1:16–20 and the twelve mentioned later, and a number of unnamed others, this meant traveling as itinerant preachers. They were a common phenomenon in early Christianity (see, e.g., Matt. 10 and Luke 10:1–20 [incorporating material from Q]; 1 Cor. 9; 3 John).[21] In Mark, the emphasis is on Jesus' call and election and on the obedience of those who followed him as well as of those who were sent on a special mission. The latter share in his authority. Like their master, they preach the message of repentance; they have the authority to cast out demons and to heal sick persons. In a somewhat different context (Mark 9:37) we find the fundamentally Jewish idea that the envoy of a person acts as that person and is to be treated as that person himself. In Matt. 10:40 and par. Luke 10:16 (a text from Q), a similar saying is applied to traveling preachers: "He who receives you receives me, and he who receives me receives him who sent me" (cf. John 13:20). Mark would no doubt agree: the words and actions of those who are sent out by Jesus are in conformity with those of Jesus himself. Jesus too wanders from village to village and from city to city, and has no permanent abode. In fact, he meets with unbelief in his hometown (6:1–6). His family regards him as insane (3:20–21), and when they arrive to call on him, he looks at the crowd around him and replies: "Here are my mother and my brothers! Whoever does the will of God is my brother, and sister, and mother."[22]

Jesus was a teacher/preacher, he exorcised demons, and he healed. This becomes immediately clear when Mark, in 1:21–45, describes Jesus' activity in Capernaum and surrounding villages, bringing together a representative sample of stories he had at his disposal. People are "astonished at his teaching, for he taught them as one who had authority, and not as the scribes" (v. 22); after the exorcism of a man with an unclean spirit they are amazed and say: "What is this? A new teaching with authority! He commands even the unclean spirits and they obey him" (1:27, punctuation alt.). The reaction of the people of Capernaum is typical of the reaction of the people in Galilee in general. So in 6:2 the initial reaction in the synagogue in his hometown is: "Where did this man get all this? What is the wisdom given to him? What mighty works are wrought by his hands!" In 7:37, after the healing of a deaf-mute, people are completely astonished: "He has done all things well; he even makes the deaf hear and the dumb speak."

Jesus teaches (Mark 1:21; 2:13; 4:1f.; 6:2, 6, 34) and is called "teacher" (4:38; 5:35); he preaches (1:(14), 38f.—there is little or no difference in the use of these words); he heals (1:32–34, 40–45;

2:1–12; 3:1–5, 10–11; 5:25–34; 6:55f.; 7:31–37; 8:22–26), and exorcizes demons (1:23–27; 1:39; 3:22–27; 5:1–17; 7:24–30; 9:14–29); he even brings Jairus's daughter back to life (5:21–24, 35–43). People recognize his authority: a direct authority, quite unlike that of the scribes, who derived it from their acquaintance with the traditional exposition of the law of Moses.

This authority is to some extent explained and specified by Jesus in two stories in this section of the Gospel.[23] In the story of the healing of a paralyzed man in Mark 2:1–12 the central event is not the healing but the remission of the man's sins. In a discussion with the scribes, who point out that only God is able to forgive sins, Jesus declares that "the Son of man has authority on earth to forgive sins." He designates himself as "Son of man"—an expression that does not disclose his identity (see above), but implies that he has received direct and exclusive authority from God to speak and act as he does.[24]

Next, Mark describes a controversy over Jesus' exorcisms with scribes who had come down from Jerusalem (3:22–27). The issue is whether he casts out the demons by God's power or by that of the chief of demons. The answer is that here is someone at work who, in God's power, is stronger than Satan. Mark continues with a few verses speaking about the Holy Spirit (3:28–30), stating that there is only one unforgivable sin: to say that Jesus is inspired by an evil spirit whereas it is clearly God's Holy Spirit who is working in him. His opponents do not accept his claim; on the contrary: in 2:1–12 he is accused of blasphemy (after two Sabbath incidents, in 2:23–28 and 3:1–5, the Pharisees are said to have begun planning Jesus' death, 3:6), and in 3:22–30 they clearly remain convinced that he is an associate of Satan.

In this section the story of Jesus' teaching, healing, and exorcisms is one of partial understanding at most, and of gross misunderstanding. In between the parable of the sower (Mark 4:1–9) and its explanation to the disciples (4:13–20), Jesus tells his disciples that to them "the secret of the kingdom of God" has been given; outsiders will not really perceive what is to be seen or understand what is to be heard (4:10–12). Indeed, the kingdom of God is like the seed sown in a field (4:26–29), or like a mustard seed, the smallest seed in the world (4:30–33). It is extremely inconspicuous, but those who know the secret will wait confidently for the full revelation of God's sovereign rule.

Yet even the disciples to whom the secret of the kingdom of God has been entrusted are rebuked for their lack of faith and real insight. They too need to have the parable of the sower explained to them, and they indeed receive explanations also of other parables (Mark

4:34). Still, on the evening of the same day they are afraid when their boat is in danger of sinking in a storm; they are rebuked for their lack of faith, and still can do no better than ask the question: "who then is this, that even wind and sea obey him?" (4:35–41). They fail to understand the meaning of the feeding of the five thousand (6:52), and even after Jesus has again shown his miraculous powers in the feeding of the four thousand, they show a lack of understanding (8:14–21, ending with Jesus' question in v. 21: "Do you not yet understand?"). Between Peter's confession in 8:27–30 and 8:14–21 Mark inserts the story of the healing of the blind man in Bethsaida (8:22–26), presumably a symbolic story. The blindness of outsiders and insiders has to be taken away before anyone can comprehend who Jesus really is.

This theme of the misunderstanding of Jesus by "those outside" (Mark 4:11), and even by the disciples, was clearly introduced by the author of the Gospel himself. In his second section (8:27–10:52), Mark continues to emphasize that the disciples still have much to learn, and will only be able to tell the full story about Jesus after the resurrection (8:30; 9:9—see also the second section of this chapter). In the last days in Jerusalem they desert Jesus (14:50), and Peter denies him (14:54, 66–72). Present at the crucifixion were the women who had followed Jesus in Galilee; they, along with many other women, watched from a distance (15:40–41). It is they who see where Jesus is buried and who hear the message of the resurrection when they go to the tomb to anoint Jesus' body (15:47–16:8). Peter and his colleagues will get a new chance only after a new meeting with their master in Galilee.

Another clearly Markan editorial element in this section of the Gospel is the reactions of the demons. What human beings suspect, but do not and cannot put into words, is unambiguously expressed by the demons that Jesus casts out: "I know who you are, the Holy One of God" (Mark 1:24); "What have you to do with me, Jesus, Son of the Most High God?" (5:7). In a summary of events Mark tells us: "And whenever the unclean spirits beheld him, they fell down before him and cried out, 'You are the Son of God' " (3:11; cf. 1:34). The demons recognize who Jesus is, whereas the people in their amazement keep asking who he might be. The relationship between the cries of the demons and the questions is contrapuntal. The following pattern may be detected: demonic cry (1:24), question (1:27), demonic cries (1:34), question (2:7), demonic cries (3:11), question (4:41), demonic cry (5:7), question (6:3).[25] In Mark's story these cries are systematically suppressed by Jesus (1:25, 34; 3:12), or do not get out because no other people besides Jesus and the demoniac are present (5:1–13). Consequently, human beings continue to ask the question, the answer to which has been given by the demons. In Mark's opinion, these demons have spoken out of turn.

The reactions of the people, the scribes, the disciples, and the demons clearly play an important role in the overall story that Mark wants to tell his readers. He has disclosed to them in advance who Jesus is—a man endowed with the Holy Spirit (Mark 1:7–8, 9–11); the unique Son of God (1:9–11); one who conquered Satan (1:12–13); the one who preached the gospel of God and inaugurated the kingdom of God (1:14–15). This is the man whom Peter and his fellow disciples confessed as Christ/Messiah (8:27–30) after all they had seen, heard, and experienced in Galilee. The readers know that the demons are right, and that the scribes are wrong when they speak of an evil spirit or the chief of demons in Jesus and do not recognize the Holy Spirit. Jesus has indeed a very special authority, and he does not blaspheme; when he calls himself "Son of man" this designation is later amply explained by the evangelist. Also when people compare Jesus with John the Baptist, or regard him as Elijah (6:14–16; 8:28), the reader realizes that Jesus does have traits of an eschatological prophet, but is more than that. This is made very clear in the story of the transfiguration and the conversation thereafter between Jesus and his disciples (9:1–13), and in the controversy between Jesus and the Jewish leaders in 11:27–33 (plus 12:1–12), where the question of the source of Jesus' authority is answered definitively.

We find, then, that Mark incorporated ancient traditions about Jesus' teaching/preaching, healing and exorcisms in his Gospel, but made them subordinate to his own picture of Jesus. This makes it difficult to say anything with certainty about the Christology of this narrative and related material before they were integrated into Mark's book.[26] Immense effort has been spent on this Gospel and the material incorporated into it by literary critics and form and tradition critics (see the Introduction). Nevertheless we know very little about the explicit or implicit Christology of the individual narratives and pronouncements in their earliest form or about early collections of them.

It is clear that Mark could report on Jesus' activity in Galilee because he had access to a lot of relevant material. More of this is found in the common source of Matthew and Luke (Q), which will be treated in the next chapter; moreover, there is the material found only in Matthew, Luke, and John. All these traditions were transmitted because they were relevant to the groups and persons who transmitted them. Evidently Jesus was regarded as a teacher/preacher, healer and exorcist, of great—even unique—authority. His followers had to take seriously that they were his disciples, and therefore had to take his examples and directions seriously. He was the one whose authority stood behind the itinerant preachers and their message and exorcisms. Whether this unique authority was already spelled out in terms like prophet, Son of man, Son of God, Christ/Messiah, we are not able to tell on the basis of the material preserved in Mark alone. We shall have to postpone our conclusions until, in the next chapter, we have analyzed the traditional material handed down through that other channel, Q, the common source of Matthew and Luke.

Mark's Christology in Its Context

Summing up the most important findings of this chapter, we first emphasize that Mark took up the terms "the gospel of God," "the gospel of (Jesus) Christ" or "the gospel" without any further qualification—terms found in Paul, and, in all probability, already used before Paul. For Mark, "the gospel of God" was first proclaimed by Jesus, and to him it is essential that "the gospel of Jesus Christ" (*the* gospel, in fact) cannot be preached without the narrative about Jesus' activity in Galilee and Judea before his death and resurrection.

Particularly in the analysis of Mark 8:27–16:8 we noted that Mark was acquainted with Christological formulas which were also known from the writings of Paul. He gives his own variant of a double formula dealing with Jesus' death and resurrection; perhaps this has to be connected with the probably pre-Markan, traditional picture of Jesus as the righteous sufferer to be vindicated by God, as found in the narrative of the crucifixion. Mark twice tells his readers that Jesus "died for us," once in 10:45, where the expression "to give his life as a ransom for many" occurs in a word of Jesus, and once in the Markan version of Jesus' words at the last supper (14:22–25). Mark takes for granted that the disciples of Jesus confess him as the Christ/Messiah, but regards it necessary to define this title vis-à-vis "Son of David." He prefers the title "Son of God," which figures prominently in certain places in his book (9:7; (13:32); 14:61; 15:39; also 3:11; 5:7; and perhaps in 1:1). "Christ" and "Son of God" are also found in various traditional statements used by Paul; in Rom. 1:3–4 there is the expression "descended from David." At the time Mark wrote his Gospel it had become necessary to explain what the designations "Christ," "Son of God," and "Son of David" mean when used in connection with Jesus.

For Mark—like Paul and many later authors—general expressions like those used in Rom. 1:2 ("promised beforehand through his prophets in the holy scriptures") and 1 Cor. 15:3–4 ("in accordance with the scriptures") no longer sufficed. He quotes specific texts from the scriptures to prove his point. We have noticed in particular the quotation from Isaiah in Mark 1:2–3; Ps. 110:1 in 12:36; and may add Ps. 118:22–23 in 12:10–11, besides numerous allusions to parts of scripture. Here we should mention in particular Dan. 7:13, alluded to in 13:26 and 14:62 in connection with Jesus' use of the designation "Son of man." This expression, though probably traditional (we shall meet it again in the next chapter), is not found in Paul or in traditional material used by him.

All along Mark makes it clear that Jesus' teaching and actions before his death and resurrection form an integral part of "the gospel." In particular he emphasizes the nonpolitical nature of Jesus' kingship (ch. 15), and the differences between Jesus and other messiahs and prophets (ch. 13).

It is commonly assumed that Mark was written a little before or immediately after the destruction of Jerusalem and the temple in A.D. 70. The picture found in Mark 13 may well reflect the tribulations in and before the war between the Jews and the Romans in A.D. 66–70 and its aftermath. It is not difficult to imagine the grueling situation in which the followers of Jesus Christ found themselves. It was necessary for them to realize that Jesus the Christ/Messiah was one who suffered, was brought to death, was vindicated in the resurrection, and would come again to reign as king in God's kingdom. Sticking to this basic kernel of the gospel concerning Jesus Christ, they would be able to stand firm and defend themselves—against those, for instance, who insisted that they believed in a false messiah because Jesus had not done what was expected from a true Son of David—or against those who accused them as "messianists" secretly plotting against the authorities. After all, they were followers of a man who, in the days of Pilate, had been crucified as a rebel. Finally, they would be able to resist the temptations of false messiahs and false prophets, particularly those who presented themselves as Jesus the Christ who had returned (Mark 13:5–6). You know better! Mark assures his readers. There are many who are led astray, but you belong to the elect who are preserved by God (13:20, 22, 27)!

In the difficult circumstances around 70, Mark had to remind his readers of the central points of the early Christian convictions about Jesus Christ, and to set out unambiguously why he was condemned to death. In order to do so effectively, he also had to report at least some essential elements of Jesus' teaching and of his actions.

We may go further back in time. The existence of a pre-Markan passion narrative, whatever it may have contained, or of at the very least a collection of stories about the events leading up to the crucifixion, points to the need to tell outsiders and to instruct new members in the Christian communities about what had happened. One could not mention the crucifixion without recording how and why Jesus was rejected and condemned to death. Celebrating the Lord's Supper in the inner circle in order to commemorate the Lord's death, one could simply refer to "the night when he was betrayed" (1 Cor. 11:23–26). But if one had to explain to those who did not belong to the initiated why one believed in a master who had suffered such an ignominious death, more had to be said. One had to make clear that God had vindicated him in the resurrection, and an explanation of what had preceded his trial was equally necessary. Of course the story could not simply begin with what happened in Jerusalem immediately before Jesus' arrest. Speaking about Jesus' mission and message would necessarily arouse interest in the teaching and actions of Jesus during the whole of his public ministry.[27]

That Mark (and others) had access to narrative traditions and sayings material about or by Jesus shows that these stories and sayings had been relevant for the groups of his followers and itinerant preachers all along.

We shall come back to this last point in the next chapter. Then we must also look again at the picture of Jesus as the herald of the kingdom of God, appearing when the time was fulfilled (Mark 1:14–15), and at the use of *euaggelion* and related words in this connection. Also the connection between John the Baptist and Jesus (see 1:2–3) will again require our attention. We have already pointed to the pre-Lukan tradition behind Acts 10:34–43 as a possibly embryonic form of "gospel."

3
The Sayings of Jesus in Q

The Common Material in the Gospel of Matthew and the Gospel of Luke

The relationship between Mark, Matthew, and Luke is most easily explained by the theory that the latter two evangelists used the Gospel of Mark more or less in the form in which we know it. Matthew and Luke also have in common material not found in Mark. This is generally thought to have been taken from a written source called Q (a designation probably derived from the German *Quelle,* "source"). We do not have this source in our hands; it has to be reconstructed. Consequently, as handbooks on "Introduction to the New Testament" show, there is much disagreement about the nature and the exact content of this source.

We begin by assuming that Q contains all non-Markan parallel material in Matthew and Luke. But there is a wide range in parallelism, from sayings that are almost word-for-word the same to others that have much in common but are also significantly different. Scholars may differ as to where to draw the line. Next, Matthew and Luke have inserted this material in their Gospels in quite different ways; so the question of the order of the Q material arises. There are, however, sufficient verbal or near-verbal parallels, and sufficient agreements, to support the theory of the existence of a written common source.

Theoretically, Q may have contained more than the parallels just mentioned. It is possible that some Q sayings were preserved by either Matthew or Luke alone; nor is it to be ruled out that Mark knew and was influenced by Q in some cases. Yet Mark, Q, the specific material preserved in Matthew, and that transmitted by Luke alone all draw on a common stock of oral and/or written traditions concerning Jesus. Consequently, similarities and agree-

71

ments can be explained in other ways than by postulating an expanded Q.

We shall have to admit that Q cannot be analyzed in the same way we analyzed Mark. Yet we are interested in knowing what views of Jesus are found in the common material used by Matthew and Luke, and whether certain views are characteristic of Q as a collection. Q consists mainly of sayings of the earthly Jesus that were handed down because they were regarded as authoritative and relevant. Now independent sayings are notoriously difficult to interpret. In different literary and historical contexts they may have been understood and have functioned differently. But Q often connects sayings with specific incidents in the ministry of Jesus. It also contains traditions about John the Baptist, records the story of the centurion in Capernaum (Luke 7:1–10), and in general gives, or at least suggests, a picture of Jesus as one who speaks and acts with great authority. It is a risky enterprise to attempt to go further back to possible earlier forms of these sayings or their original meanings. We are on safer ground when we ask whether there is any consistency in the Christology of the Q collection.

Athanasius Polag, the author of an important and careful monograph on the Christology of Q,[1] thinks there is. In his view, Q's Christology is implicit rather than explicit. It is not dependent on titles or fixed concepts, nor is it a Christology of statements about Jesus' work and words. It may best be described as a "Christology of appeal." Jesus' teaching claims to be of decisive importance for the life of those it addresses. It requires response, decision, and total commitment.

Polag, however, goes further than this. He finds traces of at least two redactions of Q. At the level of the first redaction we find a frequent use of "Son of man" for Jesus, and a connection between Jesus' mission and that of God's Wisdom on earth (we shall return to this later). But there is as yet no development of designations in the direction of titles. At this stage the basic underlying conviction is that the appeal, promise, and threat laid down in the words of the earthly Jesus for his contemporaries are still valuable and valid. The presupposition is that Jesus, who died, lives with God and will come again to realize God's kingdom on earth.

Later, according to Polag, new material was added to the already existing collection, including, for instance, the story of Jesus' temptation in Luke 4:1–13 (par. Matt. 4:1–11) and that of Jesus' thanksgiving in Luke 10:21–22 (par. Matt. 11:25–27). At this final stage we find an extra emphasis on Jesus' direct and unique relationship with God and the use of the designation "Son of God" / "Son." Also passages from the scriptures are quoted and applied to John the

Baptist and Jesus. The initial collection clearly led to a search for additional material in the tradition, and invited further reflection and comment.

It may well be that Polag, notwithstanding the great care and caution applied throughout his analysis, wants to prove too much. In the present investigation I have used with great profit his reconstruction of Q, divided into a number of groups of sayings, and his comments on the various pericopes. I shall restrict myself, however, to a survey of the most prominent elements in the Christology of Q, and I shall not try to distinguish between different redactions of the material.

Jesus and John the Baptist

We shall start with an analysis of Q's view of the relation between Jesus and John the Baptist. Here we may consult a group of sayings in Luke 7:18–35 (par. Matt. 11:2–19). In the background is the picture of John the Baptist in Luke 3:1–18 (par. Matt. 3:1–12), where elements from Q are combined with material derived from Mark.

In Luke 7:18–23 (par. Matt. 11:2–6) we find three central elements. First, there is the question of John the Baptist, transmitted to Jesus by John's disciples: "Are you he who is to come, or shall we look for another?" Second, there is Jesus' reply, which explicitly refers to his actions and preaching: "Go and tell John what you have seen and heard: the blind receive their sight, the lame walk, lepers are cleansed, and the deaf hear, the dead are raised up, the poor have good news preached to them." Finally, John (like all those who are in doubt) has to realize that he needs to come to a decision regarding Jesus: "And blessed is he who takes no offense at me."

John is said to be in prison (so Matt. 11:2; cf. Luke 3:19–20). The expression "he who is to come," which he uses, is not very specific, but there seems to be a clear reference to Luke 3:16–17 (par. Matt. 3:11–12). In the Q version, "he who is mightier than I," whose coming is announced by John, is one who will bring judgment on earth. John, in his imprisonment, is portrayed as puzzled if not disappointed by what he hears Jesus is doing. Jesus' answer in Luke 7:22 (par. Matt. 11:5) consists of allusions to prophecies from the book of Isaiah (e.g., 29:18f.; 35:5f.; 42:7, 18; 26:19; and 61:1). In "the poor have good news preached to them," which forms the climax of the series, we encounter again the term *euaggelizesthai*. Jesus' preaching is characterized as "good news," and it is directly connected with his healings: what the prophets promised has now become reality. Luke makes Jesus give his answer to John's messengers just after he has healed many of diseases and plagues and evil spirits, and restored sight to blind persons. John's disciples do indeed have something essential "to hear and see." (Just before, in Luke 7:11–17, the evangelist has told his readers how Jesus raised the son of a widow in Nain.) Matthew, who tells us that John, in prison, heard "about the deeds of the Christ" (Matt. 11:2), prepares his readers in advance for Jesus' answer to John by bringing together a collection of miracles in chapters 8 and 9.

For Q, Jesus is not just any messenger, any preacher of good news; he brings the good tidings of the fulfillment of the promises of the prophets. In his actions this fulfillment is visible and tangible. It is now up to John, and to all others who meet Jesus, to recognize who he is, and to put their trust in him. We may add another beatitude addressed to the disciples: "Blessed are the eyes which see what you see! For I tell you that many prophets and kings desired to see what you see, and did not see it, and to hear what you hear, and did not hear it" (Luke 10:23–24; the parallel in Matt. 13:16–17 is slightly different). There are also the four beatitudes in Luke 6:20–23 (expanded in Matt. 5:3–12), beginning with "Blessed are you poor, for yours is the kingdom of God." These beatitudes occupy an important place in Q, because they form the beginning of Jesus' teaching.

Luke 7:18–23, together with 6:20, points to the same view of Jesus as is found in Mark 1:14–15 (discussed early in chapter 2). We should note that Q does not seem to be interested in titles, as Polag has emphasized. Matthew speaks of "the deeds of the Christ (= Messiah)," and Luke quotes Isa. 61:1 in full in the story of Jesus preaching in the synagogue of his native town, Nazareth (4:16–30), which occupies a prominent place in Luke's Gospel. For Luke, Jesus is the Christ because the Lord has anointed him by the Spirit, in accordance with the first lines of Isa. 61:1 (cf. Acts 10:38). In Q, however, the title "Messiah" is not mentioned explicitly; already John's "he who is to come" is intentionally "open."[2] But Jesus *is* the one who was to come; in his preaching and actions a decisive new beginning has been made.

To this central pericope about John and Jesus a number of further sayings have been added. In Luke 7:24–28 (par. Matt. 11:7–11) John the Baptist is called a prophet, "and more than a prophet." A composite quotation of Mal. 3:1 and Ex. 23:20 (found in nearly the same form in Mark 1:2) calls him "my messenger before thy face, who shall prepare thy way before thee." John is more than a prophet, he is the messenger who announced the coming of Jesus. Jesus himself, who is speaking here, is evidently regarded as belonging to an altogether different category. Luke 7:28 (par. Matt. 11:11) adds, with some emphasis, "Among those born of women none is greater than John; yet he who is least in the kingdom of God is greater than he."

The first half of this saying is clear; the translation and meaning of the second half are disputed. Whoever may be referred to by "he who is least" (literally: "he who is less")—perhaps any of Jesus' followers, perhaps Jesus himself—the emphasis is on the fact that after the arrival of the kingdom in Jesus' words and actions, customary standards no longer apply.

Matthew now adds another saying about John the Baptist and the kingdom (11:12–13) to which there is a shorter, and in many ways different, parallel saying in Luke 16:16. In Luke it runs: "The law and the prophets were until John; since then the good news of the kingdom of God is preached, and every one enters it violently." In Matthew it reads: "From the days of John the Baptist until now the kingdom of heaven has suffered violence, and men of violence take it by force. For all the prophets and the law prophesied until John." Because of uncertainties about the exact wording of this saying in Q, its interpretation is even more difficult than that of the preceding saying. Again, the kingdom constitutes a completely new beginning. John the Baptist's preaching marks the dividing line between the old dispensation (characterized by "the law and the prophets") and the new one. From Jesus onward the good news of the kingdom is preached *(euaggelizetai)*. Luke, who uses this phrase, may take the following Greek word *(biazetai)* as meaning "is forced into it, is urgently invited to take part." In Matthew, however, the verb most likely refers to violence done to the kingdom. John's fate and that of Jesus, as well as the messengers after Jesus, illustrate that their contemporaries in Israel did not and do not listen, but want to have their share in God's kingdom in their own way. This obscure saying may refer to persecution, and even to all sorts of activities of zealous Israelites in the difficult years before the capture of Jerusalem.[3] In any case it stresses that God's kingdom has begun with Jesus.[3]

The following Q section, Luke 7:31–35 (par. Matt. 11:16–19) uses a parable to emphasize that both John and Jesus were rejected by their contemporaries. The latter are qualified by the words "the men of this generation"—an expression often used in Q (see, e.g., 11:29–32, 50–51), always in connection with a negative response. The people of this generation rejected John because he abstained from bread and wine; they rejected Jesus, called "Son of man" in this saying, because he came eating and drinking even with tax collectors and sinners (cf. Mark 2:14–17). Jesus' table fellowship with outcasts clearly annoyed many people. This short pericope ends with the words: "Yet wisdom is justified by all her children" (thus Luke; Matthew: "by her deeds").[4] Very probably the meaning of this saying is that both John and Jesus are seen as representatives of God's Wisdom on earth; both share in the fate of the messengers sent out into the world by Wisdom (cf. Luke 11:49–51). Those who accept the message are "children of Wisdom" (cf. Prov. 8:32; Wisd. of Sol. 7:27; Sir. 4:11) and, as such, compare favorably with "the people of this generation."[5] We shall return to the Wisdom concept presently.

This group of sayings shows that for Q as for Mark (and compare Acts 10:37), John and Jesus are closely connected. Although John is clearly described as Jesus' forerunner, and the new dispensation in God's dealings with Israel and the world only begins with Jesus, there is no indication that John is expressly relegated to an inferior position. John was important for those who composed the Q collection, and there was no need to put groups of disciples of John (Luke 7:18) right concerning the true status of their master.

Jesus and the Kingdom

We continue now with a short survey of Q texts about the kingdom of God. We have already mentioned the first beatitude in Luke 6:20, as well as Luke 7:28 plus 16:16 in connection with John the Baptist. There is a certain emphasis on the presence of the kingdom: "But if it is by the finger of God that I cast out demons, then the kingdom of God has come upon you" (Luke 11:20; par. Matt. 12:28).[6] This saying is found in the Q version of the Beelzebul pericope (compare Mark 3:22–27); here also the victory of God's reign over that of Satan is emphasized. The kingdom is preached by the disciples sent out by Jesus, and as they heal people they are told to say, "The kingdom of God has come near to you" (Luke 10:9; cf. Matt. 10:7–8).[7]

At the same time the kingdom has yet to become full reality. In Luke 6:20–24 "yours is the kingdom of God" is followed by "you *shall* be satisfied" and "you *shall* laugh." The disciples are told not to be anxious about their lives (Luke 12:22–32; see also 33–34; cf. Matt. 6:25–34). They are urged to seek God's kingdom now; then the things necessary for life will be theirs as well. Luke says explicitly: "Fear not, little flock, for it is your Father's good pleasure to give you the kingdom" (Luke 12:32). The kingdom is a dynamic, growing entity. After the parable of the mustard seed, which stresses the tremendous growth of a tiny seed into a huge plant (Mark 4:30–32 par.), Luke 13:20–21 (par. Matt. 13:33) adds the parable of the leaven. The kingdom of God is like "leaven which a woman took and hid in three measures of flour, till it was all leavened."

Jesus taught his disciples to pray "Thy kingdom come" (see the Lord's Prayer in Luke 11:2–4; par. Matt. 6:9–13). In Luke 13:28–29 (par. Matt. 8:11–12), the kingdom of God is pictured as an eschatological banquet; Abraham, Isaac, and Jacob (and all the prophets, according to Luke) will be present; many will come from the four winds and will be admitted. Some of Jesus' contemporaries, who expect to be present at this occasion, will not be allowed to attend (see the context in Luke 13:22–30; Matthew puts the saying in the context of the Q story of the non-Israelite centurion of Capernaum— see Matt. 8:5–13 (par. Luke 7:1–10). We may compare here the parable of the great feast, which we have in two different versions (Luke 14:16–24 and Matt. 22:1–10), both introduced by a reference to the kingdom of God (Luke 14:15; cf. Matt. 22:2). There is also Jesus' promise to the disciples in Luke 22:28–30: those who have stayed with him in his trials will eat and drink at his table in his kingdom, and will sit on thrones to rule over the twelve tribes of Israel (cf. Matt. 19:28).

To sum up: God's kingdom is present in Jesus' preaching and in his actions. Those who meet Jesus, or meet his disciples sent out to heal and to preach, are confronted with a choice. If they believe and accept what is offered to them, they may share in the dynamic reality of the kingdom, until the supreme moment at which it encompasses the entire creation. If they do not pay heed to the message and the claim inherent in it, they will be excluded forever. Jesus' mission is an integral part of the realization of the kingdom. Yet this claim is not expressed or explained by any explicit Christological statement.

Jesus as Son of Man

We may now turn to those statements in Q in which we find "Son of man" as the self-designation of Jesus. We have already dealt with Luke 7:34 (par. Matt. 11:19), which clearly refers to the earthly Jesus. The same applies to the saying in Luke 9:58 (par. Matt. 8:20) about the Son of man who has nowhere to lay his head (and expects his followers to give up family life too). In Luke 11:30 (Matt. 12:40 is different), the Son of man, Jesus, is compared to Jonah. The people of this generation seek a sign but will receive no other sign than the Son of man. They compare unfavorably with the men of Nineveh, who accepted Jonah's prophetic message. Luke 11:32 says explicitly: "The men of Nineveh will arise at the [final] judgment with this generation and condemn it; for they repented at the preaching of Jonah, and behold, something greater than Jonah is here" (par. Matt. 12:41).

In these three passages the Son of man is sent by God with authority and expects people to give heed to his message. Some people give up everything and follow him; "this generation" rejects him. His public appearance is, however, to some extent also incognito. According to the difficult saying Luke 12:10 (par. Matt. 12:32) a word

against the Son of man will be forgiven, whereas he who blasphemes
against the Holy Spirit will not be forgiven. Significantly, however,
Luke connects this saying with 12:8–9: "And I tell you, every one
who acknowledges me before men, the Son of man also will acknowledge before the angels of God; but he who denies me before men will
be denied before the angels of God." People acknowledge Jesus or
deny him; their decision determines their future destiny. The title
"Son of man" is here clearly connected with the future judgment; yet
it is also clear that the future Son of man is the "I" who is speaking
(the parallel in Matt. 10:32–33 uses the first person singular throughout).

The future Son of man is also found in Luke 12:40 (par. Matt.
24:44), where the disciples are told to be ready: the Son of man will
be coming at an hour they do not expect. Luke (17:22, 24, 26, 30)
speaks about the sudden arrival/revelation of the Son of man on his
day (in his days). Matthew, in 24:27, 37, 39, speaks consistently of
the *"parousia* of the Son of man" (cf. also Matt. 10:23 and 19:28).
The context of these sayings is one of threatening catastrophe: the
situation of the people before the arrival of the Son of man is compared with that of the people before the Flood, and, only in Luke,
with that in the days just before Lot left Sodom.

The activity of the Son of man in the catastrophic events at hand
is not specified. It is clear that Jesus' disciples are to remain watchful
and prepared for the sudden arrival of the Son of man; they should
not be like the indifferent "people of this generation," who continue
their human pursuits without realizing what lies ahead.

Q's picture of the future Son of man is not directly connected
with Dan. 7:13, as is that in Mark 13:26; 14:62. Further, it is the
evangelist who, after "so will the Son of man be in his day," adds
in Luke 17:25: "But first he must suffer many things and be rejected by this generation." This verse is obviously modeled after
the passion predictions in Mark, which are taken over, with
changes, by Matthew (16:21–23; 17:22–23; 20:18–19) and Luke
(9:22; 9:44; 18:31–33; cf. 24:6–7). In the Q collection itself we find
no reference to the suffering, death, and resurrection of the Son of
man. Q does stress, however, that the earthly Son of man is not
accepted by the people of this generation (Luke 7:34; 11:29–32).
On the day of the Son of man it will become clear that they are
doomed. Those who acknowledge Jesus (Luke 12:8–9) and follow
the Son of man (Luke 9:57–62) will have to give up everything and
face persecution (Luke 6:22, "Blessed are you when men hate you,
and when they exclude you and revile you, and cast out your name
as evil, on account of the Son of man!").[8] But they will be vindicated at the end, when the Son of man acknowledges them before

the angels of God (Luke 12:8). When the Son of man will sit on his glorious throne, those who have followed Jesus will also sit on twelve thrones, judging the twelve tribes of Israel (Matt. 19:28, the Matthean version of Luke 22:30 that connects the sitting on the thrones with participating in the eschatological banquet).

Jesus as the Envoy of Wisdom and as Son of God

The group of sayings on John the Baptist and Jesus, discussed above, ends with the saying "Yet wisdom is justified by all her children" (Luke 7:35). In the context provided by Q the most likely interpretation is that John and Jesus are envoys of God's Wisdom on earth. In the short discussion devoted to Luke 7:35 we mentioned Luke 11:49–51 (par. Matt. 23:34–36), a difficult passage that requires further attention. This saying belongs to a group—including Luke 6:22–23 (par. Matt. 5:11–12); Luke 11:47–48 (par. Matt. 23:29–32); and Luke 13:34–35 (par. Matt. 23:37–39)—that emphasizes the rejection of Jesus and his followers by Israel. It views this rejection in the light of Israel's negative response to God's messengers in the past (see also 1 Thess. 2:14–16 and the discussion on these verses in chapter 1). The passage that concerns us here belongs to a group of sayings that severely criticize the Pharisees and the lawyers as representative leaders of Israel. Likewise, Luke 13:34–45 (par. Matt. 23:37–39) is addressed to "Jerusalem," characterized as "killing the prophets and stoning those who are sent to you." The rejection and persecution of Jesus and his followers is typical of what the leaders of Israel have always done. "This generation" (Luke 11:50; Matt. 23:36) will have to pay the price for all these crimes. "Fill up, then, the measure of your fathers," Jesus exclaims in the Matthean addition to Q in 23:32 (but see also 1 Thess. 2:16).

The saying in Luke 11:49 is introduced with the words "Therefore also the Wisdom of God said"; in Matt. 23:34–36 the saying is by Jesus himself. Wisdom declares that she " 'will send them prophets and apostles, some of whom they will kill and persecute,' that the blood of all the prophets, shed from the foundation of the world, may be required of this generation." In the Lukan version all prophets and envoys are meant; already in Q John, Jesus, and the Christian messengers were included. The personified Wisdom of God calls people to share in her blessings, but they refuse. She sends out her envoys, but they are rejected (cf., e.g., Prov. 1:20–33; 8:1–21, 32–36; 9:1–6; Sir. 24:19–22, 30–34; Baruch 3:9–4:4; *1 Enoch* 42). Matthew, who restricts the envoys to the "prophets and wise men and scribes" sent out by Jesus, and who speaks of the treatment they will receive from their fellow Jews, clearly narrows the scope of the saying. We should note that in the order of Luke, which is very likely also the order of Q, the saying follows rather closely after the pericope about "the sign of Jonah" and the rejection of the Son of man (Luke 11:29–32),[9] and is followed by a saying in 11:52 that reproaches the lawyers for having taken away "the key of knowledge."

In Luke 13:34–35 (par. Matt. 23:37–39) Jesus speaks of himself in the future in words derived from Ps. 118:26: "Blessed is he who comes in the name of the Lord!" The reference in Q is clearly to his coming as judge at his *parousia.* Jerusalem will not see this messenger from God until he returns in a different role, and until it is definitely too late to make amends (cf. Luke 13:25–27 = Q). Jesus' mission to a Jerusalem that kills the prophets, and stones those who are sent to her, is expressed in loving terms: "How often would I have gathered your children together as a hen gathers her brood under her wings, and you would not!" (Luke 13:34). This terminology may be inspired by the tradition of Wisdom, who continually calls people to share in her blessings and wants her children to remain near her (Prov. 8:32–35; contrast v. 36; Sir. 4:11–19).[10] There is no indication, however, that Jesus is portrayed here as more than a bearer of God's Wisdom.

At the same time, Jesus and the messengers who go out in his name are definitely the last ones in a long series. God's efforts to bring Israel back on the path of righteousness, through Wisdom and otherwise, have reached a climax, and therefore the rejection of Jesus by the leaders of Israel is an extremely serious affair. God's final judgment and condemnation of the sinners is at hand.

The next pericope to be discussed, Luke 10:21–22 (par. Matt. 11:25–27), is also directed against the leaders and teachers in Israel and their earthly wisdom. Jesus thanks his Father that in his good pleasure he has hidden "these things" from the wise and understanding and revealed them to little children. "God addresses himself to the poor and simple who are prepared to listen to him because they have no wisdom of their own," says I. H. Marshall,[11] who points to Sir. 3:19 and Wisd. of Sol. 10:21, among other texts. Baruch 3:9–4:4 stresses that many people who might be expected to know Wisdom have not found her. In Dan. 2:20–23, Daniel, the truly wise man who knows what remains hidden from the wise men among the Chaldeans, thanks God for his revelation: "He gives wisdom to the wise and knowledge to those who have understanding; he reveals deep and mysterious things." In our passage, however, those who are supposed to know the God of Israel on the basis of their study of the scriptures are classified among those who are wise only according to human standards. The same line of thought is taken up by Paul, when he speaks of the folly of the message of the cross, which is not understood by the wise of the earth, Jews and Greeks alike (1 Cor. 1:18–31).

God's revelation takes place in and through Jesus, who as Son stands in a unique relation to the Father. "All things have been delivered to me by my Father; and no one knows who the Son is except the Father, or who the Father is except the Son and any one to whom the Son chooses to reveal him" (Luke 10:22). The Son chooses to reveal the Father to his disciples. They are the ones who, in the Q saying that follows in Luke 10:23–24, are blessed: "Blessed are the eyes which see what you see!" The disciples are allowed to see and to hear what many prophets and kings (Matt. 13:17, "righteous ones") longed to see and hear.

In Wisd. of Sol. 2:13 and 16–18 the truly righteous man is called a son of God; he may call God his father. When he is vindicated by God after having been condemned to a shameful death by his adversaries, the latter see him "among the sons of God" (5:5—see also p. 62). In Wisdom passages the close connection between Wisdom and God is repeatedly stressed (Job 28:12–28; Prov. 8:22–31; Sir. 1:1–10; Baruch 3:29–38 [3:29–4:1aE]; Wisd. of Sol. 8:3–4; 9:9). For Q, Jesus is more than a wise and righteous man par excellence or the ideal representative of Wisdom. His unique and exclusive relationship with God as a son with his father is without precedent; it surpasses human imagination and imagery. It is this relationship that is in view; this passage does not aim at introducing a specific Christological title, "Son of God," nor does it make the title the object of special revelation.

This leads us to a few short remarks on the temptation story found in Luke 4:1–13 (par. Matt. 4:1–11). Both Luke and Matthew go beyond the short notice in Mark 1:12–13 and give a story of three (though not in the same order) attempts of Satan to seduce Jesus. As in Mark, the purpose of this longer version of the temptation story, which is derived from a common source, very probably Q,[12] is to assure the hearers/readers that Jesus once and for all proved his superiority over the devil. Strikingly, the devil addresses Jesus twice as "Son of God." The reference, in both Matthew and Luke, is to the story of Jesus' baptism. Their version of the baptism story is so close to that of Mark, however, that it is impossible to tell what Q had on this point. And when we look at the temptation story itself we notice that Jesus' absolute obedience to God is stressed. The only words he speaks in reply to the devil's temptations are words from the scriptures, in fact from Deut. 8:3; 6:13; and 6:16. Whereas Israel was disobedient and put its Lord to the test, the Son of God refuses to use the power and authority given to him by the Father for any other purpose than that for which he was sent. If the designation

"Son of God" was stressed at all in Q, it may have been inspired by the use of this term for Israel (and "children of God" for the Israelites) in the Old Testament (see, e.g., Deut. 32:5–6 and 18–19).[13]

Jesus, His Disciples, and Israel

Many sayings in Q are concerned with the consequences of following Jesus. In Luke 9:57–62 Jesus' followers are told to be prepared to leave their homes and families and join the company of the Son of man, who has nowhere to lay down his head. The proclamation of the kingdom of God must have absolute priority over family obligations (cf. also Luke 14:26–27 [par. Matt. 10:37–38], which adds: "whoever does not bear his own cross and come after me, cannot be my disciple"). On the other hand, those who seek the kingdom before all else will find that God takes care of them in all worldly matters (Luke 12:22–32; par. Matt. 6:25–34).

Luke 10:1–12[14] tells how Jesus sends out his disciples as laborers into a plentiful harvest. Yet they go as lambs in the midst of wolves. They should carry no purse, no bag, no sandals; they will have to accept the food, drink, and lodging offered them. If a town receives them, they are to heal the sick and to declare: "The kingdom of God has come near to you" (10:9). If they are not received, they must sever all ties. It should be clear to everyone that "He who hears you hears me, and he who rejects you rejects me, and he who rejects me rejects him who sent me" (Luke 10:16; par. Matt. 10:40).

As representatives of Jesus the disciples must reckon seriously with rejection and persecution. They will often meet with a negative response. Between their sending, in Luke 10:1–12, and their return, in 10:17, we find the woes against Chorazin and Capernaum. If the mighty works done in those towns had been performed in Gentile Tyre and Sidon, these cities would have repented! In the final judgment it will be more tolerable for Tyre and Sidon than for these towns in Galilee (Luke 10:13–15; par. Matt. 11:20–24). There is an unmistakable link between these words, the passage on the sign of Jonah in Luke 11:29–32, and the woes against the Pharisees and lawyers in 11:37–54 (discussed above).

Q contains many hortatory sayings relevant in many situations; for example, Luke 6:20–7:1, the so-called "Sermon on the Plain" (the nearly all-Q counterpart of Matthew's Sermon on the Mount), and Luke 11:1–13 on praying. But passages that comfort, encourage, and admonish Jesus' disciples, who have to stand firm in situations of stress and temptation, seem to predominate, together with sayings that announce the coming judgment and the full realization of God's sovereign rule.[15]

Q's Christology in Its Context

The sayings in Q were collected and handed down by people who saw their lives and mission in direct continuity with Jesus' ministry. They regarded themselves as his disciples. They felt called to preach the good news of the kingdom and to perform the "mighty deeds" accompanying it. They were prepared to suffer and even to undergo martyrdom. Some people may have had to accept the consequences held out to them in Luke 9:57–62. Some were itinerant preachers after the fashion of Luke 10:1–12. Many of these disciples had experienced rejection and unbelief but were firmly convinced that they were sustained by God's fatherly care and would be vindicated on the day of the Son of man. The important thing now was to give heed to his admonitions and to persist in faith, love, and hope.

There is a clear correlation between the picture of Jesus and the picture of his disciples. Yet Jesus is distinctly different from God's messengers before him, John the Baptist included; in his words and work the kingdom of God has come. Those who come after him are in fact sent out by him to preach his message of the kingdom, and to heal and exorcize as he did. The words of the earthly Jesus are handed down as authoritative for his disciples as well as for those whom his disciples approach with the good news. They are authoritative because in the experience of these disciples they are relevant and effective.

Polag is right when he states that Q's Christology is implicit rather than explicit. The designation "Son of man" implies authority in the present, and certainly later, at the *parousia.* But it retains an aspect of incognito. The designation "Son" / "Son of God" is undoubtedly not used as a title, but as a means of expressing Jesus' unique relation to his Father and his complete obedience to God. All along Jesus is portrayed as a unique envoy of God who has inaugurated a new era in God's relation with Israel and the world. His appeal, his promise, and his claim on people, as well as their response to him, continue to be of crucial importance. Once this is accepted an implicit Christology suffices.

It is extremely unlikely, however, that the communities in which the sayings of the Q collection were handed down knew no other traditions about Jesus' life, death, and resurrection/exaltation. Q's implicit Christology cannot have represented the whole understanding of Jesus in any Christian congregation.[16] For one thing, one could not speak of Jesus' rejection by Israel's leaders without telling what happened afterward. One had to explain why the kingdom of God was a present dynamic reality and not an illusion of people who did not want to admit that their master had deluded both them and himself. Those who handed down the Q material believed in a God who had vindicated Jesus, his work and his message, and they believed that he would come again to share with them the full bliss of the kingdom of God. Thus the words with which G. N. Stanton concludes his article "On the Christology of Q" are appropriate:

> In view of the fact that both Matthew and Luke (and presumably also their communities) had access to two different and originally separate kinds of material about Jesus (Q and Mark), is it not at least possible that the Q community also had two different kinds of material? If so, we might envisage traditions which set out the teaching of Jesus, but underlined the grounds of his authoritative words and actions, being used in instruction of those within the community and also in an evangelistic context. And, alongside Q, traditions which told the story of the ultimate rejection of Jesus by men, but proclaimed his vindication by God—such traditions being used primarily in the worship of the community.[17]

It is significant that the Q traditions were preserved for us only in the books of Matthew and Luke, which are modeled on the pattern of the Gospel of Mark. As time went on, the originally separate Q collection could only survive after having been incorporated into a more complete presentation of Jesus' ministry, death, vindication, and *parousia*.

There is a marked contrast here with the Gospel of Thomas, a collection of 114 sayings of Jesus discovered as part of the Nag Hammadi library. It must have been composed prior to A.D. 200 and is often dated around A.D. 140. Its history is disputed; the collection probably went through various editorial stages where different theological perspectives were incorporated.[18] In its present form it is still a collection of sayings not unlike Q, often introduced only by "Jesus said." It does not contain any narrative about the ministry or the passion of Jesus. Its opening words and the first sayings indicate the purpose of the collection: to provide esoteric teaching of Jesus leading to true knowledge and immortality: "These are the secret sayings which the living Jesus spoke and which Didymus Judas Thomas wrote down. (1) And he said: 'Whoever finds the interpretation of these sayings will not experience death.' "[19] Here the tradition of sayings detached from Jesus' concrete ministry and death has led to a view on humanity, God, and Jesus which differs completely from that preserved in Q through Matthew and Luke, and in Mark.

Q and Mark

Apart from material on the events leading up to Jesus' crucifixion and resurrection, brought together in chapters 11–16, Mark used existing traditions on Jesus' ministry in Galilee that can now be found in 1:16–8:26 and in chapters 9 and 10 of his Gospel. We do not know whether Mark used all the material he found, or whether he selected what suited his purpose. When we compare what he incorporated with the collection of Q as it can be reconstructed from Matthew and Luke, we note that he has more miracle stories (in Q only Luke 7:1–10 [par. Matt. 8:5–10, 13]; cf. Luke 11:14 [par. Matt. 12:22]). He has many pronouncement stories, both in debates with opponents and in discussions with disciples, and relatively few groups of individual sayings. There are instances where Mark and Q have preserved the same traditions, as any Synopsis of the Gospels will show. Although influence from Q on Mark cannot be excluded, we may, on the whole, assume that in these cases traditional material has come down to us through two independent channels.

Although it is often a complicated task to reconstruct the exact wording of sayings and stories in Q, the fact that we possess a Matthean and a Lukan version enables us to distinguish between the redactions and the material that was redacted. In the case of Mark it is much more difficult to distinguish between Markan redaction and the source material before it was incorporated into Mark. Comparison between Mark and Q, however, makes it possible to draw some conclusions about the pre-Markan stage of the material on Jesus' ministry found in Mark. It is likely that it was collected and handed down for the same reasons as was the Q material. Both collections aim at encouraging and admonishing disciples, and both presuppose the activity of itinerant preachers; both collections record controversies with the Jewish leaders and alienation of Jesus and his followers from their families and friends. The pre-Markan collection, too, may have been marked by an implicit rather than an explicit Christology: Jesus was the man who spoke and acted with direct authority. His words remain authoritative, and his message is to be proclaimed by his followers, who may heal and exorcize in his name.

A closer comparison, taking into account the margin of uncertainty existing with regard to both the pre-Markan and the Q material, would be interesting. We restrict ourselves to a brief review of the corresponding views of Jesus in Q and Mark. There is, first, an emphasis on the close relation between John the Baptist and Jesus, both in the introductory passages to Mark and Q and later. In Mark, the passages on John are found in different places. He is portrayed as an eschatological prophet (6:14–16; 9:11–13) sent by God (1:2–8; 11:27–33), and he is identified with Elijah, who had to come first to restore all things (9:11–13). Jesus is the one who preaches the good news of the kingdom and inaugurates it (1:14–16); he is the Christ (8:29), the Son of God (12:1–9). Q, as we have seen, devoted a whole section to John and Jesus in Luke 7:18–35 (par. Matt. 11:2–19). Here John is more than a prophet, but there is no explicit identification with Elijah. Jesus is, again, the one who preaches and inaugurates the kingdom (see especially Luke 7:18–23). Q does not seem to need a Christological title in this context to explain why Jesus is greater than John. Mark and Q agree in stressing that both John and Jesus are rejected. Q ranges both of them in a succession of divine messengers (see Luke 7:35 and the Wisdom texts discussed above). Mark states specifically that John was arrested ("delivered up," 1:14) and put to death like Jesus (6:16–29).

On the basis of this comparison, we may conclude that Mark was in line with a broader pre-Markan tradition, also extant in Q, when he connected John and Jesus and characterized Jesus as the one who preached the good news of God and inaugurated the kingdom of God. We argued that this same tradition may be supposed in Acts 10:34–43 (see p. 57). At a very early time Jesus' teaching, preaching, healing, and exorcizing must have been understood in terms of the announcement of the good news of the kingdom and the inauguration of it in his words and works.

Another interesting feature is that both Mark and Q use the term "Son of man," strange to Greek ears, as a self-designation of Jesus for his earthly activity and for his decisive intervention in the future. In Q, as in Mark, the term is not used as a title by Jesus' disciples or adversaries. In Mark we find the traditional use of this designation in connection with Jesus' death and resurrection (8:31; 9:31; 10:33; 9:9–12) or his death alone (14:21, 41). This is clearly due to the incorporation of the material on Jesus' ministry into a fuller story, in which the death of Jesus and the events leading up to it played an important part. But then the use of the term in Mark 2:12, 28 for Jesus as a person with authority on earth, and in 8:38; 13:26; 14:62 for his future coming in glory, goes back to earlier conceptions also preserved in Q. In Mark there is a link between the Son of man and the future kingdom of God (in 8:38 and 14:62) that is not made explicit in Q. Nor is there in Q a clear link with Dan. 7:13–14.

It is difficult to say anything with certainty about the use of the expressions "the Son" and "Son of God" in Mark in comparison with the important function of the terms in Q. In Mark 1:14; 9:7; 13:32 ("the Son"); and 12:6 (in the context of a parable), a unique relationship between the Son and the Father, including trust and obedience, is indicated. In 9:7 ("listen to him") and 12:6 the importance of the Son's mission and message are emphasized. In these respects Mark agrees with Q. The exclamations of the evil spirits in 3:11 and 5:7, however, do not seem to fit into the picture, and in 14:61–62 (in connection with 12:35–37), royal connotations of the term "Son of God" seem to play a role. We shall have to come back to this in our discussion of the term "Son of God" in chapter 10.

Q, Mark, and Paul

Looking back at the traditional material found in the letters of Paul, we are again struck by the scarcity of references to the earthly life and teaching of Jesus. This material is predominantly concerned with his death, resurrection, and *parousia,* as well as with his being sent by God. In 1 Cor. 11:23–26 his betrayal is mentioned briefly in connection with the last meal with his disciples. In 1 Thess. 2:14–16 Paul mentions the killing of Jesus in the context of an ancient tradition of Israel's persecution of messengers of God, which we have also found in Q and Mark. And as to his teaching, we already noted that Paul knew a collection of "words of the Lord" on which he draws occasionally.

As to common elements in Q and Mark, we should add that the terms *euaggelion* and *euaggelizesthai* are very important in Paul's letters. In Rom. 10:15 the apostle uses Isa. 52:7 (cf. Nahum 2:1 [1:15E]), "How beautiful are the feet of those who preach good news!" (changing Isaiah's singular to the plural) to characterize Christian preachers. Their message was about Jesus Christ, but clearly Paul wants to indicate that their mission corresponds with Jesus Christ's own mission and continues it. And although the term "kingdom of God" is not frequent in Paul's letters, he does use it. In particular, in 1 Cor. 6:9–10; 15:50; and Gal. 5:21 he speaks of inheriting, or failing to inherit, the kingdom, and in 1 Cor. 4:20 he emphasizes the dynamic character of the kingdom.

A careful scrutiny of Paul's letters has brought to light a number of further allusions to words of Jesus, e.g., in Rom. 12:14, 17; 13:7; 14:3, 4; 1 Thess. 5:2, 4, 15; 1 Cor. 13:2.[20] There are relatively many allusions to Luke 6:27–38 and Mark 9:33–50. In 1 Cor. 9 we find several references to the missionary discourse material in Mark 6:6b–13; Matt. 10:1–6; Luke 9:1–6. This suggests that Paul may have been acquainted with (at least) blocks of words of Jesus to which he occasionally referred implicitly. There is no reason to assume that his knowledge was limited to what we are now able to trace. Paul's letters are writings addressed to particular groups of Christians on particular occasions. In his correspondence Paul used the Jesus tradition where necessary; there was no reason why he should transmit that tradition or representative samples of it more or less systematically in the context of his letters.[21]

It may seem that Paul, who so often emphasizes the crucial importance of Jesus' death and resurrection, is not interested in more than the fact of Jesus' death. But, apart from 1 Cor. 11: 23–26 and 1 Thess. 2:14–16, just mentioned, could Paul really speak about Jesus' death "for us" and use it in a hortatory context (Rom. 15:9; 1 Cor. 8:11; 2 Cor. 5:15) without having any further knowledge of the one who gave his life? In Gal. 2:20 he speaks about the Son of God "who loved me and gave himself for me." In 2 Cor. 10:1 he mentions "the meekness and gentleness of Christ." In Rom. 15:3, again in a hortatory context, he reminds his readers that "Christ did not please himself"; in Rom. 15:8 he calls him "a servant to the circumcised." In 2 Cor. 8:9 Paul describes Jesus: "though he was rich, yet for your sake he became poor, so that by his poverty you might become rich." He speaks about the preexistent Lord, but cannot possibly have bypassed his earthly ministry; he appeals to Jesus Christ's attitude as he encourages the Corinthians to contribute liberally to the collection for Jerusalem. In Phil. 2:6–11 Paul uses the humiliation-exaltation motif in a clearly hortatory context. Of course he includes Jesus' preexistence, incarnation, and final glorification; but his admonitions would be unconvincing if he did not also refer to the readiness of the earthly Jesus to give up everything.

We must conclude, then, that Paul did know Jesus' teaching and was acquainted with traditions about his ministry. The differences between Paul, Mark, and Q in their transmission of early traditions about Jesus' life and teaching are to be explained by the differences in the situations for which they wrote, by their selecting relevant material, and by the differences in literary genres they chose to convey their message.

PART II
Continued Response to Jesus

The preceding three chapters were devoted to a search for the earliest Christian response to Jesus. We studied the earliest written documents and tried to locate early Christological material, looking for clear indications in the text and for possibilities of comparison with other texts.

But may there not be more evidence? After all, the gospel had to be preached to outsiders all the time, new aspirant members wanted instruction, baptism was administered and the Lord's Supper was regularly celebrated, controversies necessitated defense against attacks from opponents. For all these (and numerous other) situations one had to draw on what was handed down in oral tradition and written documents.

We have noticed a great variety in the wording of the traditional expressions used by Paul and others, and also a great diversity of statements, patterns, and concepts. Both the variety and the diversity have to be explained as the outcome of a process of living tradition in which continuity and continual change presuppose one another. The very fact that the traditional material proved authoritative and relevant also in later, different situations led to its transmission, sometimes with adaptations, in later writings. We noticed, when we were looking into formulas used by Paul, that they are also found in other letters of the New Testament, in and outside the Pauline tradition. Q did not survive independently, but was incorporated into the later Gospels of Matthew and Luke, which also used the Gospel of Mark extensively (including thereby a number of pre-Markan Christological concepts).

It is evident that the nature of the early Christian writings calls for a description of Christology in terms of continuation and development. We have been able to discern with some degree of certainty statements, patterns, and concepts belonging to the earliest stages of Christological thinking. We shall now attempt to trace how they continued to be used and were developed or combined with other concepts, old and new. We shall also have to see whether the use of certain terms and patterns of thought was discontinued, and whether new responses to Jesus gave rise to different approaches.

We will only be able to sketch the main features of a very complex process of transmission in continually changing circumstances, a process that is only partly reflected in the written documents at our disposal. But if we proceed with due caution an interesting picture emerges.

In the following chapters the main characteristics of the Christology of the writings preserved in the New Testament will be sketched, with special attention to the old as well as the possibly new elements in it. We shall take up the documents in the following order:

First, Matthew and Luke-Acts will be analyzed with special emphasis on what they did with the views on Jesus which they found in Mark and Q. After determining typically Lukan Christological traits we will be able to make some remarks on possible pre-Lukan elements in the Acts of the Apostles, which, after all, purport to give a picture of the life and teachings of early Christianity.

Next, we will turn again to the letters of Paul in order to analyze especially Paul's own contribution to Christology. A chapter on Paul's "school" and the letters of which Pauline authorship is disputed follows. Discussions of the epistle to the Hebrews, 1 Peter, and Revelation are given in the next chapter. Finally, we shall have to pay attention to the Gospel and the epistles of John as documents stemming from a particular group of communities with great concern for, and much strife about, the right Christology in changing circumstances.

A few writings not yet mentioned will be treated in appendices (James in the chapter on Matthew and Jude, and 2 Peter after the section on 1 Peter). On the whole the various sections will have to be brief and restricted to what is prominent, and to what is essential for a better understanding of the complex process of continuation and development in early Christology.

4
The Christology
of Matthew

Jesus as the Unique Teacher

Almost half of the Gospel of Matthew has a parallel in Mark, and a little over a quarter has a parallel in Luke (and may, therefore, with some degree of certainty be assigned to Q). The rest consists of verses peculiar to Matthew; part of this material may be older than Matthew, but we cannot be sure.

On the whole, Matthew follows the story found in Mark, but he tends to bring the material pertaining to Jesus' teaching together into blocks. Of particular importance are the Sermon on the Mount in Matt. 5–7, the commissioning of the disciples in chapter 10, the collection of parables in chapter 13, the regulations for life in the Christian community in chapter 18, the woes to the scribes and Pharisees in chapter 23 just before the apocalyptic discourse (24:1–44), and a group of parables about the *parousia* and a description of the final judgment (24:45–25:44) just after it.

For Matthew, Jesus is first of all the supreme teacher, who addressed the crowds and his disciples on a mountain, like Moses (Matt. 5:1), and taught them with an authority surpassing that of the scribes (7:28–29, taking up Mark 1:22). He did not come to abolish the law and the prophets, but to fulfill them (5:17–20); he asks his disciples to do and to teach all commandments, in accordance with his interpretation of them (5:21–48). True righteousness exceeds that of the scribes and the Pharisees (5:20). Children of God must be perfect ("whole," "single-minded") as their heavenly Father is perfect (5:48).

Jesus came to establish a new community of people completely committed to doing the will of God. People are called upon to seek first God's kingdom and *his righteousness* (Matt. 6:33). Jesus proclaims, "Blessed are those who hunger and thirst for righteousness" (5:6), and he warns, "Not every one who says to me, 'Lord, Lord,' shall enter the kingdom of heaven, but he who does the will of my Father who is in heaven" (7:21).

Jesus' ministry in the name of God is portrayed as the fulfillment of prophecies and other statements in the scriptures. Matthew's Gospel abounds with quotations from the Old Testament, many of them introduced with a special quotation formula which runs (with variations): "This was to fulfil what was spoken by the prophet ..." (see 1:22; 2:5, 15, 17, 23; 4:14; 8:17; 12:17; 13:35; 21:4; 27:9–10). Matthew and his readers clearly belonged to a community of believers who, meditating on Jesus' life and ministry, tried to interpret it in the light of relevant passages from the scriptures. Only Matthew has the saying of Jesus, "Therefore every scribe who has been trained for [or: has become a disciple of, TEV] the kingdom of heaven is like a householder who brings out of his treasure what is new and what is old" (13:52).

Matthew wrote in the time after the destruction of Jerusalem (22:7). He is aware of the rejection of Jesus' message by the leaders of Israel, and he tends to underscore this fact (ch. 23; 27:25; cf. 28:11–15). He preserves a number of statements which restrict Jesus' missionary activity and that of his disciples to Israel (15:24; 10:5–6, 23), but at the same time he speaks of "their scribes," "their (your) synagogues" (4:23; 7:29; 9:35; 10:17; 12:9; 13:54; 23:34). At the time of the writing of this Gospel the Christian community which Matthew had in view had become separated from Israel. The evangelist concludes his version of the parable of the wicked husbandmen with a solemn declaration by Jesus: "Therefore I tell you, the kingdom of God will be taken away from you and given to a nation producing the fruits of it" (21:43).

In two evidently redactional passages Jesus' ministry is characterized as "teaching in their synagogues and preaching the gospel of the kingdom and healing every disease and every infirmity" (Matt. 4:23; 9:35). Here, and in 4:17 ("From that time Jesus began to preach, saying, 'Repent, for the kingdom of heaven is at hand' "), Matthew follows Mark; but the terms "kingdom of heaven" and "gospel of the kingdom" are his.[1] The third time he speaks about "the gospel of the kingdom," he emphasizes that in the time between Jesus' resurrection and his *parousia* it "will be preached throughout the whole world, as a testimony to all nations" (24:14; cf. 26:13).

Jesus' preaching and teaching are continued in the message and instruction of his disciples worldwide. The Gospel of Matthew ends with an encounter between Jesus and the remaining eleven disciples in Galilee, significantly again on a mountain (28:16–20). Jesus' resurrection has made evident what his disciples were allowed to understand and confess all along (cf., e.g., 13:10–17; 14:22–33; 16:13–19, especially vs. 17–19), however imperfectly: "All authority in heaven and on earth has been given to me. Go therefore and make disciples of all nations, baptizing them in the name of the Father and of the Son and of the Holy Spirit, teaching them to observe all that I have commanded you; and lo, I am with you always, to the close of the age."

The emphasis is obviously on Jesus' authority, in his union with the Father and with the Holy Spirit, after as well as before his resurrection. The disciples of the resurrected Jesus are sent on a worldwide mission, making new disciples, teaching them to observe all that Jesus has commanded them. The teaching of the earthly Jesus (incorporated in Matthew's book) remains, therefore, of utmost importance to those living in the period between Jesus' death and resurrection, on the one hand, and his *parousia* with the complete realization of God's kingly rule ("the close of the age," cf. 16:28), on the other.

Matthew's church (he alone among the evangelists uses the Greek word *ekklēsia* in 16:18; 18:17) is a closely knit community. It strives for righteousness, a right relationship to God and one another according to Jesus' commandments that claim to bring out the true meaning of the law of Moses. The community studies the scriptures of Israel in view of their fulfillment in Jesus' life and teaching and leads a life of its own, alongside and often over against the Israel led by the scribes and Pharisees. It is committed to hand down Jesus' teaching in a worldwide mission, in which Jesus' followers represent their Lord.

Special Aspects of Matthew's View of Jesus

In view of what has just been said, it does not come as a surprise that Matt. 28:18–19, strategically placed in the Gospel, is of great importance for the understanding of Matthew's Christology.[2] The threefold baptismal formula[3] underscores what is told in the stories of Jesus' baptism (3:13–17) and temptation (4:1–11) and sheds new light on 11:25–27, followed in Matthew by verses (28–30) reminiscent of Sir. 51:23–27. By adding this, the evangelist seems to identify Jesus implicitly with personified Wisdom.[4] Jesus' union with the Spirit is also emphasized in the quotation from Isa. 42:1–4 in 12:18–21, which is followed by the dispute about the nature of Jesus' exorcisms, ending with the statement: "But if it is by the Spirit of God that I cast out demons, then the kingdom of God has come upon you" (12:22–28; cf. 43–45).[5]

Special attention should be given to the two opening chapters of the Gospel. Here the Holy Spirit is mentioned as active in the conception of Jesus (Matt. 1:18, 20). Jesus is not called "Son of God" here (but see 2:15, which applies Hos. 11:1 to him). The evangelist emphasizes, however, that Isa. 7:14 was fulfilled: " 'Behold, a virgin shall conceive and bear a son, and his name shall be called Emmanuel' (which means, God with us)" (1:23). The link between this verse and 28:16–20 (via 18:20) is obvious.

All along Matthew emphasizes Jesus' unique authority, grounded in his special union with the Father. By way of example we may point to Matthew's version of Jesus' walking on the water (Matt. 14:22–33), which ends with the confession of the disciples: "Truly you are the Son of God." In 16:16 Peter's confession is: "You are the Christ, the Son of the living God." In the following verses Jesus declares that this insight into Jesus' true identity can only be achieved by revelation of God. This insight has been granted to Peter as the leader of the church (vs. 17–19). Another instance of Matthew's emphasis on Jesus' divine sonship is found in 27:39–43, where the title "Son of God" is used twice by those who deride Jesus, once in v. 40 and once in v. 43, where the reference to Wisd. of Sol. 2:18–20 is made explicit in the words of the Jewish leaders: "He trusts in God; let God deliver him now, if he desires him, for he said, 'I am the Son of God.' "[6]

Matthew 1 and 2 not only disclose the "Emmanuel" as the essence of Jesus' being and ministry,[7] they also stress that Jesus is the Messiah / Son of David. Matthew knows Jesus Christ as a double name (1:1, 16, 18; 27:17, 22), but he explains to his readers that "Christ" denotes the Messiah, Son of David, the king of the Jews (2:1–6). He employs the word a few times more than Mark (11:2; 16:20; 23:10; 26:68). The political overtones of the expression "king of the Jews," found in the story of the trial before Pilate narrated in Mark 15, recur in Matt. 27. They are already found in Matt. 2, where it is clear that Herod's interpretation of the term is inadequate and completely wrong. While Gentiles worship the newborn "king of the Jews" (2:9–12; they are the first to do so!), Herod tries, in vain, to destroy a potentially dangerous political opponent (2:13–18).

Matthew makes it clear that Jesus was the true "king of the Jews" as Son of David. Jesus enters Jerusalem as a humble king on the back of an ass (Zech. 9:9 is quoted in 21:5), and he is greeted with the words "Hosanna to the Son of David!" (21:9; also in v. 15). Matthew pays much attention to the latter designation—it occurs not only in the genealogy at the beginning of his Gospel (1:1; cf. vs. 6, 17) and in the story of the announcement of Jesus' conception (1:20), but in particular in stories of healings by Jesus. In four cases (9:27–31; 12:22–23; 15:21–28; 21:14–17) the use of the title is peculiar to Matthew; only in the story of the healing of the blind man at Jericho in 20:29–34 do we have a parallel in the Bartimaeus story in Mark 10:46–52 (and Luke 18:35–43). Some remarks have to be added here about the term *Kyrios* = "Lord." In Matthew it is often used in the vocative by the disciples and people who come to Jesus in the belief that he can heal and save.[8] Evildoers address Jesus as eschatological judge with the words "Lord, Lord" (7:21, 22). In 24:42 the warning "Watch therefore, for you do not know on what day your Lord is coming" introduces a number of parables in which the relation between the believers and Jesus as the one who is to come back is portrayed as that between servants and Lord (see 24:43–25:46). The term *Kyrios* is clearly both "relational" and "confessional"; it is used by people who recognize Jesus' authority, now and in the future, as an authority derived from God himself[9]—the term is, of course, also used several times to denote God.[10] In view of this frequent use of *Kyrios* in connection with Jesus we may assume that Matthew attached the same meaning to it in 3:3 (par. Mark 1:3); 21:3 (par. Mark 11:3); and 22:41–46 (par. Mark 12:35–37)—cases where the word does not receive any emphasis in Mark.[11] On this point, Matthew's Christology is evidently more advanced than that of Mark.

In his use of the terms "Son of man" and "kingdom of God/heaven," Matthew does not substantially differ from Mark and Q. "Son of man" is still used exclusively by Jesus, and never taken up by believers to confess their faith, nor by opponents to dispute Jesus' claims. In the Matthean parable of the taxes and its explanation (13:24–30, 36–43) we find some new nuances. The Son of man is the one who, in the final judgment, separates the righteous from the evildoers, but he also is the one who "sows the good seed" (v. 37), that is, he puts "the sons of the kingdom" in the world. By implication he is portrayed as active in the time between his earthly ministry and his *parousia* and judgment.

In Matt. 13:41–43 a distinction is made between "the kingdom of the Son of man" (from which the evildoers are removed) and "the kingdom of their Father," where only the righteous will shine as the sun. In 16:28 Matthew, changing the reference to the coming of the kingdom of God with power (Mark 9:1), speaks of "the Son of man coming in his kingdom." We may conclude with J. D. Kingsbury: "The idea which the term Kingdom of the Son of Man appears to express for Matthew is that following Easter God reigns over the world in the person of Jesus Son of Man and, beyond the parousia, will continue to reign through his agency."[12]

Jesus is portrayed above all as the Son who operates in union with the Father. In Matt. 1 this is connected with Jesus' divine origin: he was conceived through the power of the Holy Spirit. By and large Matthew uses the same titles as Mark, but more frequently and with less reserve. He attaches special importance to *Kyrios* as a term both relational and confessional. All titles serve to emphasize the abiding importance and authority of Jesus' teaching. Similar teaching is found in the epistle of James, to which we now turn briefly.

Note on the Christology of the Epistle of James

The ethical teaching in the epistle of James has many things in common with similar exhortations in Jewish Wisdom literature and in the works of popular Hellenistic philosophers. On first sight there is little that is typically, let alone exclusively, Christian. On closer inspection it becomes clear, however, that James has drawn from a tradition of sayings of Jesus which have also been preserved in the Synoptic Gospels and which he has subsumed under a single principle, the law of love of one's neighbor.[13] Some scholars have found a specific affinity with Q sayings in their Matthean form.[14] The explicit Christological statements in the letter are few. "Jesus Christ" is used as a double name; there is a distinct preference for the title *Kyrios.* It is used in James 1:1; 2:1 ("the Lord of glory"); and 5:7–8, where "the coming of the Lord" is said to be at hand. Because the Lord as the eschatological judge is near, the brethren whom the author addresses have to remain patient and steadfast. A similar eschatological emphasis is found in 2:5, where the poor in the world are called "rich in faith and heirs of the kingdom";[15] the rich, on the contrary, are heading for "the day of slaughter" (5:1–5). Finally, in 5:13–16 the author exhorts his readers to call for the elders of the church in case of illness; they will pray over the one who is ill and anoint him or her with oil "in the name of the Lord." We may compare here the reference to baptism in 2:7 ("the honorable name which was invoked over you").[16]

5
The Christology of Luke-Acts

Jesus' Ministry and That of the Apostles

The author of the writing we know as "the Gospel of Luke" also wrote the Acts of the Apostles (see Luke 1:1–4 and Acts 1:1–2). The first book deals with "all that Jesus began to do and teach, until the day when he was taken up, after he had given commandment through the Holy Spirit to the apostles whom he had chosen" (Acts 1:1–2). Acts, the second book, tells the story of the mission of the apostles. In 1:8 Jesus' last words to them are: "But you shall receive power when the Holy Spirit has come upon you; and you shall be my witnesses in Jerusalem and in all Judea and Samaria and to the end of the earth." In the first volume Luke makes use of Mark and Q. We should note, however, that he leaves out about 30 percent of the material of Mark, and that about one third of the Gospel consists of material not transmitted elsewhere. Three major features of this Gospel are peculiar to it. (a) Chapters 1–2 provide a long "overture," dealing with the birth of Jesus and that of John the Baptist. (b) Luke 9:51, "When the days drew near for him to be received up, he set his face to go to Jerusalem," introduces a long "travel account," 9:51–19:27. Its first part (9:51–18:14) is composed of material derived from Q, plus other, specifically Lukan material; the second part (18:14–19:27) follows Mark. (c) Especially important is the last chapter, Luke 24, which gives an account of the meetings of the resurrected Jesus with his disciples, and his departure to heaven. Verses 13–32 describe his encounter with two of his disciples on the road to Emmaus. He explains what has happened and why it had to happen: " 'Was it not necessary that the Christ should suffer these things and enter into his glory?' And beginning with Moses and all the prophets, he interpreted to them in all the scriptures the things concerning himself" (vs. 26–27). This point returns in the story of the meeting with the eleven and a number of people assembled with them in Jerusalem that follows (vs. 44–46). Two further elements are added. In verses 36–43 we are told that the risen Jesus eats a piece of broiled fish and thereby demonstrates that he really is the one they know, and not a spirit. In verses 47–49 Jesus explains that it is written of the Christ in the scriptures that "repentance and forgiveness of sins should be preached in his name to all nations," and he appoints the disciples as his witnesses. They are to stay in the city until they receive "power from on high."

Luke 24 ends with the account of Jesus' farewell (vs. 50–51). He leads his disciples out of the city as far as Bethany, blesses them, parts from them, and is carried up into heaven.[1] The disciples return to Jerusalem, to the temple, where they bless God unceasingly.

The beginning of Acts (1:3–11) takes up the main themes of Luke 24 but introduces a number of changes. Jesus' meetings with his disciples are extended over a period of forty days. Jesus' departure, at the end of the period, is described as follows: "he was lifted up, and a cloud took him out of their sight" (1:9). Two angelic messengers of God in white robes tell the disciples that the Jesus who has just been taken up from them into heaven will come back in the same way as he went to heaven (1:10–11).

Luke shares the expectation of Jesus' *parousia* (see, e.g., 21:27, 36); twice he specifies that Jesus will return as judge—"of the living and the dead" (Acts 10:42), indeed of the entire world (Acts 17:31). In 1:3–11 the emphasis is, however, on the time between Jesus' final appearance to his disciples[2] and the *parousia.* During those forty days, Jesus spoke to the apostles "of the kingdom of God" (v. 3). His hearers (and, probably, also at least some of Luke's readers) thought that this meant the speedy restoration of a kingdom for Israel (v. 6),[3] but Jesus told them to leave the fulfillment of that expectation to the Father. For the time being they have to wait, not for the arrival of the kingdom, but for the gift of the Spirit promised by the Father (vs. 4–5; 7–8). Jesus, after having entered into his glory (Luke 24:26), or (to put it differently) after being exalted at the right hand of the Father (Acts 2:33; 5:31; cf. 7:56), does indeed pour out the Holy Spirit (Acts 2:33; cf. 2:17–21).[4] Guided and strengthened by this Spirit, the apostles and their followers preach the message, first to the Jews, then to the Samaritans, and finally to Gentiles all over the world. Paul, the major witness of the gospel from chapter 13 onward, finally carries it to Rome. How he fared in the emperor's court of appeal we do not learn. But the last words in Acts tell us that he lived in Rome "two whole years in his own hired dwelling, and welcomed all who came to him, preaching the kingdom of God and teaching about the Lord Jesus Christ quite openly and unhindered" (28:30–31, RSV margin). With this open and unimpeded preaching and teaching to all and sundry (in particular to the Gentiles—see 28:23–28) in the center of the Roman Empire, the story of Luke-Acts has reached its goal.

This rapid survey of the Gospel of Luke and the book of Acts makes clear that the two writings have to be studied together. In Luke's view of God's dealings with Israel and with humanity in general, the period of Jesus' ministry should be understood in the perspective of the continuation of that ministry by the apostles and the church. What Jesus said and did is related to the tasks, the problems, and the hopes of the community of his followers scattered around the eastern part of the Mediterranean, from Jerusalem to Rome: Jews and Gentiles who confess Jesus as their Lord try to find their way in the Hellenistic world and to live peacefully with other groups, keeping on the right side of the Roman administration. They have a keen interest in what Jesus taught and who he was, long ago in the land of Israel—a country distant in many ways from many of his later believers. They want to know even more who he is now, this living Lord who guides them. The Christological answers given in Luke-Acts reflect the situation they address, as we see at once if we look somewhat more closely into the nature of the continuity between Jesus' ministry and that of his disciples.

First, in the book of Acts (as we have just seen) and in the Gospel of Luke, the Spirit plays an important part. In the two first chapters the Spirit (as in Matt. 1:18–22) is active at Jesus' conception. Gabriel announces to Mary in Luke 1:35:

The Holy Spirit will come upon you,
and the power of the Most High will overshadow you;
therefore the child to be born will be called holy,
the Son of God.

In a different way the Spirit will fill and guide John the Baptist from his mother's womb (1:15, 17; cf. v. 80). Elizabeth and Zechariah are filled by the Holy Spirit (1:40, 67), who later on leads Simeon to the temple to meet "the Christ of the Lord," whom, according to a promise by the Spirit, he would see before his death (2:25–27). As for Jesus himself, Luke (3:22) recounts Jesus' baptism as do the other Synoptics, and immediately afterward (4:1) calls him "full of the Holy Spirit." "In the power of the Spirit" he returns to Galilee, where he teaches in the synagogues (4:14–15). Then follows the story of Jesus' teaching in Nazareth (4:16–30), which occupies a prominent place in Luke. Jesus reads from Isa. 61:1–2a, which begins, "The Spirit of the Lord is upon me, because he has anointed me to preach good news to the poor." We met this passage in chapter 3 when we discussed Q's description of Jesus' ministry in Matt. 11:2–6 (par. Luke 7:18–23). It is important as an illustration of the meaning of the verb *euaggelizesthai* (to preach good news) for Luke, who tends to avoid the noun *euaggelion* (which he uses only in 15:7; 20:24). Luke employs the verb to characterize Jesus' ministry (4:18, 43; 7:22; 8:1; [16:16]; 20:1) and that of his disciples (Luke 9:6, and no less than fourteen times in Acts).⁵ In 4:18 (cf. Acts 10:36), however, Luke emphasizes the first two clauses of this passage from scripture in order to explain that Jesus was the *christos* because he had been anointed (Greek *chriein*) with the Holy Spirit. Luke not only wants to show that Jesus is the Christ, but also to explain why he could be called so. In fact, he is the only Christian writer in the earliest period who gives such an explanation, clearly because it was helpful for the Gentiles among his readers. Finally, in 10:21–22, Luke introduces the well-known Q saying about the intimate relationship between the Son and the Father⁶ with the words, "In that same hour he rejoiced in the Holy Spirit and said . . . ."

Next, something must be said about the ministry of Jesus and the apostles and the promises to Israel. In Luke's view, Jesus' ministry should be connected, not only with the period of the church that follows it, but also with the period of Israel that precedes it. This may be illustrated with a few examples. Time and again, it is clear that Jesus' ministry and that of the apostles must be seen as the fulfillment of the promises to Israel. It cannot be confined to Israel, however, but is a matter of worldwide concern.

The overture to the Gospel in chapters 1 and 2 begins in the temple of Jerusalem, where Zechariah receives the angel's message about the birth of John the Baptist (Luke 1:8–23), and where Jesus is brought by his parents in accordance with the law of Moses (2:22–38). There, Joseph and Mary meet with Simeon and Anna, righteous and devout Israelites "looking for the consolation of Israel" (2:25) and "the redemption of Israel" (2:38). Likewise, in the beginning of Acts, the apostles and the community around them remain in Jerusalem and meet regularly in the temple (Acts 2:46; 3:1–4:4; 5:12–42). The twelve stay in Jerusalem. We do not hear about them anymore after the important meeting on the conditions for admission of Gentiles to the church in chapter 15, but at the end of his missionary journeys in Asia Minor and Greece Paul goes up to the city and the church there led by James, the brother of the Lord (20:18–38; 21:15–26). He is apprehended in the temple and arrested by the Romans—an arrest that leads eventually to his journey to Rome.

The announcements of the births of John the Baptist and Jesus, as well as the hymns of Mary and Zechariah in Luke 1, are steeped in biblical language and announce the coming change in the fate of Israel. The story of Jesus' birth in Bethlehem (2:1–20) leads up to the announcement by an angel of the arrival of a savior, who is Christ the Lord, in the city of David, a source of great joy for all the people (2:10–11). But Jesus is clearly portrayed as the counterpart of the emperor Augustus, who was hailed as the one who had brought peace to the empire. The angels, therefore, sing God's praise with these words (2:14):

Glory to God in the highest,
and on earth peace among men with whom he is pleased.

When Jesus is brought to the temple, he is recognized by Simeon and Anna. Simeon hails him as "a light for revelation to the Gentiles and for glory to thy people Israel" (2:32). The reference to Isa. 42:6 and 49:6 is obvious; significantly, the Gentiles are mentioned before Israel. Simeon adds that "this child is set for the fall and rising of many in Israel" (2:34).

In the story of his teaching at Nazareth Jesus quotes the saying "No prophet is acceptable in his own country" and continues to compare himself with Elijah, who healed only the son of a widow in the land of Sidon; and with Elisha, who healed Naaman the Syrian (4:23–27). The Nazareth episode ends with an attempt to kill Jesus (4:28–30). In the Lukan form of the parable of the great supper (14:15–24) there is a double invitation after the refusal by the original guests: the servants are first sent out to the streets and lanes of the city, and afterward "to the highways and hedges" outside the town (clearly symbolizing the mission to the non-Jews).

It is evident that the book of Acts views the preaching of the message about Jesus as a worldwide affair (Acts 1:8; 2:1–21). Important stages are Philip's preaching to the Samaritans (8:1–25); his conversation with the Ethiopian eunuch (8:26–32); the story of the conversion of the Roman centurion Cornelius (10:1–11:18; note the last verse); and the meeting in Jerusalem about the participation of Gentiles in the church (ch. 15) after the first missionary journey of Paul. We should note that Paul, the witness to the Gentiles par excellence, addresses the Jews before turning to the Gentiles. In Acts 13:46–47 he does so while quoting Isa. 49:6, "I have set you to be a light for the Gentiles, that you may bring salvation to the uttermost parts of the earth" (cf. Luke 2:32). In Acts 28:17–28 Paul, after his arrival in Rome, visits the local leaders of the Jews for a discussion. Acts tells us, "He expounded the matter to them from morning till evening, testifying to the kingdom of God and trying to convince them about Jesus both from the law of Moses and from the prophets," but he is able to convince only a few of them. Paul quotes Isa. 6:9–10 and announces that "this salvation of God has been sent to the Gentiles; they will listen." It is on this note that the book of Acts ends.

We now turn to the description in Luke-Acts of the contents of Jesus' preaching and that of his disciples. We have already noted the frequent use of *euaggelizesthai* (to preach good news) in Luke and Acts. A number of times it is used with "the kingdom of God" as subject: see Luke 4:43; 8:1; 16:16 (of Jesus); and Acts 8:12 (of his followers; also Luke 8:1 and 16:16 by implication). The expression "the kingdom of God" figures prominently in the preaching of Jesus in Luke, and also in that of the disciples (9:2; 10:9 [Q], 11; and Acts 8:12; 14:22; 19:8; 20:25; 28:23, 31). By and large, Luke's view of the dynamic presence and future of God's kingdom is that found in Mark and Matthew. A few aspects receive special emphasis. Besides Luke 11:20 (Q), "But if it is by the finger of God . . . then the kingdom of God has come upon you," we note Luke 17:21, "Behold, the kingdom of God is in the midst of you," a saying of Jesus directed against the Pharisees who ask him when the kingdom of God will come. In 19:11–27 the parable of the pounds is told for those who expect the immediate arrival of the kingdom because Jesus is near Jerusalem. We have already noted similar criticism by Jesus of the disciples' impatient question in Acts 1:6: "Lord, will you at this time restore the kingdom to Israel?"

"The kingdom of God" is used as a more or less technical term to denote the content of the preaching of missionaries in Acts; in 8:12 and 28:31 preaching the kingdom and preaching/teaching Jesus Christ are directly connected. In 14:22 we meet the traditional expression "to enter the kingdom of God."

Other favorite words of Luke to describe the content of the message are "peace," "life," and "salvation." For "peace" we may mention the song of the angels in Luke 2:14: "Glory to God in the highest, and on earth peace . . ." (cf. 19:38; 11:21; 14:32; 19:42; and Acts 10:36 [Isa. 52:7]). For "life" we may point to Luke 10:25; Acts 5:20; 11:18; 13:46, 48; and the designation "the one who leads to life" (TEV), used for Jesus in Acts 3:15.[7] "Salvation" figures prominently in Luke 19:9, "Today salvation has come to this house, since he (= Zacchaeus) is also a son of Abraham"; and in Acts 4:12, "And there is salvation in no one else, for there is no other name under heaven given among men by which we must be saved" (cf. Acts 13:26, 47; 16:17). Not only God (Luke 1:47) but also Jesus is called "Savior" (Luke 2:11; Acts 5:31; 13:23).

The Gospel of Luke pays much attention to Jesus' message and activity for persons who are held in low esteem by the leaders of the Jewish people. It frequently mentions tax collectors: besides Levi and his colleagues (Luke 5:27–30) there is also Zacchaeus (19:1–10). Luke is the only one to give the story of the Pharisee and the tax collector (18:9–14). In 3:12 and 7:29 he notes the positive reaction of the tax collectors to the message of John the Baptist. In 15:1 the protest of Pharisees and scribes against Jesus' association with tax collectors and sinners forms the introduction to the parables of the lost sheep, the lost coin, and the prodigal son. Among the "sinners" especially mentioned in Luke are the sinful woman (7:36–50) and the prodigal son (15:11–32). Luke's interest in the women who were helped by Jesus and who followed him is well known: the widow of Nain (7:11–17); the sinful woman (7:36–50); women followers in Galilee (8:2–3); Martha and Mary (10:38–42); the crippled woman, healed on a Sabbath (13:10–17). On his way to the cross Jesus addresses the women of Jerusalem in particular (23:27–31). Women also figure in Lukan parables (15:8–10; 18:1–8).

Finally, Luke takes special interest in the poor: see the speech in Nazareth (4:18); also 6:20, a beatitude directed to the poor (*not* "the poor in spirit" as in Matt. 5:3); and 7:22 (Q). Next there is the parable of the rich man and Lazarus (16:16–31). Also we find the praise of the poor and the commendability of giving to the poor in 14:13; 18:22 (also in Mark); and 21:1–4 (also in Mark). This emphasis on God's gifts to the poor has as its counterpart severe criticism of the rich (see, e.g., 6:24–25; 12:16–21; and 16:16–31).

If we now turn to Acts, we find a distinct emphasis on the founding of Christian communities separate from the Jewish synagogues and apart from other groups and movements in the Hellenistic world. Typical of this emphasis is Paul's farewell speech to the elders of Ephesus at Miletus, found in Acts 20:17–38. The topic of the disciples' preaching is very often called "the word of God" (or "the word of the Lord"), or simply "the Word," or summed up in terms like "Jesus," "Christ," and "Christ Jesus." All this reflects common Christian usage. In a number of cases the preaching of the apostles concentrates on "repentance and forgiveness of sins . . . to all nations" (Luke 24:47; see also Acts 2:38; 5:31; 10:43; 13:38; 22:16; 26:18, 20; cf. 3:19; 9:35; 11:21; 14:15; 15:19; 17:30). Those who repent are baptized; baptism functions without further explanation as a rite of admission to the church (2:38, 41; 8:12–13, 16; 9:18; cf. 22:16; 10:47–48; 16:15, 33; 18:8; 19:1–7). The true baptism is a baptism in the name of Jesus Christ (2:21; 10:48), or of the Lord Jesus (8:16; 19:5).[8] This picture of the various Christian communities in Acts no doubt corresponds with the situation regarded as normative and desirable in the circles in which Luke-Acts originated.

Special Aspects of Luke's Views on Jesus

The designation *christos* occupies a prominent place in Luke-Acts. Specifically Lukan phrases are "the Lord's Messiah" (Luke 2:26, RSV: the Lord's Christ; Acts 4:26; RSV: Anointed) and "God's Messiah" (Luke 9:20; 23:35; RSV: the Christ of God), where the genitive refers to the One who anoints (as in the Old Testament; cf., e.g., 1 Sam. 24:6).[9] The expression "Jesus Christ" occurs several times in Acts as a double name, sometimes combined with the designation "Lord" (11:17; 15:26; 28:31). "Christ" and "Lord" occur in parallel position in Luke 2:11, "a Savior, who is Christ the Lord," and in Acts 2:36, "God has made him both Lord and Christ." As Messiah Jesus is Son of David (Luke 1:32; 2:11; 3:31; cf. 1:69), but this designation does not receive much emphasis.[10] "Christ" has the connotation of King of Israel (or: King of the Jews); this is brought out very clearly in Luke 23, where the Jewish leaders explicitly accuse Jesus of "forbidding us to give tribute to Caesar, and saying that he himself is Christ a king" (23:2; cf. vs. 3, 37–38; and 19:38, as well as Acts 17:7). Of course Luke also denies the political nature of Jesus' kingship. This is pertinent to the situation he addresses, as the description of events in Thessalonica in Acts 17:1–9 shows. Here Paul and his friends are accused of "acting against the decrees of Caesar, saying that there is another king, Jesus" (Acts 17:7). Luke stresses that Jesus' kingship is of an entirely different nature. There will be no end to his reign (Luke 1:32–33, 69); when one of the two who are crucified with Jesus asks him, "Jesus, remember me when you come in [or: into] your kingdom" (23:42, RSV margin), the answer is, "Truly, I say to you, today you will be with me in Paradise" (v. 43), with a clear reference to Jesus' exaltation in heaven.

As we have already seen, Luke connects the title "Christ" with "anointing through the Spirit," by way of Isa. 61:1. He is also at pains to show that Jesus is a suffering Messiah. We have already mentioned the use of the double formula "that the Christ should suffer these things and enter into his glory" in Luke 24:26, in a context which speaks of the interpretation of the scriptures. The same theme is repeated in a similar context in Luke 24:46, "Thus it is written, that the Christ should suffer and on the third day rise from the dead"; and it is also found in Acts 3:18; 17:3; 26:23 (cf. 25:19). We have here a typical Lukan variant of the double formula,[11] using *christos* and the verb "to suffer," and making a general reference to the scriptures to bring out the divine necessity of Jesus' suffering. In Acts 17:1–3 Paul, whose teaching in the Jewish synagogues is characterized a few times as testifying "that the Christ was Jesus" (Acts 18:5) or "that Jesus was the Christ" (9:22; cf. v. 20), is portrayed as arguing with the Jews in Thessalonica "from the scriptures, explaining and proving that it was necessary for the Christ to suffer and to rise from the dead." On this basis it is possible to say, "This Jesus, whom I proclaim to you, is the Christ" (Acts 17:1–3).[12] Luke here gives an account of the typical subjects for argumentation in discussions between the Christians of his time and the Jews. He and his fellow Christians would have used ancient arguments, but we are not in a position to know whether the Lukan form of the double formula just mentioned is older than Luke.

Furthermore, Luke tells us that the designation "the Christians" was first used for the followers of Jesus in Antioch (Acts 11:26; cf. 26:28 and 1 Peter 4:16). This implies that the Jesus people had formed a separate group, and that they were called after one who was commonly designated as *christos.*[13]

Little needs to be said about the use of *Son of God* in connection with Jesus. As in Matthew, Jesus is Son of God on the strength of his conception (Luke 1:32, 35); the child that Mary will conceive and bear will be a Son of David *and* a Son of God.[14] The stories of Jesus' baptism (3:21–22), the temptation (4:1–13), the transfiguration (9:28–36), and the pericope in 10:21–22 (par. Matt. 11:25–27) do not call for further comment, nor do two utterances by demons (4:41; 8:28). We should note, however, that at the trial before the Sanhedrin the high priest's question found in Mark and Matthew has been replaced by two parallel questions from the members of the Sanhedrin: "If you are the Christ, tell us," and "Are you the Son of God, then?" (22:66–71). The second question follows on Jesus' answer to the first one, in which, significantly, he does not mention his *parousia* but only his exaltation: "But from now on the Son of man shall be seated at the right hand of the power of God." The reference to Ps. 110:1 leads to speculation on Jesus being Son of God (cf. Luke 20:41–44). In fact, he *is* Son of God, in his own way; then as God's representative on earth, now as the living Lord of the church.

In Acts 9:20 and 22 "Christ" and "Son of God" are also used together; in 13:33 there is an explicit quotation from Ps. 2:7, "Thou art my Son, today I have begotten thee," connected with Jesus' resurrection. We are reminded here of the ancient formula in Rom 1:3–4.[15]

There was reason to believe that in Matthew the designation *Servant of God* should be subsumed under "Son of God."[16] It occurs a few times in Acts (3:13, 26; 4:27, 30), and here the matter is not so simple. In Acts 4:23–31 not only Jesus but also David is called "servant of God," in a context which quotes Ps. 2:1–2, ending with the words "against the Lord and against his Anointed." As Davidic Messiah, Jesus is "thy holy servant . . . whom thou didst anoint."

The title seems to recall passages from the Old Testament in which David is called "servant of God" (see, e.g., Pss. 78:70; 89:3, 20, 39; 132:10) and the Davidic king "son of God." After all, the Greek word *pais* used here may be translated "child" as well as "servant" (see, e.g., Wisd. of Sol. 2:13, 18). In the other two instances the connection with David is not obvious, and it is just possible that the designation was also intended to remind Luke's readers of the central figure in the Isaianic Servant Songs (Isa. 42:1–7; 49:1–7; and 52:13–53:12 in particular). We have already noticed the reference to Isa. 42:6 or 49:6 in Luke 2:32. Jesus quotes Isa. 53:12 at the last supper (22:37). Philip meets the Ethiopian dignitary while reading Isa. 53:7–8, a passage about the sheep being led to its slaughterers, and he applies this passage to Jesus (Acts 8:32–33).[17]

We should note in passing that Jesus is called *the Holy and Righteous One* immediately after being called "servant of God" (Acts 3:14; cf. 3:13). We may compare here Acts 4:27 ("thy holy servant"); Luke 4:34 (par. Mark 1:24); and Acts 2:27. In Luke 23:47, the centurion at the cross declares: "Indeed, this man was righteous" (= "was innocent," RSV). In Acts 22:14 Paul receives the privilege of seeing the Righteous One and hearing a voice from his mouth.

More prominent in Luke's portrait of Jesus are *the prophetic elements.* The people of Nain glorify God after Jesus has raised the son of a widow from death, saying, "A great prophet has arisen among us!" (Luke 7:16). A Pharisee, thinking that Jesus is not aware of the sort of woman touching him, says to himself: "If this man were a prophet . . ." (7:39). As in Mark and Matthew, "the people" think that Jesus is a prophet (9:7–8, 19). And (as in Mark and Matthew) at the trial before the Sanhedrin Jesus is asked to prophesy (22:64). What is more important is that Jesus calls himself a prophet and draws a parallel between himself and Elijah[18] and Elisha in the Nazareth pericope (4:14–30), and that in another passage he declares that "it cannot be that a prophet should perish away from Jerusalem" (13:33). This exclusively Lukan pronouncement is followed by the Q passage, which accuses Jerusalem of "killing the prophets and stoning those who are sent to you" (13:34–35; cf. 11:49–51).[19] In Acts 3:22–23 and 7:37 Moses' prophecy concerning "a prophet from your brethren" whom God will raise up "as he raised me up" (see Deut. 18:15–18) is applied to Jesus.

The title *Lord* is frequently used in Luke-Acts for God and Jesus; in Acts 25:26 the governor Festus uses it to denote the emperor. As we have seen, it is used together with *christos* in Luke 2:12 and Acts 2:36. In Luke 1:43 Elizabeth calls Mary "the mother of my Lord." In Luke 24:34 the disciples announce: "The Lord has risen indeed, and has appeared to Simon!"[20] Very frequently Luke speaks about "the Lord" when referring to Jesus in narratives in the Gospel (see Luke 7:13, 19; 10:1, 39, 41; 12:42a; 13:15; 17:5–6; 18:6; 19:8, 31, 34). We may add, no doubt, the cases where "Lord" occurs in the vocative in the mouth of Jesus' disciples and of people who ask for his help.[21] In Acts, "the Lord" is a common designation of the exalted Jesus, and sometimes it is difficult to know whether the author refers to him or to the Lord God.

We should single out for mention here the use of the expression "to call upon the name of the Lord" in Acts 2:21, where Joel 2:32 is quoted (cf. Acts 9:14, 21; 22:16). On p. 46 we found that this reflects pre-Pauline usage. There we mentioned also the use of "the Lord" in baptismal formulas in Acts 8:16 and 19:5. "The Lord," "the Lord Jesus," and "the Lord Jesus Christ" are often used where the content of the Christian message and faith receive some emphasis (Acts 4:33; 7:59; 8:25; 9:28, 35, 42; 11:17, 20; 13:12, 44, 48–49; 14:3, 23; 15:11, 26, 35–36; 16:31–32; 18:8, 25; 19:10, 13, 17, 20; 20:19, 21, 24; 21:13; 28:31). Jesus the Lord is the supreme authority for the communities scattered over the Roman Empire; he governs and guides them, and it is him they have to obey, not any human official, however popular and powerful.

Also in the Gospel of Luke the designation *the Son of man* is only found on the lips of Jesus. Of the passages found in Luke only, we may mention Luke 19:10, "For the Son of man came to seek and to save the lost," which serves as a concluding comment on the story of Zacchaeus. "Nevertheless, when the Son of man comes, will he find faith on earth?" serves as conclusion to the parable of the unjust judge (18:8). Luke's version of the Synoptic Apocalypse ends with an exhortation to watch and pray in order that one may have strength "to stand before the Son of man" (21:36).[22]

Acts 7:56 forms a special case, because the expression is used here not by Jesus, but by Stephen just before he is stoned to death: "Behold, I see the heavens opened, and the Son of man standing at the right hand of God." The exalted Jesus is here portrayed as advocate for his disciple who acknowledges him before men. The reader is reminded here of the Q saying Luke 12:8–9 (par. Matt. 10:32–33), which refers to the *parousia.*[23] In this case the emphasis is on the activity of the exalted Lord at the death of the martyr. This does not come unexpectedly, after Luke's version of Jesus' answer before the Sanhedrin, in 22:69, and after his word to the penitent criminal crucified with him, in 23:43.

Ancient Elements in Acts?

In Acts a number of speeches of Peter and Paul directed to the Jews figure prominently (2:14–39; 3:12–26; 4:9–12; 5:29–32; 10:34–43; 13:16–41). These and many further speeches addressed to other audiences are recorded at significant moments in the story to explain to the readers the meaning of the events. In this respect, Luke follows the custom prevalent in Greek and Hellenistic historiography.[24] These speeches should, therefore, first of all be regarded as Lukan compositions, reflecting Luke's idealized picture of the beginning of the Christian movement inspired and led by the Holy Spirit.

Yet, however many later elements may have been incorporated in these speeches, Luke purports to recount what the Christians of the first generation believed and preached. Do his speeches contain ancient elements?

The only way to delineate those elements is to compare (parts of) the speeches with the evidence found elsewhere, in particular in Mark, Q, and Paul. We have already noted, for instance, that the pre-Pauline formula in 1 Thess. 1:9–10 is reflected in Paul's speeches to Gentiles in Acts 14:15–17 and 17:22–31.[25] Are we able to find similar ancient elements in the speeches directed to the Jews?

As might be expected, these speeches show many variations because they are adapted to the specific audiences and situations they address. In the longer speeches we notice the use of passages from the scriptures, some of which are also used elsewhere in the New Testament. Here too there is variation. Among the constant elements we find a basic pattern in the preaching about Jesus' death and resurrection, in which the contrast between the acts of human beings and God's activity is stressed. In its shortest form we find it in Acts 4:10, where Peter declares that a healing has taken place "by the name of Jesus Christ of Nazareth, whom you crucified, whom God raised from the dead."

The Jews in Jerusalem "have crucified and killed [Jesus] by the hands of lawless men" (Acts 2:23; cf. v. 36); they "delivered [him] up and denied [him] in the presence of Pilate" (3:13; cf. v. 15); they "killed [him] by hanging him on a tree" (5:30; also 10:39). In 13:27–29 we find an elaborate description of the activities of the Jerusalem Jews and their leaders in Paul's speech in the synagogue in Antioch in Pisidia, where people did not know the facts. God, on the contrary, "raised him up, having loosed the pangs of death" (2:24; cf. vs. 32, 36); "glorified his servant Jesus" (3:13); "raised [him] from the dead" (3:15; cf. 5:30; 10:40; 13:30).

If we study the speeches in detail, we shall note that many elements of the crucifixion story as we know it from the Synoptic

Gospels are interspersed, and that in the traditional material a few Christological elements receive special emphasis.

Jesus is said to have been exalted at God's right hand (Acts 2:33; 5:31; compare his position as judge in 10:42). He gave the Spirit (2:33; cf. 5:32); and he appeared to select witnesses (3:15; 5:32; 10:41f.; 13:31). Once (10:40) it is specified that Jesus appeared "on the third day," and several times that all this happened in accordance with the scriptures. (See 2:23, "Jesus, delivered up according to the definite plan and foreknowledge of God"—illustrated by the quotation of several passages from the Old Testament; see also 10:43, which mentions the witness of the prophets; and 13:29, "when they had fulfilled all that was written of him"; cf. v. 33.)

It is clear that in these speeches Luke has brought together much traditional material, the exact origin and date of which cannot be determined, unless we are able to compare it with evidence outside Luke-Acts. But even so, much remains uncertain. Let us look for a moment at the basic "contrast pattern" underlying these speeches to the Jews. The emphasis is clearly on God's initiative and activity in Jesus' resurrection. This corresponds with the pre-Pauline single resurrection formulas,[26] but not with any of the double formulas found in Paul; nor with the predictions of passion and resurrection in Mark, nor with those found elsewhere in Luke. Equally, the hostile activity of the Jews (in Jerusalem) receives emphasis. This corresponds partly with the passion predictions in Mark, but there passive verbs are used, with Jesus as the grammatical subject. The closest parallel is found in the passages transmitted in 1 Thessalonians and Q, in which Jesus accuses the Jews of being killers of the messengers sent by God.[27] It would seem, then, that we have here a specific form of a double formula about passion and resurrection, either formed by Luke or taken over from earlier preaching, which combines two elements found separately in two early formulas about the resurrection and about Jesus' death.

It has often been remarked that the positive effects of Jesus' death are not mentioned. The only time, in fact, that Luke mentions that Jesus' death was "in behalf of us/you" is in his version of the institution of the Holy Supper, and then in connection with the bread: "This is my body which is given for you" (Luke 22:19).[28] The absence of this expression in the Lukan contrast pattern (and in Luke 24:26, etc.) is not too surprising. It is not found in the passion-resurrection predictions in Mark, and it is not at all common in the double formulas found in the letters of Paul.

We have to ask one further question: Do individual speeches contain or reflect ancient traditions? Three passages are important enough to call for special comment: Acts 2:36; 3:18–21; 10:36–38.

In Acts 2:22–39 the contrast formula is found in verses 23–24, but embedded in a much larger argumentation. Not only does the earthly life of Jesus receive attention in verse 22, but also Jesus' resurrection, exaltation, and his gift of the Spirit are dealt with at great length; many passages from the scriptures are quoted in support. We have here, after all, Peter's first speech, immediately after the startling events at Pentecost. In this speech 2:36 forms a climax. Before urging his hearers to repent and be baptized (see vs. 38–39, after the question from the audience, "What shall we do?"), Peter solemnly declares, "Let all the house of Israel therefore know assuredly that God has made him both Lord and Christ, this Jesus whom you crucified." As we have seen, the parallelism between "Lord" and "Christ" is very probably Lukan. The title "Lord" is here derived from Ps. 110:1, quoted in verses 34–35 in connection with Jesus' exaltation at the right hand of God (cf. Luke 22:66–70). In view of the parallel between verse 36 and verses 23–24 it is probable that "God has made him both Lord and Christ" is thought of as having taken effect when God raised Jesus from death. Without any doubt, in Luke's view Jesus was Christ and Lord already during his life. In the context of the speeches in Acts, however, the decisive event which proves that God is on Jesus' side is the resurrection.[29] The ad hoc formulation emphasizes this too, in the tradition of the pre-Pauline formulas Rom. 1:3–4 and Phil. 2:9–11.

The following speech by Peter in Acts 3:12–16 combines a number of kerygmatic themes. We find the contrast scheme in verses 13–16; the Lukan theme, "What God foretold by the mouth of all the prophets, that his Christ should suffer, he thus fulfilled," follows in verse 18. The fulfillment of prophecy is also the theme of verses 22–23, where Jesus is portrayed as the prophet predicted by Moses in Deut. 18:18–19. Peter's Jewish audience is urged to repent and give heed to the message of all the prophets (vs. 24–26). Between verses 18 and 22–23 we find a separate unit, verses 19–21, which also urges repentance in view of the coming of "the times of refreshing" or the arrival of "the time for establishing all that God spoke by the mouth of his holy prophets from of old." The exact meaning of these and other terms in this difficult passage is disputed.[30] The emphasis on the need of repentance when this is still possible in the time before the *parousia* is found in Acts 17:30f. (and, differently, in 10:42f.), but the way Jesus' *parousia* is announced is peculiar: "and that he may send the Christ appointed for you, Jesus, whom heaven must receive until ..." (vs. 20f.). In the New Testament the Greek verb translated by "appointed" is found only in Acts, namely in 22:14 and 26:16 in connection with Paul. The emphasis here is clearly on God's preordained plan according to which all things happen; there is, again, no doubt that for Luke, Jesus was Christ/Messiah during his life on earth (see the immediately preceding verse 18). Yet it is at least suggested that Jesus' Messiahship becomes fully manifest only when a new dispensation is "established"[31] in the world. Again we find an ad hoc formulation; it has no parallel elsewhere in the Christian tradition, so we cannot determine whether Luke took over an existing Christological expression.

The last passage, 10:36–38, was discussed early in chapter 2, where we tried to show that here Luke used traditional material about Jesus' preaching, healing, and exorcisms that was already subsumed under the heading "God's good news by Jesus Christ." He avoids the noun, but uses the verb *euaggelizesthai,* and brings out the connection with Isa. 52:7. Ignoring his own "overture" in Luke 1–2, he makes the Jesus story begin in Galilee after the baptism by John.

6
The Christology of Paul

The Decisive Change in Paul's Life

In chapter 1 we studied a number of Paul's letters to find out which of the apostle's views on Jesus were shared with his readers. Only in a few cases may we be sure that the formulas and patterns of thought employed by him are actually pre-Pauline. It became evident, however, that early Christianity before and around Paul had already developed a great variety of more or less fixed formulations to express the many aspects of its belief in Jesus. Paul appealed to this common Christology in his attempts to bring a number of special points home to his readers.

In the present section we will look for what is specifically Pauline in Paul's thinking about Jesus. For obvious reasons we start with the decisive change that took place in his life when he, a persecutor of the community of Christians in Jerusalem, was called to become an apostle of Jesus Christ.[1] In Gal. 1:15–16 Paul describes this change as a prophetic call (Isa. 49:1; Jer. 1:5) when he writes, "But when he who had set me apart before I was born, and had called me through his grace, was pleased to reveal his Son to me, in order that I might preach him among the Gentiles, I did not confer with flesh and blood. . . ." In the Galatian situation he strongly emphasizes that he received this gospel through a revelation of Christ and not from any human authority (1:1, 11–12). In 1 Cor. 15:1–11 he describes his call in terms of an appearance of the risen Christ to him. It came as something altogether unexpected (Paul calls himself "one untimely born"), yet Paul's apostleship is no different from that of the other apostles. "Am I not an apostle? Have I not seen Jesus our Lord?" he asks in 1 Cor. 9:1. In 1 Cor. 15:3–5, as we have seen, the content of his gospel is expressed in commonly accepted terms.

In Phil. 3:2–6 (compare also Gal. 1:13–14) Paul describes his life as a pious Jew, linking the persecution of the church with his zeal for the law of Moses and the traditions of the fathers. Paul was (vs. 5–6) "as to the law a Pharisee, as to zeal a persecutor of the church, as to righteousness under the law blameless." However, "because of the surpassing worth of knowing Christ Jesus my Lord," Paul said, "I have suffered the loss of all things, and count them as refuse, in order that I may gain Christ and be found in him, not having a righteousness of my own, based on law, but that which is through faith in Christ, the righteousness from God that depends on faith" (Phil. 3:8–9).

Before his call, then, Paul lived a strict life in obedience to law and tradition, as a Pharisee, and persecuted those who followed Jesus the Messiah. After his call he gave up everything in order to know Christ Jesus, his Lord, and to preach God's Son among the Gentiles so that they, like himself, might find themselves in the right relationship to God through faith in Christ.

Glimpses of what made it impossible for Paul the Jew to believe in Jesus, and what led him to persecute Jesus' followers, may be perceived in 1 Cor. 1:23, "but we preach Christ crucified, a stumbling block to Jews and folly to Gentiles," and in Gal. 3:13, where the apostle quotes Deut. 21:23—a passage in the law that curses "one who hangs on a tree"—and applies it to the crucified Jesus.[2] Before his conversion, Paul and many other Jews must have concluded that the crucified teacher Jesus could not possibly be the Messiah. Those who followed Jesus, and who claimed to have found the right way to God through him so as to neglect certain aspects of the law,[3] had to be punished. However, after his confrontation with Jesus as the living Lord, as Son of God vindicated by God, Paul came to the conclusion that the law, not Jesus the Christ, was proved wrong. God so arranged things that Christ, in complete solidarity with those who believe in him, took the curse of the law upon himself ("having become a curse for us") in order to free them from the curse. For those who accept Jesus Christ, the struggle for a perfect obedience to the commandments of the law is over, and they stand in the right relationship to God through faith. The Gentiles who accept Jesus as their Lord stand side by side with the Jews who believe in him.

The confrontation with the living Lord assured Paul of the truth of the confession expressed in 1 Cor. 15:3–5. If Jesus was raised from the dead and is alive, one has to accept him as Lord and Son of God. Then he is, indeed, the Messiah, and then his death "for us," "for our sins in accordance with the scriptures" (and not contradicting them), is meaningful; it has removed all stumbling blocks on the road between God and the faithful. And as the radical thinker that he is, Paul concludes that we do not need any other help in our relationship to God. In Gal. 2:20–21 he writes, "I live by faith in the Son of God, who loved me and gave himself for me. I do not nullify the grace of God; for if righteousness were through the law, then Christ died to no purpose" (RSV margin). Here Paul uses common traditional formulas to express his own very specific views on God, Jesus, and the believers.

A few words on the terms "Christ," "Lord," and "Son of God" in Paul are in order. The apostle uses the term "Christ" very frequently, alone and in the combinations Jesus Christ, Christ Jesus, Jesus Christ the Lord. Although Paul the Jew knew, of course, what the term meant to Jews, and his readers, too, must have known that it had very specific connotations, yet Paul never stresses Jesus' Messiahship. Even in Rom. 9:5 ("to them [i.e., the Israelites] belong the patriarchs, and of their race, according to the flesh, is the Christ"), where the titular use is evident, the point is equally valid for those readers of this passage who would take the Greek *ho Christos* as a simple reference to Jesus.[4] All along, the designation/name Christ "receives its content not through a previously fixed conception of messiahship but rather from the person and work of Jesus Christ."[5] Jesus Christ, in Paul, becomes a double name, as, for example, the very frequent use of the expression "Jesus Christ the Lord" shows.

Also, apart from that expression, the title "Lord" is used very often in Paul's letters. For the Hellenistic world it was a better term to express Jesus' royal authority than the unusual word *Christos.* "Lord" is used for the earthly Jesus (1 Cor. 9:5; Gal. 1:19; 1 Thess. 1:6; 2:15); the resurrected one (1 Cor. 9:1),[6] very often for the one who now reigns and guides the believers in life and death (e.g., Rom. 14:4–8).[7] Paul looks forward to the day on which the Lord will come to judge the world and to call all true believers to share in his glory (e.g., 1 Cor. 1:7–8; 1 Cor. 5:5; Phil. 3:20; 4:5; 1 Thess. 2:19; 3:13; 4:13–18; 5:2).[8]

The term "Son of God," prominent in Gal. 1:16 as well as in Rom. 1:9 ("the gospel of his son"; cf. 2 Cor. 1:19), is found relatively seldom in Paul's letters. In chapter 1 we discussed 1 Thess. 1:10; Gal. 2:20 and Rom. 8:32; also Gal. 4:4–6 with Rom. 8:3. And we considered Rom. 1:3–4, where the ancient formula stated that the resurrection made it evident that Jesus was appointed Son of God (in power). Paul, however, stresses that Jesus was already God's Son during his sojourn on earth, and he ends the statement with a reference to "Jesus Christ our Lord" who sent him as an apostle to the nations "to bring about the obedience of faith" (Rom. 1:4b–5). In Rom. 5:10 (and 8:32) Paul emphasizes that Jesus' death was the death of God's Son. In 8:29 the emphasis is on the future: the believers as sons of God are predestined to be conformed to the image of his Son, in order that he may be "the first-born among many brethren" (cf. 8:14,

19 and 1 Cor. 1:9). The Son is God's supreme representative and agent on earth, yet he remains subordinate to God. "When all things are subjected to him, then the Son himself will also be subjected to him [God] who put all things under him" (1 Cor. 15:28).

Jesus Christ's Death, Resurrection, and Parousia, and Their Effects on the Believers

Speaking about Jesus is for Paul never a theoretical affair. He wants to show how what God has done, is doing, and will do to and through Jesus, the crucified Messiah, the living Lord, and the triumphant Son of God at the turn of the ages, affects the believers—in fact all human beings (Israel *and* the Gentiles), even the entire creation. His readers, living in small communities alongside the Jewish synagogues in cities that hosted numerous similar social and religious groups, had to be reminded of who they were in God's great plan for the world. The situation in the various communities differed, and therefore there are significant differences in the way Paul presents his case in his letters. Yet all he says fits into an overall view of God's dealings in history.

The various aspects of God's activity are intimately interconnected. We cannot believe in the saving effect of Jesus' death unless we are convinced that God made him conquer death and the forces of evil in the resurrection. For Paul, the resurrection of Jesus means the inauguration of a new period in God's dealings with the human race. People should realize that the period of the law and of the dominion of "the elemental spirits of the universe" is past, as Paul declares in the Galatian controversy (see, e.g., Gal. 3:1–4:11). When the time had fully come, God sent his Son to set free those who were under the law and to make them children of God. The Spirit who allows them to pray "Abba! Father!" is there to prove it (see Gal. 4:4–7). At the same time Paul knows that one can only speak of a proleptic presence of the New in the Old, and that the definitive change, affecting the entire cosmos, is yet to come. So he says in Rom. 5:1–2: "Since we are justified by faith, we have peace with God through our Lord Jesus Christ. Through him we have obtained access to this grace in which we stand, and we rejoice in our hope of sharing the glory of God." Paul knows that Christians have to suffer, like Christ and with Christ; he exhorts them to hold on, trusting in God's love and relying on the guidance of the Spirit, which assures them that they are and remain children of God; he urges them to look out for their final deliverance. Christians, according to Paul, live in the period between the ages. On the one hand, God's promises have become reality in Jesus Christ, for those who believe in him and live in communion with him. It is the time of the "already" corresponding with the "no longer." On the other hand, sin has not been expelled, and death has not yet been destroyed; suffering, hardships, and persecution may be expected any time. It is the time of the "not yet," but just because of what has "already" been granted, we all the more eagerly await the final consummation of God's purpose with the world.

Paul's emphasis on the decisive change brought about when God raised Jesus from the dead explains why in his letters he concentrates on the implications and effects of the basic gospel message about Jesus' death and resurrection and pays relatively little attention to Jesus' mission in Galilee and Jerusalem. To quote J. C. Beker, "The manner in which the one gospel of 'Christ crucified and risen' in its apocalyptic setting achieves incarnational depth and relevance in every particularity and variety of the human situation . . . constitutes Paul's particular contribution to theology."[9] Beker emphasizes that Paul is a coherent thinker who manages to give contingent interpretations of the one gospel in answer to specific situations. The letter to the Galatians, for instance, stresses what is decisively new in Christian life and thought (see the example just given from Gal. 3 and 4). Yet in Gal. 5:5 he says, "For through the Spirit, by faith, we wait for the hope of righteousness," and he continues with exhortations. Those who have received the Spirit should walk by the Spirit and not gratify the desires of the flesh (5:13–6:10). In this hortatory context Paul mentions the kingdom of God as a future reality. After summing up a number of vices to be avoided, he writes, "I warn you, as I warned you before, that those who do such things shall not inherit the kingdom of God" (5:21).

How do people get involved in God's saving activity through Jesus Christ? In our discussion of Gal. 3 and 4 in chapter 1 we noticed that Paul uses "faith-language" as well as corporate notions. The emphasis on faith, i.e., complete trust in Christ and in all that God effected through him, is typical of Paul. The theme of the letter to the Romans is expressed in Rom. 1:16–17 with the words, "For I am not ashamed of the gospel: it is the power of God for salvation to every one who has faith, to the Jew first and also to the Greek. For in it the righteousness of God is revealed through faith for faith; as it is written, 'He who through faith is righteous shall live.' " With the help of faith-language Paul stresses the necessity of a human decision, a positive response to God in Christ. The supreme example of one who unconditionally put his trust in God is Abraham (Gal. 3; Rom. 4). Abraham's true children are those who have faith, Gentiles as well as Jews.

Once the bond with God in Christ is established, it has to be maintained. Paul expresses this in terms of "being in Christ," "remaining in Christ."[10] In chapter 1 we ventured the suggestion that the many elaborations of the theme of "the corporate Christ" in Paul go back to earlier notions about baptism. In any case this theme is very central to him where he wants to emphasize the power of God as manifested in the living Christ who, through the Spirit, guides and permeates the lives of those who are incorporated into him.[11] So Paul in Phil. 3:10–11, after expressing his joy at having obtained righteousness through faith in Christ, writes of his purpose "that I may know him and the power of his resurrection, and may share his sufferings, becoming like him in his death, that if possible I may attain the resurrection from the dead." Or, to mention yet another example, in Rom. 8:9–11, Paul, speaking about the continuing reality of sin, says:

> But you are not in the flesh, you are in the Spirit, if in fact the Spirit of God dwells in you. Any one who does not have the Spirit of Christ does not belong to him. But if Christ is in you, although your bodies are dead because of sin, your spirits are alive because of righteousness. If the Spirit of him who raised Jesus from the dead dwells in you, he who raised Christ Jesus from the dead will give life to your mortal bodies also through his Spirit which dwells in you.

One will notice the close relationship between the resurrected Christ and the Holy Spirit, and the neat balance between the "already" and the "not yet." The quotation is to be read, of course, in its context, which assures the readers that the righteous demands of the law are fully satisfied in those who live according to the Spirit. God himself, sending his own Son in the likeness of sinful flesh to do away with sin, has made it possible for those who are "in Christ," Jews and Gentiles, to live in that way (see 8:1–4). They should then act accordingly (8:5–8, 12–13).

Space does not permit showing in detail the many different ways Paul's views on Jesus interacted with his ideas about salvation. A few important passages must, however, be mentioned briefly. In all cases his concern that non-Jews and Jews are allowed to share in Christ's gifts on the same level comes out very clearly. His readers have to remember this in order to maintain unity and harmony in the congregations which he founded.

In Rom. 3:21–26, a crucial passage in this important letter, Paul speaks about the manifestation of God's righteousness apart from the law. This is both a saving event, justifying all who have faith in Christ (i.e., bringing them into the right relationship to God), and an event which shows that God punishes people for their shortcomings. Jesus' death is viewed as a sacrifice that brings expiation,[12] i.e., removes the sins which form an obstacle on the road between God and man. Paul also speaks about "redemption which is in Jesus Christ" (cf. Rom. 8:23; 1 Cor. 1:30), by which he refers to the liberation from the oppressing force of sin (or, in 8:21, from the bondage to decay to which people are subjected).[13] It is God himself who manifests that he is righteous, restores the right relationship, redeems, and provides the means of expiation; all have sinned, Jews and Greeks, all receive his grace as a gift.[14]

In Rom. 5:6–11 Paul, commenting on what it means that "Christ died for us," stresses that those for whom Christ died ("we") were yet helpless (weak) and sinners when this happened. Consequently, the justification by Christ's blood may be described as reconciliation: "Since, therefore, we are now justified by his blood, much more shall we be saved by him from the wrath of God. For if while we were enemies we were reconciled to God by the death of his Son, much more, now that we are reconciled, shall we be saved by his life. Not only so, but we also rejoice in God through our Lord Jesus Christ, through whom we have now received our reconciliation." Reconciliation is the removal of hostility or estrangement between human beings (1 Cor. 7:11) or between God and sinners. God in his love took the initiative. We are no longer enemies of God thanks to Jesus' death; we shall be saved when the final judgment comes (cf. 1 Thess. 1:10; 5:9), thanks to our communion with the living Lord.

"Reconciliation" recurs in 2 Cor. 5:14–21, where Paul comments on "one [Christ] has died for all" and "he who for their sake died and was raised" (see vs. 14–15).[15] Here Paul combines the notion of "dying for" with corporate language; he concludes, "therefore all have died" (v. 14). This implies the ethical obligation "that those who live might live no longer for themselves but for him who for their sake died and was raised" (v. 15). "If any one is in Christ, he is a new creation" (v. 17).[16] "For our sake he made him to be sin who knew no sin, so that in him we might become the righteousness of God" (v. 21; cf. Gal. 3:13 and Rom. 8:3). Between the two verses just quoted Paul speaks about the ministry of reconciliation entrusted to him and his colleagues, which speaks about God who reconciled humanity to himself through Christ. "All this is from God, who through Christ reconciled us to himself" (v. 18). "That is, in Christ God was reconciling the world to himself, not counting their trespasses against them" (v. 19). Transgressions are no longer counted; God wants to have a good relationship with everybody. Those who have already accepted it, who are already a new creation because for them "the old has passed away, behold, the new has come" (v. 17), have to bring the message of reconciliation to the entire world. They are ambassadors for Christ, through whom God makes his appeal (v. 20).

We now turn briefly to two passages on Adam and Christ. Romans 5:12–21 describes humanity as subject to the power of death because of Adam's transgression which brought death to him and his off-spring. (Paul adds, however, in verse 12, that all sinned individually.) Adam's disobedience is more than compensated by the obedience of Christ. All those who accept him will share in what he brought about. "If, because of one man's trespass, death reigned through that one man, much more will those who receive the abundance of grace and the free gift of righteousness reign in life through the one man Jesus Christ" (v. 17). In Rom. 5 the effects of Jesus' obedience are described as present and future; also in the second passage, 1 Cor. 15:20–57, we find these two aspects, but the emphasis lies on the future state of the believers. In this chapter Paul speaks about the central importance of the resurrection of Christ. If Christ has not been raised, our faith is futile and we are still living our old life in sin. Then those who have fallen asleep "in Christ" have perished (vs. 17–18). "But in fact Christ has been raised from the dead, the first fruits of those who have fallen asleep. For as by a man came death, by a man has come also the resurrection of the dead. For as in Adam all die, so also in Christ shall all be made alive" (vs. 20–22).

This will take place at Christ's *parousia,* as is shown by Paul in the difficult passage 1 Cor. 15:24–28. Christ rules as king[17] until he hands over his rule to God the Father and the kingdom of God becomes full reality (vs. 24, 28). First he has to subdue all (cosmic) rulers, authorities, and powers; finally death as the last enemy is destroyed. Paul advances as proof a reference to Ps. 110:1; he takes the second clause of this verse, "till I make your enemies your footstool," and combines it with Ps. 8:6, where the glory of man is said to exist in the fact that God has put all things under his feet. In Christ's victory over God's enemies these two passages of scripture are fulfilled. It is God who has commissioned him and given him the power to carry out his commission; Christ remains subordinate to God.

Somewhat later, Paul continues with a long disquisition on the nature of the resurrected body in 1 Cor. 15:35–57. In the course of this he returns to the antithetic parallelism between Adam and Christ, this time calling Christ "the last Adam": "Thus it is written, 'The first man Adam became a living being' [Gen. 2:7]; the last Adam became a life-giving spirit" (v. 45). "The first man was from the earth, a man of dust; the second man is from heaven" (v. 47). "Just as we have borne the image of the man of dust, we shall also bear the image of the man of heaven" (v. 49). Paul envisages the *parousia* of Jesus Christ as the appearance of the true man, created in the image of God, after his likeness (Gen. 1:26).[18] He is heavenly and spiritual; those who belong to him will all be changed—those who are alive at his coming as well as those who have already died will be raised imperishable (vs. 50–57; cf. 1 Thess. 4:13–18, discussed early in chapter 1).[19]

The idea of a change of the earthly existence of those who belong to Christ so as to conform to him in his divine glory is also found in Rom. 8:29, "For those whom he foreknew he also predestined to be conformed to the image of his Son, in order that he might be the first-born among many brethren."[20] There is also Phil. 3:20–21, "But our commonwealth is in heaven, and from it we await a Savior,[21] the Lord Jesus Christ, who will change our lowly body . . . by the power which enables him even to subject all things to himself." This text leads us to 2 Cor. 3:18, where Paul in a complex disquisition about the fading splendor of the old covenant of Moses praises the glory connected with the new covenant of Christ, and concludes: "And we all, with unveiled face, beholding the glory of the Lord, are being changed into his likeness from one degree of glory to another; for this comes from the Lord who is the Spirit."[22] He returns to this in 4:4, when he speaks about "seeing the light of the gospel of the glory of Christ, who is the likeness [or: image] of God." Paul is probably thinking again of Gen. 1:26, for in verse 6 he refers to the creation story in Gen. 1: "For it is the God who said, 'Let light shine out of darkness,' who has shone in our hearts to give the light of the knowledge of the glory of God in the face of Christ."[23]

In all these passages[24] the notion of Jesus Christ as the counterpart of Adam, as the last Adam, the true eschatological Man who shares God's glory and bears God's image, serves to ensure the complete "glorification" of those who as children of God belong to him as his brothers and sisters. This will become full reality at the time when all evil forces will be subjected and God will hold the entire cosmos under his sway.

Jesus Christ and God Before Jesus' Mission on Earth

In the passages just mentioned all attention is centered on Jesus Christ's glory to be manifested in the future—a glory that he has possessed since the resurrection, and now possesses, while he reigns as Lord. It stands in contrast to Jesus' earthly life, about which Paul does not speak very often, but which is characterized by his death for those who believe in him, and by his suffering. In Phil. 3:10 Paul speaks about sharing Christ's sufferings and about becoming like him in his death (cf. 2 Cor. 4:10, "carrying in the body the death of Jesus"; 2 Cor. 1:5; 13:4). The question remains: Does the future glory of Jesus Christ perhaps correspond to a glory that he had before he

shared human suffering and died a human death?
Here we have to return to Gal. 4:4–6 and Rom. 8:3, where Paul,
following an ancient pattern of thought, relates that God sent his
Son.[25] He specifies that this Son was "born of woman,"[26] born under
the law"; this was necessary to redeem those who were under the law,
so that they might receive adoption as sons. Paul explains the nature
and the source of the mission of the Son, but does not tell us where
Jesus was before he was born. There is, however, at least a strong
suggestion that he was with God and stood in a special relationship
to God before he was sent.[27] In Rom. 8:3, too, the fact that God sent
"his own Son in the likeness of sinful flesh" suggests that before his
birth he had a different status.

Philippians 2:6–11 and 2 Cor. 8:9 should receive attention next.
The first passage has already been mentioned briefly in chapter 1 in
discussing the confession of Jesus Christ as Lord, with which it
closes. For our present purpose it is important to note that the hymn,
in its first line, declares that Christ Jesus was "in the form of God."
He "did not count equality with God a thing to be grasped [or: to
be held on to]," but he humbled himself, became like a man, "became
obedient unto death, even death on a cross." For that reason God
highly exalted him. Many interpreters[28] find here an implied contrast
between Adam and Christ. Christ, like Adam, bore the image of God
and was like God (Gen. 1:26). Contrary to Adam, he was not
disobedient in that he wanted to be like God (Gen. 3:5). He "walked
the path of obedience all the way to death—his death on the cross"
(Phil. 2:8, TEV), and received "the name which is above every name"
(v. 9) and which is beyond the reach of disobedient Adam. In any
case Christ, "who, though he was in the form of God," was not
simply an ideal human being, a perfect example of what God intended man to be; it was only later that he assumed a human form
and became like man (v. 7, TEV). Before that, he must have existed
in a form more than human, in a "form of God." This is also
suggested by 2 Cor. 8:9, where Paul, while exhorting his readers to
contribute liberally to a collection for the Christians in Jerusalem,
speaks about "the grace of our Lord Jesus Christ who, though he was
rich, yet became poor for your sake, so that by his poverty you might
become rich" (RSV adapted).

In chapter 1 we have also already discussed 1 Cor. 8:6, where,
among other things, the Lord Jesus Christ is said to be the mediator
of creation. As we have seen, this aspect is not prominent; yet it is
mentioned, and, as we shall see in chapter 12, it suggests that Paul
and his predecessors here think of Jesus Christ in terms of personified
Wisdom associated with God and active at the creation. This implies
that Jesus Christ existed with God before the creation of the world.

In 1 Cor. 1:24, where Paul calls Christ "the power of God and the wisdom of God," and in 1:30, where he speaks of Christ Jesus "who became wisdom for us from God, and righteousness, and sanctification, and redemption" (my trans.), this is not implied. Over against the Corinthians, who seem to have held power and human wisdom in high esteem, Paul stresses that it is only in the foolishness and weakness of the crucified Jesus and the proclamation of the message of the cross that God's power and God's wisdom are revealed and have become operative.[29] In 1 Cor. 2:6–10 Paul goes a little further when he speaks about "a secret and hidden wisdom of God, which God decreed before the ages for our glorification." The present age is dominated by cosmic powers, called "rulers of this age." God's wisdom remained hidden from them; if they had understood it they would not have crucified Jesus. He is "the Lord of glory" whose glory the believers will one day share. They are the ones to whom the Spirit reveals what "the rulers of this age" could not comprehend; the latter "are doomed to pass away" in any case. The wisdom here is God's mysterious plan of salvation (see also 1 Cor. 2:1 (RSV margin); 4:1; 13:2; 14:2; 15:51); as such it is preexistent, to be revealed at the appropriate time to those who are allowed to recognize Jesus as the Lord of glory through the Spirit.[30]

In 1 Cor. 10:4, however, we have again an implicit identification of Christ and Wisdom. Describing what happened during Israel's sojourn in the desert in terms that bring out the parallels with the situation of the Christian community of his days, Paul describes how the Israelites "all ate the same spiritual food and all drank the same spiritual drink" (vs. 3–4). He adds, "They drank from the spiritual Rock which followed them, and the Rock was Christ" (twice RSV margin). This is, of course, an ad hoc identification, fitting into Paul's overall approach to the biblical stories about Israel in the desert in this passage. Yet it presupposes knowledge of Jewish traditions concerning the one well in the rock accompanying the Israelites, and Hellenistic-Jewish speculations about the rock as the Wisdom of God.[31]

Paul speaks very highly of Jesus Christ, the living Lord, who, as supreme agent of God's saving work and as central authority for all who serve him, stands very near to God in the experience of those who believe in him. "Grace to you and peace from God our Father and the Lord Jesus Christ" is the usual greeting at the beginning of Paul's letters. Yet it is clear that Jesus Christ remains subordinate to God. He is the one who is sent and not the Sender, he is the Son of the Father; those who worship him as Lord do so to the glory of God the Father (Phil. 2:11), and when the end comes, he delivers the kingdom to God the Father (1 Cor. 15:24, 28). In Rom. 9:5, therefore, the translation "and of their race, according to the flesh, is the Christ. God who is over all be blessed for ever," found in the text of RSV, is to be preferred to ". . . Christ, who is God over all, blessed for ever," found in RSV margin.

7
Documents
of the Pauline School

Paul's views on Jesus Christ continued to direct the life and thought of the group of congregations which owed their existence to the indefatigable labors of the apostle to the Gentiles. When forced to answer questions arising in or outside their communities, they went back to what Paul had said, just as they took up the traditional formulas used in preaching, teaching, and liturgy, developing them in order to meet the needs of the moment. The most important of these developments are mentioned here.

2 Thessalonians

In 2 Thess. 2:1–12 we find an author using Paul's name who writes on the subject of "the coming [*parousia*] of our Lord Jesus Christ and our assembling to meet him" (2 Thess. 2:1; cf. 1 Thess. 4:13–18). People have maintained that "the day of the Lord has come" (v. 2), and the author now wants to remind his people of all that has to happen before the Lord will indeed appear. Because he uses apocalyptic language and refers to knowledge shared by him and his readers (vs. 5–6), his exposition is not as clear as we might wish. Two things, however, stand out clearly. The *parousia* of Jesus Christ will be preceded by the appearance of an apocalyptic opponent, called "the man of lawlessness," "the son of perdition" (v. 3), "the lawless one" (v. 9). In him all rebellion against God and Christ culminates. Inspired by Satan, he will show his power in signs and wonders that will deceive all who do not believe in truth and have pleasure in unrighteousness (vs. 9–12). He will pose as a divine being and even take his seat in the temple of God, proclaiming himself to be God (v. 4). He will be destroyed by the Lord Jesus, who "will slay him with the breath of his mouth and destroy him by his appearing and his coming" (v. 8). He is not there yet, although "the mystery of lawlessness is already at work" (v. 7). There is a force that restrains

him temporarily (v. 6); in v. 7 the author speaks of "one who restrains him" (my trans.). His readers know what he means, but we
are left guessing. The picture of the Lord's apocalyptic opponent can
be understood against the background of Jewish prophetic and
apocalyptic ideas about God's opponent(s) in history and just before
God's final and decisive intervention on earth. There are also parallels in 1 John ("you have heard that antichrist is coming," 2:18), and
Rev. 13 (the beast rising out of the sea and the beast that rose out
of the earth). In none of the Jewish or Christian parallels, however,
do we find a force or a person comparable to the "one who restrains
him" in 2 Thessalonians.[1]

Colossians

The letter to the Colossians is directed to a Christian congregation
that is in danger of being carried away by false ideas and practices
which can only partly be reconstructed from the author's argument
in 2:6–23.[2] They seem to favor ascetic practices and celebrate feasts,
new moons, and sabbaths (Col. 2:16, 21), in the context of worship
of angels (or: in order to participate in the angels' worship in heaven,
v. 18).[3] The author regards them as victims of "philosophy and
empty deceit, according to human tradition, according to the elemental spirits of the universe" (v. 8), and reminds them of the fact
that "with Christ you died to the elemental spirits of the universe"
(v. 20).

There is much to be said in favor of the theory that this letter is
a forceful reminder of the salvation brought about by baptism and
the ethical requirements resulting from it (see Col. 2:9–15, 20; 3:1–4;
and 3:5–4:5). The emphasis is on what has been changed in the lives
of Christians. The author even says, "If then you have been raised
with Christ, seek the things that are above, where Christ is" (3:1; see
also v. 2).[4] Besides the "already" there is also the "not yet": "For you
have died, and your life is hid with Christ in God. When Christ who
is our life appears, then you also will appear with him in glory"
(3:3–4). And because believers are not yet perfected, they have to put
to death what is earthly in them (v. 5) and to put on all sorts of
virtues as God's chosen ones. The code of domestic behavior in
3:18–4:6[5] supplements these exhortations connected with baptism.

Also in Col. 1, the emphasis is on the totally new life already
accorded to "saints and faithful brethren in Christ" (v. 2): the Father
has qualified them "to share in the inheritance of the saints in light.
He has delivered us from the dominion of darkness and transferred
us to the kingdom of his beloved Son, in whom we have redemption,
the forgiveness of sins" (vs. 12–14). This is underscored with a

Christological hymn in verses 15–20, which portrays the Son as "the image of the invisible God"; mediator at the creation of the universe, including all thrones, dominions, principalities, and authorities; the head of the church (as well as "head of all rule and authority," 2:10). He is, of course, the agent of redemption. In fact, in him "all the fulness of God was pleased to dwell [see 2:9–10], and through him to reconcile to himself all things, whether on earth or in heaven, making peace by the blood of his cross."

This hymn—probably taken over and adapted by the author of Colossians[6]—stresses the cosmic implications of the work of Christ.[7] The author, who emphasizes Christ's death on the cross in verse 20 (as well as in 1:22, 24; 2:14–15), draws the consequences for the life of the congregation of believers, who are to preserve their unity, holding on to the Lord who brought them together (1:21–23 and 1:24–2:7; cf. 2:19). He includes references to the divine dynamics of apostolic activity among the Gentiles, and uses the "hidden-revealed" pattern (also found in 1 Cor. 2:6–10) in 1:25–28 (cf. 2:2–3).

All these notions and patterns of thought are prominent in Paul's letters, and are now developed so as to meet the challenges inherent in the situation of the recipients of the letter. It cannot be excluded that Paul himself, faced with a new situation, brought out the consequences of his way of thinking in this way in this particular situation. In view of the development of ideas and the difference in style and vocabulary, however, many scholars consider a non-Pauline origin more plausible.

Ephesians

The letter to the Ephesians has a number of ideas in common with that to the Colossians, but because it lacks the involvement in a situation of crisis it reads more like a tractate than a letter. Particularly in the long, involved sentences of the opening doxology (Eph. 1:3–14) and the two sections that follow (1:15–23 and 2:1–10), we meet again the emphasis on the cosmic dimensions of the work of Christ in behalf of the church. See, for example, 1:9–10, "For he has made known to us in all wisdom and insight the mystery of his will, according to his purpose which he set forth in Christ as a plan for the fullness of time, to unite all things in him, things in heaven and things on earth,"[8] and 1:20–23, which speaks of God who raised Christ from the dead "and made him sit at his right hand in the heavenly places, far above all rule and authority and power and dominion, and above every name that is named, not only in this age but also in that which is to come; and he has put all things under his feet and has made him the head over all things for the church,

which is his body, the fulness of him who fills all in all."
Essential to the argument is the unity of the church. In Eph.
2:11–21 this becomes very clear: the central saving act is the unification of Jews and Gentiles and their joint reconciliation to God; the
section ends with a proliferation of images for the church. Also in
4:1–16 the unity of the church stands central (vs. 4–6, "There is one
body and one Spirit, just as you were called to the one hope that
belongs to your call, one Lord, one faith, one baptism, one God and
Father of us all, who is above all and through all and in all"). We
may compare here 1 Cor. 12:4–13, 27–31, and should note that in
Eph. 4:11, as in 1 Cor. 12, officers of the church are mentioned whose
most important task consists in building up the body of Christ. One
cannot help feeling that the organization of the church is further
developed and regularized here than in Corinth. The apostles and
prophets mentioned here are called the foundation of the church in
Eph. 2:20, alongside Christ Jesus, the cornerstone, and it is to them
that "the mystery of Christ, which was not made known to the sons
of men in other generations" (3:4–5), has now been revealed by the
Spirit.[9]

We pass over other views of Christ and salvation which Ephesians
shares with Colossians. However, three passages of special significance are specific to the present letter. First, Eph. 5:1 expands a
traditional formula:[10] "Christ loved us and gave himself up for us,
a fragrant offering and sacrifice to God." Next, there is 5:14, which
reads like a quotation from a baptismal hymn: "Awake, O sleeper,
and arise from the dead, and Christ shall give you light." And finally,
we note an expansion in the section of the "household code" dealing
with wives and husbands (5:21–33). At several places we find references to Christ as a bridegroom, and to the church as his bride, for
whom he gave himself up "that he might sanctify her, having
cleansed her by the washing of water with the word" (v. 26). The
author mentions this image of the relationship between Christ and
the church in order to give special depth to the exhortations to wives
and husbands.[11]

The Pastoral Epistles

When we turn to the pastoral epistles we realize that we are even
further removed from the ideas found in the genuine letters of the
apostle. The "Paul" of these letters emphasizes his special charge to
preach the gospel (apart from 1 Tim. 1:1; 2 Tim. 1:1 and Titus 1:1,
see also 1 Tim. 1:11–14; 2:7; 2 Tim. 1:11; 4:17; Titus 1:3) and his
suffering for it (2 Tim. 1:12; cf. v. 8). Above all, however, he is the
guardian of sound doctrine, of a godly life, and of right order in the

congregation at a time when false teachers propagate wrong ideas and a reprehensible style of life. "Follow the pattern of the sound words which you have heard from me, in the faith and love which are in Christ Jesus; guard the truth that has been entrusted to you [literally: your splendid trust] by the Holy Spirit who dwells within us" (2 Tim. 1:13–14).

The author holds on to what has been handed down to him, and indeed we find Christological statements in keeping with what we found in earlier chapters. In 1 Tim. 2:6 Christ Jesus is called the one "who gave himself as a ransom for all"; and in Titus 2:14 we read that he "gave himself for us to redeem us from all iniquity and to purify for himself a people of his own who are zealous for good deeds." In 2 Tim. 2:8 the author uses terminology reminiscent of Rom. 1:3–4: "Remember Jesus Christ, risen from the dead, descended from David," and in 2 Tim. 2:11–13 we find an ancient saying, the first word of which is clearly modeled upon the pattern, dying with Christ—living with Christ.

Apart from that, the author quotes other units which received their fixed form at some time before the writing of the letter; for lack of parallels, however, we cannot determine how old they are. One such text is 1 Tim. 2:5–6:

For there is one God,
and there is one mediator between God and men,
the man Christ Jesus,
who gave himself as a ransom for all,
the testimony to which was borne at the proper time.

Here we note the term "mediator," used in Gal. 3:19–20 for Moses, and in Heb. 8:6; 9:15; 12:24 for Christ as the mediator of a new covenant. Next there is the hymn in 1 Tim. 3:16, presented as "the mystery of our religion":

He was manifested in the flesh,
vindicated in the Spirit,
    seen by angels,
preached among the nations,
believed on in the world,
    taken up in glory.

The emphasis is here clearly on the glorification of Jesus. The pastoral letters often use the noun *epiphaneia,* a typically Hellenistic term for the manifestation of the gods, and the corresponding Greek verb to denote the glorious appearance of Jesus Christ. Mostly, they refer to the *parousia* (1 Tim. 6:14; 2 Tim. 4:1, 8; Titus 2:13),[12] but they are also used for his first appearance on earth (2 Tim. 1:10; Titus 2:11; 3:4). Another term that is frequently used, for Jesus Christ as well as for God, is "Savior." Here, too, we may assume Hellenistic influence: see 1 Tim. 1:1; 2:3; 4:10; 2 Tim. 1:10; Titus 1:3–4; 2:10, 13; 3:4, 6, and compare 1 Tim. 1:15; 2:4; 2 Tim. 1:9; 4:18; Titus 3:5, where the saving activity of God and Jesus is emphasized.

In these and other texts we notice a close relationship between God's plan and its execution in and by Jesus: see 1 Tim. 6:13–15; 2 Tim. 2:8–10; Titus 3:4–7. Another example is Titus 2:11–13 (RSV margin), quoted here in full (we have already quoted v. 14, attached to it):

> For the grace of God has appeared for the salvation of all men, training us to renounce irreligion and worldly passions, and to live sober, upright, and godly lives in this world, awaiting our blessed hope, the appearing of the glory of the great God and our Savior Jesus Christ.

As in Rom. 9:5,[13] the meaning of the last phrase is disputed. It is not clear whether "our Savior Jesus Christ" is mentioned here in close connection with God, or whether he himself is called God. In view of the overall Christological picture in the Pastorals the first interpretation seems the most likely one.

There is little emphasis on Christ's preexistence; it is implied in 1 Tim. 1:15; 3:16 (first clause); and 2 Tim. 1:9–10 (cf. Titus 2:11; 3:4). References to the story of Jesus' life on earth are rare: "Christ Jesus who in his testimony before Pontius Pilate made the good confession" (1 Tim. 6:13). Christ's present reign in heaven is implied in 1 Tim. 5:21, "In the presence of God and of Christ Jesus and of the elect angels I charge you . . ." (cf. 1 Tim. 6:13; 2 Tim. 4:1). Above all, the author emphasizes Christ's final appearance on earth as bringer of salvation (1 Tim. 1:2; 2 Tim. 1:2; Titus 1:2–3; 2 Tim. 2:11–13; 4:18; Titus 2:13; 3:7) and as judge (1 Tim. 6:14; 2 Tim. 4:1, 8). He will guard those who belong to him until the final day (2 Tim. 1:12; cf. Titus 3:5–7).

8
Other Letters
and Revelation

The Epistle to the Hebrews

The oldest manuscripts of the New Testament transmit the so-called epistle to the Hebrews together with the Pauline letters. It is not so much a letter as a "word of exhortation" (see the closing passage, Heb. 13:22–25); it is a lengthy "sermon" on a number of passages from scripture that aims at strengthening a group of Christians who are in danger of losing sight of the essentials of the faith. The address "to the Hebrews" is found for the first time in the early third century; it was probably added because it was thought that only people of Jewish descent could be interested in the difficult expositions on scripture found in this document.

Much remains uncertain. The anonymous author does not express points of view typical of Pauline circles; he and his readers belong to a second generation of Christians (Heb. 2:3). His readers have suffered in the past (10:32–34), and are still in the middle of a period of testing (12:4–11). They are exhorted to hold on (10:36). The author is firmly convinced that those "who have once been enlightened, who have tasted the heavenly gift, and have become partakers of the Holy Spirit, and have tasted the goodness of the word of God and the powers of the age to come" will not receive a new opportunity for repentance and divine forgiveness when they apostatize (6:4–8; cf. 10:26–27).

In this situation it is necessary once more to tell the people addressed who Jesus is: "Jesus Christ is the same yesterday and today and for ever" (Heb. 13:8). In his exposition the author combines a number of earlier Christological strands with a number of lines of argument into a very complicated and highly individual Christology.[1] All along he uses texts and themes of the Old Testament (which he quotes in the Greek version) to prove his case. For him it is the word of God. One should realize, however, that "the law has but a shadow of the good things to come" (10:1; cf. 8:5; 9:23). Jesus is the mediator of a new and better covenant (8:6; 9:15; 12:24). After a long quotation of Jer. 31:31–34 in 8:8–12 (cf. 10:16–17), the author concludes: "In speaking of a new covenant he treats the first as obsolete. And what is becoming obsolete and growing old is ready to vanish away" (8:13). If the addressees are possibly tempted to turn to Jewish beliefs and ceremonies (and 9:9–10; 12:15–17; 13:7–17 may suggest that), they should know that they revert to what is already outdated.

First and foremost, Jesus is the Son of God. The author quotes Ps. 2:7 twice in a prominent place in his argument (Heb. 1:5; 5:5) in order to emphasize Jesus' present Lordship over all powers in the universe (see the entire passage 1:5–13). Psalm 2:7 is directly connected with Ps. 110:1, a passage traditionally used to stress Jesus' exaltation and his sitting at God's right hand. It is quoted in 1:13 and used in 1:3; 8:1; 10:12; 12:2. In their temptations, followers of Jesus Christ should realize that they can rely on their Lord who sits at the right hand of God and is more powerful than all his (and their) enemies, who will someday be annihilated forever.

The Son, however, took part in God's creation. In words reminding us of 1 Cor. 8:6; Col. 1:16; and John 1:3, the author stresses that God has spoken to us in these last days by a Son, "whom he appointed the heir of all things, through whom also he created the world" (Heb. 1:2). "He reflects [or: radiates] the glory of God and bears the very stamp of his nature, upholding the universe by his word of power" (1:3; see also the quotation of Ps. 45:6–7 in vs. 8–9). This Son, powerful from the beginning and victorious at the end, takes upon himself a human existence of suffering and death. In 1:3 the author continues: "When he had made purification for sins, he sat down at the right hand of the Majesty on high." In 10:5–10 we read that he accepted a human body, and that it was this body that was offered in behalf of others. And in a singular comment on the Greek version of Ps. 8:4–6^2 it is said, "for a little while [he] was made lower than the angels, crowned with glory and honor because of the suffering of death, so that by the grace of God he might taste death for every one" (2:9). In the next verse (2:10) Jesus is called "the one who leads them to salvation" (TEV); the Greek term is *archēgos,* which is used here and in 12:2 and also occurs in Acts 3:15; 5:31 (in the latter case in connection with Jesus' exaltation at the right hand of God).

In Heb. 2:9–18, as in 4:14–16 and in 5:5–10, the emphasis is not only on the effects of Jesus' death but also on the fact that he was perfected in the sufferings which he shared with his brethren, so as to become an effective helper for those who are still in a difficult situation. It is in this context that the term "high priest" is used: "For we have not a high priest who is unable to sympathize with our weaknesses, but one who in every respect has been tempted as we are, yet without sin" (4:15). As exalted high priest, the Son helps the true believers and intercedes with God for those who belong to him (see also 7:25).

From the way the author introduces the title in Heb. 2:17; 4:15; 5:5–10; and also in 3:1 ("the apostle [= the one sent by God on a special mission] and high priest of our confession") it is clear that his readers are familiar with "high priest" as a designation for Jesus. In the writings of the New Testament it is not found outside Hebrews, but *1 Clement* (61:3 and 64), probably independently of Hebrews, calls Jesus Christ "high priest and patron" in a liturgical context. This fact suggests that also the author of Hebrews knew it as a title used in early Christian worship.[3] The notion of Jesus' intercession is already found in Rom. 8:34:

> Christ Jesus, who died,
> > yes, who was raised from the dead,
> > who is at the right hand of God,
> > who indeed intercedes for us.

Paul here uses traditional language on death and resurrection;[4] it is quite possible that the two last clauses also were taken over by him from tradition. The author of Hebrews, familiar with this notion of Jesus' intercession after his exaltation, gave it special emphasis in view of the situation addressed by him.

In Heb. 5:1–11 the author, familiar with Ps. 110:1, introduces the fourth verse of this psalm: "Thou art a priest for ever, after the order of Melchizedek," immediately after Ps. 2:7. The verse speaks about "a priest," but when the author refers to it, he mentions a "high priest after the order of Melchizedek" (5:10; 6:20; 7:26–28). In chapter 7 he explains what this designation implies. Jesus Christ is high priest forever "by the power of an indestructible life" (7:16). He holds his priesthood forever, lives always to intercede for those who draw near to God (vs. 24–25; see also 26–28). Referring to the meeting of Melchizedek and Abraham in Gen. 14:18–20 in 7:1–3, the author states that Melchizedek, being "without father or mother or genealogy," "has neither beginning of days nor end of life" and in this respect resembles the Son. He was also greater than Abraham who gave him a tithe of the spoils, and his status is superior to the Levitical priesthood descended from Abraham. The priesthood after the order of Melchizedek, instituted by a solemn oath (Ps. 110:4) is of a totally different order from the Levitical priesthood and has definitely superseded it (7:26–28).

The author combines this notion of eternal, indestructible priest-hood with the notion of Christ as sacrifice (see, e.g., Rom. 3:25; 5:9; and particularly Eph. 5:2).[5] In Heb. 7:26–27 he concludes: "For it was fitting that we should have such a high priest, holy, blameless, unstained, separated from sinners, exalted above the heavens. He has no need, like those high priests, to offer sacrifices daily, first for his own sins and then for those of the people; he did this once and for all when he offered up himself" (cf. 9:14, 24–26). In a very detailed exposition in chapters 8–10 he shows the effectiveness of the perfect sacrifice of this eternal high priest, who ministers in the heavenly sanctuary (8:1; 9:11, 24; 10:19). Leviticus 16 requires the high priest of the old dispensation to enter the Holy of Holies once a year on the Day of Atonement to sprinkle blood on behalf of the sins of the people, but Christ "entered once for all into the [heavenly] Holy Place, taking not the blood of goats and calves but his own blood, thus securing an eternal redemption" (9:12, in the context of 9:6–14).[6] In this way he is the mediator of a new covenant, infinitely more effective than the first (9:15–22).[7]

In Heb. 10:19 the author returns to his exhortations. He writes: "Since we have a great priest over the house of God, let us draw near with a true heart in full assurance of faith, with our hearts sprinkled clean from an evil conscience and our bodies washed with pure water" (vs. 21–22). However complicated the Christological pattern consisting of traditional and highly individual motifs may be, its purpose is eminently practical: to strengthen the faith, hope, and love of the group of Christians addressed in this letter, to keep them on the right track in the difficult times ahead, between Christ's exalta-tion and his *parousia* ("encouraging one another, and all the more as you see the Day drawing near," 10:25; cf. vs. 32–39).

The First Epistle of Peter

The Christians in Asia Minor to whom this letter is written are portrayed as living in difficult circumstances. The author character-izes their position as "exiles of the Dispersion" (1 Peter 1:1), and urges them, as "aliens and exiles," to "maintain good conduct among the Gentiles" (2:11–12). They are "chosen and destined by God the Father and sanctified by the Spirit for obedience to Jesus Christ and for sprinkling with his blood" (1:2).[8] They have been called to be a holy people of God (1:13–17; 2:9–10) and to form a spiritual house in which God is worshiped through Jesus Christ. Christ himself is its cornerstone—the very stone which the builders rejected (2:4–8).[9] As people born anew they must lead a new life (1:22–2:3; cf. 1:3), and that is why they are now confronted with the hostility of the world, which causes suffering and has led to persecution.

The author urges his readers to remain steadfast. They may rejoice in their sufferings (1 Peter 1:6; 3:14; 4:13–14); they are being tested (1:6). A fiery ordeal has come upon them to prove them (4:12; cf. v. 17). They will be vindicated when Jesus Christ appears (1:3–9, 13; 4:17–19; 5:4). And if they share Christ's sufferings they may also rejoice and be glad when his glory is revealed (4:13; cf. 1:11; 2:21; 5:1, 9, 10–11). A detailed analysis of the expressions used to describe the situation of the suffering Christians in a hostile world would reveal that the author uses traditional language throughout.[10] In his exhortations he makes use of a number of sayings of Jesus which are known to us from the Synoptics (see, e.g., 2:1–2; 3:9, 14).[11] In 2:13–3:7 he uses material from the "household duty code" tradition (cf. Col. 3:18–4:1; Eph. 5:22–6:9), concentrating on the attitude of slaves toward their masters and the relationship between wives and husbands. He begins with a section on the attitude of subjects to the emperor (cf. Rom. 13:1–7). His warning and encouragement are summed up admirably in 4:19: "Therefore let those who suffer according to God's will do right and entrust their souls to a faithful Creator."

In three passages in particular the author explains how Christian existence is grounded in the work of Christ: 1 Peter 1:18–21; 2:22–24 (introduced by v. 21 and followed by v. 25) and 3:18–22. Here again we find traditional notions and traditional language, which has given some interpreters reason to try to reconstruct the wording of earlier hymnic compositions possibly used by our author. They have probably wanted too much; it is safer to assume that the author himself brought together Christological material familiar to his readers and used it in places where it could support his admonitions.[12]

The passage 1 Peter 1:18–21 begins with an explanation of the effect of Christ's death. The members of God's holy people living as exiles in the world should realize that they were "ransomed from the futile ways inherited from your fathers, not with perishable things such as silver or gold, but with the precious blood of Christ, like that of a lamb without blemish or spot" (vs. 18–19). The wording of verse 18a is clearly influenced by Isa. 52:3, addressed to the people of Israel about to be released from exile in Babylon. Of the passages in the New Testament concerned with redemption and ransom Titus 2:14 provides the closest parallel: ". . . who gave himself for us to redeem us from all iniquity and to purify for himself a people of his own who are zealous for good deeds." The reference to the blood of Christ as a lamb without blemish or spot is general rather than specific;[13] Heb. 9:12, 14 provides a near parallel, but in the present context a reference to the Paschal lamb (see 1 Cor. 5:7) seems likely.[14] In 1 Peter

1:20 we read that Christ "had been chosen (by God) before the foundation of the world and was revealed in these last days for your sake" (TEV, slightly altered). This is not a statement on preexistence and incarnation, but a variant of the "hidden-revealed" pattern found in the writings of Paul and his school;[15] the emphasis is on the fact that God's agelong intention has now been realized, in Christ, "for your sake." Verse 21 emphasizes the importance of Jesus' resurrection and exaltation, again using traditional language.[16]

The next passage, 1 Peter 2:21–25, begins with an exhortation to follow in the steps of Christ "because Christ also suffered for you, leaving you an example." We have already seen[17] that here and in 3:18 (RSV margin) the word "suffered" is used in a comprehensive way; it includes Jesus' death "for us." We have also noted the parallel with certain formulas in Luke-Acts.[18] The author of 1 Peter is at pains to show that Christ's suffering and death are exemplary, yet unique as a "suffering for you." He continues by explaining the "for you" by means of a number of references to the Greek version of Isa. 53 incorporated in a short hymn on Christ. He quotes Isa. 53:9 in verse 22, and refers to Isa. 53:4, 12 when he explains that Christ "himself bore our sins in his body on the tree, that we might die to sin and live to righteousness" (v. 24).[19] Changing back to the second person plural he tells his readers: "By his wounds you have been healed [cf. Isa. 53:5]. For you were straying like sheep [Isa. 53:6], but have now returned to the Shepherd and Guardian of your souls" (vs. 24–25).[20] This is an extremely interesting passage, just because it uses Isa. 53 so fully and explicitly as an explanation of the traditional "for us / for you" used in formulas speaking about Christ's death and suffering. We shall return to this in the next chapter.[21]

The third passage (1 Peter 3:18–22), too, begins with a reference to Christ's suffering: "For Christ also died for sins once for all, the righteous for the unrighteous, that he might bring us to God." This clearly takes up 2:21–25, emphasizing the "once for all" (Rom. 6:10; Heb. 7:27; 9:12, 26–28; 10:10) and the face that his death has opened the way to communion with God (Rom. 5:1–2; Eph. 2:18; 3:12; Heb. 4:16; 10:19–22; 12:22). In the next two clauses of verse 18, "being put to death in the flesh but made alive in the spirit," we find a pattern of thought also applied in Rom. 1:3f. and 1 Tim. 3:16 (cf. 4:6). They are followed by a sentence that is difficult to interpret: "in which [i.e., in the spirit, RSV; cf. "in his spiritual existence," TEV] he went and preached to the spirits in prison, who formerly did not obey, when God's patience waited in the days of Noah" (vs. 19–20a). The author clearly wants to stress that the salvation brought about in Christ's death and resurrection affects more beings than merely the Christians he addresses, but whether "the spirits in prison" refers to the disobedient contemporaries of Noah who received the good news after their death, or to the rebelling angels mentioned in Gen. 6:1–4 in the introduction of the story of the Flood, is not clear. The former interpretation takes "in the days of Noah" in verse 20a literally; it would imply a journey of Christ to the abode of the dead.[22] Yet the story of the rebellion and punishment of the angels was a popular one in the centuries around the beginning of the common era,[23] and there may be a connection with the subjection of "angels, authorities, and powers" mentioned in verse 22. In that case the disputed sentence in verses 19–20a simply reasserts Christ's proclamation to angelic opponents of God, in line with the traditional statement on Christ's exaltation in terms of Ps. 110:1 in verse 22.[24] The second interpretation seems the more likely one,[25] but a completely convincing interpretation of all details in these verses is well-nigh impossible. This also applies to verses 20b–21, which speak about the ark as a means of saving Noah's family "through water," and about baptism as corresponding with it; they form a digression on the part of the author of 1 Peter.

Note on Jude and 2 Peter

The epistle of Jude is written in defense of "our common salvation" and "the faith which was once for all delivered to the saints" (Jude 3; cf. v. 20). It warns against people who "deny our only Master and Lord, Jesus Christ" (v. 4). The readers are exhorted to "keep yourselves in the love of God; wait for the mercy of our Lord Jesus Christ unto eternal life" (v. 21).

The unknown author of 2 Peter, who at a later stage used the epistle of Jude (see 2 Peter 2) in his refutations of a different group of false teachers, also stresses Jesus' Lordship. Several times he speaks of "our Lord and Savior Jesus Christ" (1:11; 2:20; 3:[2], 18) or "our Lord Jesus Christ" (1:8, 14, 16; cf. 1:2), and once even about "our God and Savior Jesus Christ" (1:1).[26] In 2:1 Christ is called "the Master who bought them," and in 1:16–18 the author emphasizes Jesus' majesty at the transfiguration "on the holy mountain," when he received honor and glory from God the Father and heard a voice borne to him by "the Majestic Glory."

The author of 2 Peter stresses the necessity of "knowledge of him who called us to his own glory and excellence" (1:3; cf. 1:2, 4, 5–6, 8, 11), and urges his readers to shun wrong practices and false doctrines (ch. 2). They "should remember the predictions of the holy prophets and the commandment of the Lord and Savior through your apostles" (3:2; cf. 1:2). One should not despair: contrary to what false teachers suggest, the Day of the Lord *will* come, at God's time, like a thief (see esp. 3:8–10).[27] One should "count the forbearance of our Lord as salvation" (3:15).

The Revelation to John

The last book in the New Testament reflects a situation of heavy conflict between the Roman Empire, with its cult of the emperors, and the Christians in Asia Minor; it is usually dated at the end of the reign of the emperor Domitian (81–96).[28] It presents itself as a revelation of Jesus Christ through an angel to John, a visionary on the island of Patmos (Rev. 1:1–3, 9–11; cf. 22:6–21), addressed to seven Christian communities in the region (1:1, 11). John has to write seven letters to the seven churches and to recount numerous visions of "what is and what is to take place hereafter" (1:19). It is difficult to trace the continuity and coherence in the author's conceptions; details of the apocalyptic imagery and the exact meaning of the numerous allusions to texts in the Old Testament often remain obscure. There is, despite many theories proposed by modern scholars, no consensus about the overall structure of the book.[29] In view of this, we shall restrict ourselves to sketching the main lines of its views on Jesus Christ's role in the eschatological drama in which the Christian communities addressed in Revelation take part.[30]

In the introduction and in the closing passages the readers are assured that the end is near and that the Lord will soon visit the earth (Rev. 1:1, 3, 7; 22:7, 12, 20). The final section (19:11–22:5) describes Christ's final victory. In 19:11–16 he is portrayed as a rider on a white horse, followed by a heavenly army. He is called Faithful and True (v. 11; cf. 1:5; 3:7, 14; 6:10), the Word of God (v. 13; cf. Wisd. of Sol. 18:15?) and King of kings and Lord of lords (v. 16; cf. 17:4[31]). The Beast (symbol of the Roman Empire in chs. 13–17) and all the kings of the earth are killed (19:17–21), together with its prophet who had deceived all those who had received the mark of the Beast and worshiped its image (13:11–17; 16:13).[32] Satan, the force behind the Beast (ch. 12 relates, among other things, how Michael throws him out of heaven and how he wages war on earth "in great wrath, because he knows that his time is short," v. 12b!), is imprisoned in a deep pit for a thousand years (20:1–3). During that time Christ reigns together with those who were martyred "for their testimony to Jesus and for the word of God" and "had not worshiped the beast or its image and had not received its mark on their foreheads or their hands" (20:4–6). This millennium is an interlude, a period of bliss reserved for those who have gone to the utmost in their allegiance to God and Christ.[33] It is followed by a last outburst of violence on the part of Satan and the forces of evil; those who reign with Christ remain unhurt; Satan is thrown into the lake of fire where the beast and the false prophet are (20:7–10). The final judgment follows. All the dead stand before the throne and are judged by what is written in the books, by what they have done. In the end, Death and Hades are thrown into the lake of fire. "This is the second death, the lake of fire; and if any one's name was not found written in the book of life, he was thrown into the lake of fire" (20:11–15).

Revelation 21:1–22:5 mentions "a new heaven and a new earth" and describes the new Jerusalem, coming down out of heaven from God. There is no temple; everything is centered around, and everybody is directed toward, God and the Lamb who shares God's throne: "There shall no more be anything accursed, but the throne of God and of the Lamb shall be in it, and his servants shall worship him; they shall see his face, and his name shall be on their foreheads. And night shall be no more; they need no light of lamp or sun, for the Lord God will be their light, and they shall reign for ever and ever" (22:3–5).

In this last vision[34] Jesus Christ is called "the Lamb," by far the most important Christological designation in Revelation. The new Jerusalem is called "the Bride of the Lamb" (Rev. 21:2, 9; see 19:6–9 announcing the marriage of the Lamb). The twelve foundation stones of the wall of the city carry the names of the twelve apostles of the Lamb (21:14). In 21:22–27 and 22:1–5 God and the Lamb are closely connected. They share one throne and they are the source of the light for the city and its inhabitants.

The Lamb is mentioned for the first time in Rev. 5. In chapter 4 the seer beholds God on his throne in heaven, in his right hand a scroll with seven seals. No one in heaven or on earth or under the earth is worthy to open it, except "the Lion of the tribe of Judah, the Root of David,"[35] who "has conquered" (5:5). Indeed, John sees "a Lamb standing, as though it had been slain, with seven horns and with seven eyes, which are the seven spirits of God sent out into all the earth" (5:6; cf. 1:4; 3:1; 4:5), and he hears a new song (5:9–10):

Worthy art thou to take the scroll and to open its seals,
for thou wast slain and by thy blood didst ransom men for God
from every tribe and tongue and people and nation,
and hast made them a kingdom and priests to our God,
and they shall reign on earth.

This song is followed by two short hymns of praise in verses 12 and 13.

It is difficult to trace with certainty the Old Testament background of Revelation's use of the image of the Lamb (Greek *arnion*). It is unlikely that it is derived from Isa. 53:7, which portrays an entirely different servant of the Lord, and it is not impossible that it is inspired by the Passover lamb (cf. 1 Peter 1:18). But very probably the reference to the Lamb is, as in other texts of the New Testament, general rather than specific.[36] In any case the image has begun to lead its own life in Revelation. Christ is Lamb and Shepherd at the same time (Rev. 7:17). The Lamb is the antagonist of the Beast and its prophet (ch. 14 after ch. 13!). He has conquered (5:5) and he will conquer the kings who serve the Beast: "the Lamb will conquer them, for he is Lord of lords and King of kings, and those with him are called and chosen and faithful" (and will share in his victory; 17:14). The word "to conquer" plays an important part in these passages which encourage the faithful to hold on in their difficult lot. "He who conquers, I will grant him to sit with me on my throne, as I myself conquered and sat down with my Father on his throne," says Christ to the church of Laodicea at the end of the letters to the churches (3:21; cf. 2:7, 11, 26; 3:5, 12 and also 5:2; 21:7). The victorious Lamb stands near God's throne (5:6; 7:9) or shares it (17:17; 22:1, 3). He and God are light and temple (21:22–23), and he has the Book of Life (13:8), just like God (21:27).

On the other hand the Lamb's power to open the seven seals (in Rev. 6–8) and to conquer in the name of God is directly connected with his death, by which he ransomed[37] men for God from every nation (5:9; cf. 1:4–6!). When the seer beholds a great multitude from every nation standing before the throne and the Lamb he is told: "These are they who have come out of the great tribulation; they have washed their robes and made them white in the blood of the Lamb" (7:14). "The Lamb in the midst of the throne will be their shepherd, and he will guide them to springs of living water" (7:17). Elsewhere, in a hymn on the salvation and the power and the kingdom of God and his Christ after Satan's downfall from heaven in 12:10–12 (cf. 11:15–18), we hear of people who "have conquered him [Satan] by the blood of the Lamb and by the word of their testimony," for they gave up their lives. In 14:3–4 we find the hundred and forty-four thousand "who had been redeemed from the earth"; they are called those "who follow the Lamb wherever he goes; these have been redeemed from mankind as first fruits for God and the Lamb." The Christians addressed in Revelation are followers of the Lamb who died to set them free, who conquered death and will one day conquer all resistance to God's kingdom on earth. They will be persecuted, but in the end they will share in the Lamb's glory. In the visions of the book of Revelation the believers receive glimpses of the glory in which they will share, and which is essentially theirs already.[38]

9
The Christology
of the Gospel
and the Letters of John

The Johannine Point of View

The Fourth Gospel tells its own story about Jesus from its own point of view. It shows an acquaintance with Synoptic traditions, and it must have had access to sources of Jesus material not transmitted elsewhere. But everything is taken up in an independent story told in a typically Johannine way. There is a specific Johannine vocabulary that we also find in the Johannine letters, and the Jesus drama unfolds itself in a distinctly Johannine fashion. Jesus travels from Galilee to Jerusalem, and back again. In Jerusalem, in the temple, in the discussions with the leaders of the Jewish people, the secret of Jesus' mission and his relation to God is disclosed—to the disciples and to any reader open to it, but not to his opponents. The Johannine Jesus performs his deeds, which are called "signs" in this Gospel; in many cases these deeds lead up to long speeches starting with a dialogue with opponents but ending in a monologue. Within each speech, and within the Gospel as a whole, the argument circles around the various aspects of Jesus' mission. Later speeches take up earlier events and earlier points of discussion. The argument of the Gospel as a whole unfolds itself as a spiral. It begins with the witness of John the Baptist in John 1:19–34 and ends with the confession of Thomas in 20:24–29, followed by the conclusion by the evangelist in 20:30–31. A Prologue precedes the Gospel (1:1–18), and it winds up with an Epilogue (ch. 21).[1]

In John 20:30–31, the verses that conclude the Gospel, we read: "Now Jesus did many other signs in the presence of the disciples, which are not written in this book; but these are written that you may believe that Jesus is the Christ, the Son of God, and that believing you may have life in his name." Clearly, the question of the right belief in Jesus stands at the center of the Gospel. The principal witnesses to what Jesus did and said are his disciples. They do indeed play an important part in John's story.[2]

In John 20:19–20, for instance, the disciples receive the Spirit and are sent out with authority to forgive and to retain sins (vs. 21–23). They are the ones who are able to say to Thomas "We have seen the Lord" (v. 25). After eight days Thomas is allowed to join them with the confession "My Lord and my God!" (v. 28). He receives an "extra" appearance of the Lord, unlike all believers coming after him, who rely on the witness of the disciples and are blessed because they have not seen and yet believe (v. 29).

In the beginning of the Gospel the calling of the first disciples is told at length (John 1:35–51). After the story of the wedding at Cana a redactional passage states, "This, the first of his signs, Jesus did at Cana in Galilee, and manifested his glory; and his disciples believed in him" (2:11). All along, the disciples are present when Jesus wanders through Galilee and goes up to Jerusalem. They hear and see, then believe and begin to understand. Immediately after the next episode, that of Jesus cleansing the temple, we hear, however, that it was only after Jesus' resurrection that the disciples remembered what Jesus had said, and could see this and the words from the scriptures in the right perspective (v. 22, at the end of 2:13–21; cf. 12:16).

Very prominent in the Fourth Gospel are chapters 13–17, which give the story of the last meal of Jesus with his disciples, the farewell discourses, and a long prayer of Jesus. Between the account of Jesus' public ministry and the passion narrative, these chapters deal with Jesus' relationship to his disciples, in particular in the period after his departure. The disciples are here representative of all believers of all times; on the other hand they are also the ones on whose witness later generations depend: "I do not pray for these only, but also for those who believe in me through their word" (17:20).

Jesus' representative and, in a way, his successor to act among the disciples after his departure is the Holy Spirit, called "the Spirit of truth" and "the Paraclete" (RSV "the Counselor"; TEV "the Helper"). He appears several times in these chapters (John 14:16–17, 25–26; 15:26–27; 16:7–11, 12–15). He will "teach you all things, and bring to your remembrance all that I have said to you" (14:26). He does not teach anything new, but will bring out the truth of what God revealed in Jesus: "When the Spirit of truth comes, he will guide you into all the truth." He makes it possible for the disciples to hand down God's message to further generations, and to bear witness before the outside world (15:26–16:4; 16:7–10). It is within the community of the disciples (that is, those involved in a continuing process of guidance and instruction) that the Spirit operates. The Fourth Gospel claims, therefore, to give the true story about Jesus, inspired by the Spirit and told for those who want to remain in, or to join, the community of "insiders" led by the Spirit. Outside that circle, no real understanding of Jesus is possible.

The uniqueness of the insiders' knowledge is brought out in several other ways in the Fourth Gospel. In chapters 2–12 Jesus meets with much opposition and unbelief. The principal opponents are "the Jews," represented mostly by the Jewish religious authorities in Jerusalem. Time and again, they reject Jesus' claims and try to kill him (5:16, 18; 7:1, 19, 25, 30; 8:37, 40; 11:53). At the end of the account of Jesus' public ministry the evangelist complains, "Though he had done so many signs in their presence, yet they did not believe in him" (12:37, RSV alt.). Every now and then people sympathize with Jesus (e.g., 2:23–24; Nicodemus in chs. 3 and 7; other people in the crowd in chs. 7–8), but their faith does not lead to a real understanding of the secret of Jesus' ministry. Of leading figures such as Nicodemus, the author says: "Nevertheless many even of the authorities believed in him, but for fear of the Pharisees they did not confess it, lest they should be put out of the synagogue: for they loved the praise of men more than the praise of God" (12:42–43).

Jesus and his followers face a hostile world. God loved the world, sent his Son into the world, but only those who believe in him are saved and receive eternal life (John 3:16–21). In the farewell discourses Jesus says, "If the world hates you, know that it has hated me before it hated you. If you were of the world, the world would love its own; but because you are not of the world, but I chose you out of the world, therefore the world hates you" (15:18–19).

The true believers are not "of this world" (see also John 17:16), because Jesus is not "of this world" (8:23; 17:16). He is "from above" (8:23; 3:31), and the believers are "born from above" (3:3, 7; see RSV margin). The believers are "children of God" (1:12; cf. 11:52) just as he is Son of God. The true believers belong to Jesus and remain in communion with him after his return to the Father (e.g., 15:1–11). Together they face the opposition of a hostile outside world.

The Situation of the Johannine Communities

The Gospel of John reflects a situation in which controversies with the Jews have led to a break between the community of believers in Jesus and the synagogue in which "the Pharisees" are the leaders.[3] The fate of the healed man blind from birth in chapter 9 is exemplary for that of other Jews who come to believe in Jesus. He is cast out, "for the Jews had already agreed that if any one should confess him to be Christ, he was to be put out of the synagogue" (John 9:22, 34; cf. 16:1–4; 20:19). The opposition of the

Jews is representative of the hostility of the world.

In the debates recorded in the Gospel we do not find a real dialogue. Jesus takes up Jewish ideas about "the Messiah" and other eschatological hopes, and counters objections against his views and behavior. It is obvious that these are important issues for the readers, but they, like their Master in the story, clearly are no longer engaged in discussion, but at the most in occasional hostile debate. Yet the Jews and the non-Jews among the readers have to be clear why the former were thrown out of the synagogue, and in particular about which Christological views led to the break that could no longer be healed. The community knows sympathizing Jews and Christians of other groups, but is evidently inclined to think that the true insights into the secret of Jesus' ministry are found only in their own community.[4]

The Gospel is probably to be dated at the end of the first century when, after the destruction of Jerusalem in A.D. 70, Pharisaic scribes reorganized Judaism by emphasizing fidelity to the law and tradition, and enforced a strict way of life and uniformity of liturgical usages. In that period, existing estrangement between followers of Jesus and the local synagogues must have led to a definite break, and expulsion of the former. When and where exactly this happened we do not know. The situation reflected in the Fourth Gospel is that of a particular region. Traditionally, the Gospel is connected with Asia Minor and Ephesus; some scholars think of Syria and Antioch, but we have no decisive evidence one way or another.

The letters of John must be dated somewhat later than the Gospel;[5] again it is not clear where the Christians to whom they were addressed lived. The letters reflect a situation of conflict; a split has occurred, a group of Johannine Christians has separated from the group which writes 1 John (see 1:1–4), and from "the elder" who writes 2 and 3 John (1 John 2:19; 2 John 7–11. The Christological aspects of the conflict mentioned in 3 John are not evident, so we leave this letter out of account).

Both sides in the conflict claim to be led by the Spirit and to possess knowledge (this is implicit in 1 John 2:20–27). In order to be able to distinguish between false and true inspiration, one has to test the spirits to determine whether they are of God. In 1 John 4:1–6 (cf. 2 John 7) the criterion is the confession that "Jesus Christ has come in the flesh" (4:2–3; cf. 2 John 2:7 and 1 John 1:1–14); elsewhere, the emphasis is on Jesus' suffering and death (5:6–8), and on the expiation for the sins of the believers and of the whole world brought about by him (1 John 2:2; 4:10). The differences in Christology have ethical consequences (1:6–10; 2:3–9), and all along the authors of 1 John exhort their readers to stay firm in the final period before the Last Judgment (2:28–3:3; 4:17). Their opponents are clearly "spiritualists" who claim that the Son of God was "spiritual" too, and that he did not have a real body of flesh and blood; for that reason, they are usually called "docetists." They claim moral perfection, and regard their group in its spiritual and moral purity as the true claimants to the Christian heritage in the Johannine tradition. No trace of the conflict with the Jews remains; there is not even any use of arguments from the scriptures in the debate.

The Christology of the Fourth Gospel

For the Fourth Gospel Jesus is "the Christ, the Son of God"—see the conclusion of the Gospel in 20:30–31 and Martha's confession in 11:27. John the Baptist denies that he is the Messiah, or Elijah or the Prophet, and confesses Jesus as the Son of God (John 1:34). When the first disciples express their faith in Jesus they use several terms, among which are "the Messiah," i.e., "the Christ" (1:41; cf. v. 45), and in verse 49 "the Son of God," "the King of Israel." Jesus refers to himself as "the Son of man" in verse 51. In the debates between Jesus and the Jews and the discussions among people in Jerusalem, recorded in chapter 7, Jesus is called "the Christ" (7:26, 27, 31) as well as "the prophet" (7:40, plus an important variant in v. 52), but he claims that his authority is from God "who sent him" (7:11–24, 25–29)—an expression elsewhere connected with "the Father" (see below). In this light, the Davidic descent of the Messiah, and his birth in Bethlehem are irrelevant (7:40–44). In chapter 6 the feeding of a multitude in the desert leads to the reaction "this is indeed the prophet" (6:14); people want to make Jesus king (6:15). The following dialogue-monologue shows that Jesus is not "the prophet like Moses" of Deut. 18:18–19, but much more: he is himself the Bread from Heaven, sent by God in order that those who accept him may live forever. In John 9 the discussion between the healed blind man and the Pharisees is on the question whether Jesus really is a reliable prophet (9:13–17, 24–34; see Deut. 13:1–5; 18:9–22). After the man has been expelled, like all those who confess Jesus as the Christ (9:22), Jesus reveals himself to him as the Son of man (9:35–41). In 10:24 the Jews ask Jesus: "If you are the Christ, tell us plainly," but Jesus answers with a discourse on the intimate union of the Father and himself. As a final example[6] we may mention the discussion between Jesus and Pilate in 18:33–38 on Jesus' royal authority. In the story of the crucifixion we find the title "King of the Jews" (see 19:3, 12, 14, 15, 19, 21). Jesus tells Pilate that his kingship is "not from the world." His mission is "to bear witness to the truth." As king, Jesus is a prophet and more than prophet: a messenger directly from God; in 19:7 the Jews accuse him of making himself "Son of God."

Jesus is the Messiah, the true king, and the true prophet, but he is so as Son of God, Son of man, the Son sent by the Father, living in intimate union with the Father.[7] Particularly the last aspect is unacceptable to the Jews, as is evident from John 19:7 and from the conflict in chapter 5. We read in 5:18, "This was why the Jews sought all the more to kill him, because he not only broke the sabbath but also called God his own Father, making himself equal with God." In verses 19–20 and verse 30 Jesus claims that the divine authority which he possesses has been given to him by the Father, with whom he remains in close communion as he speaks and acts (the entire discourse 5:19–47 demonstrates this main point; see also the debate in 10:31–39).

The central titles in John are thus Son of man and Son of God or the Son (of the Father). The first title is, as in the Synoptics, only found in words of Jesus (and once in an echo of such a pronouncement in John 12:34). The difference between the use of this title and the other one is not great (see, e.g., 3:11–21, 31–36; 6:27; 8:28). "Son of man" is used to accentuate the heavenly origin (3:13; 6:62; cf. 1:52) and the return to heaven (3:13; 6:62; 8:28; 12:23, 32, 34; 13:31, 32) of the Son. The "Son of man" is also the one who passes judgment on behalf of God (5:27; 9:35–39; 12:31–32) and is, therefore, also the one who is able to grant life (6:27, 53; cf. 9:39; 12:32).[8] As in the Synoptic Gospels, the Son of man has to die; the cross is, however, for John an essential element in the process of Jesus' being "lifted up" (his "glorification"; 3:14; 12:23–36;[9] cf. 6:53 after 6:27).

The titles "Son of God" and "the Son" should be understood, first of all, within the context of the Johannine use of the ancient pattern of thought "God sent his Son in order that . . ." which we described in chapter 1. There we mentioned John 3:16f. (and 1 John 4:9f.): "For God so loved the world that he gave his only Son, that whoever believes in him should not perish but have eternal life. For God sent the Son into the world . . . ." The Fourth Gospel presents numerous variations on this theme. We find the expression "the Father who sent me/him" in 5:23, 37; 6:44; 8:16 (RSV margin), 18; 12:49; 14:24, and even more often: "He who sent me/him" (4:34; 5:24, 30; etc.). Elsewhere, we find the expression "whom God (or: whom he) has sent" (3:34; 5:38; 6:29; 10:36; 17:3; etc.). We should note that in all these cases active forms of the verbs concerned *(apostellō, pempō)* are used. Jesus is the one whom God has sent, as an envoy, as plenipotentiary. As Son he speaks and acts in perfect unity with the Father (4:34; 5:30, 36; 6:38; 7:16–18; 8:16, 28–29). Jesus did not merely receive his commission and instruction once for all, he continues to work in complete dependence upon the Father (5:30; cf. vs. 17, 19, 20; 8:29; 11:41–42; 16:32), in a relationship of love (3:35; 5:20; 10:17; 17:23–26).

The Fourth Gospel exhibits a close affinity with all sorts of Jewish conceptions about prophets, angels, and especially Moses,[10] but at the critical moment more is said than can be expressed in categories of sending. The Son is the perfect, unique envoy, more than "a teacher come from God" of whom it can be said that "God is with him" (Nicodemus in John 3:2); even the term "sent one" cannot properly be applied to him.[11]

The unique nature of the Son's mission and message is not only expressed with the help of the terminology just discussed, but is emphasized by the phrases "from above," "from heaven," connected with a number of terms denoting Jesus' coming from God and returning to God. At a crucial moment in the dialogue with Nicodemus Jesus says, "No one has ascended into heaven but he who descended from heaven, the Son of man" (John 3:13;[12] see also 6:62, together with the many passages in this chapter speaking about the descent of the Bread from heaven, and 20:17). In 3:31–32 we read: "He who comes from above is above all; he who is from the earth belongs to the earth, and of the earth he speaks; he who comes from heaven is above all. He bears witness to what he has seen and heard, yet no one receives his testimony"; the Son of God is a stranger from heaven. We may add 8:14, "Even if I do bear witness to myself, my testimony is true, for I know whence I have come and whither I am going, but you do not know whence I come or whither I am going" (cf. 8:21–23, 38, 42, and 7:33–36); and 13:3: "Jesus, knowing that the Father had given all things in his hands, and that he had come from God and was going to God" (cf. 13:1), and 16:28: "I came from the Father and have come into the world; again, I am leaving the world and going to the Father" (cf. 16:27, 30; 14:12, 28; 17:13).

Also these expressions serve to underline the uniqueness of Jesus' relationship to God. They refer to the way of this special envoy from God to the world, rejected by the world but accepted by believers who are of God,[13] and returning to God. The way from God to God, from heaven to heaven, is never described in mythological language. Yet the Fourth Gospel clearly could not dispense with spatial imagery. It also does not speculate about the mode of existence of the Son with the Father, yet it cannot speak about the origin of the mission without speaking about the origin of the One whom God sent. In John 17:24 Jesus speaks about "my glory which thou hast given me in thy love for me before the foundation of the world" (cf. 17:5)—a glory in which he shares again after his return to the Father.

Many further passages express the unity between Son and Father in terms which at the same time identify the two and subordinate the Son to the Father. This is the case in John 10:37–38: "If I am not doing the works of my Father, then do not believe me; but if I do them, even though you do not believe me, believe the works, that you may know and understand that the Father is in me and I am in the Father." This is Jesus' explanation of his earlier statement "I and the Father are one" (10:30; cf. 14:10–11, 20; 17:11, 21–23). In this light also Jesus' pronouncements which begin with "I am . . ." must be understood. Those with a predicate ("I am the bread of life," "I am the light of the world," etc.)[14] are all variations on the one theme: Jesus grants life on behalf of God, his gifts are unique, and gift and Giver are identical. When "I am" is used without a predicate,[15] corresponding to the revelation formula used, e.g., in Isa. 43:10 (cf. Ex. 3:14), it is clear that Jesus is able to reveal himself in the way God reveals himself, because as the Son he speaks and acts in unity with the Father. Jesus' pronouncement in John 8:58, "Truly, truly, I say to you, before Abraham was, I am," implies preexistence.

This leads us to a few short remarks on the Prologue of John, 1:1–18, which introduces the term "the Word" and speaks about it in a way analogous to the use of the term "Wisdom" in other early Christian texts.[16] The Word was in the beginning with God "and the Word was God" (1:1–2). It acted as a mediator at the creation: "All things were made through him, and without him was not anything made that was made" (v. 3). It represents and grants life and light (v. 4). In Jesus, the Word became flesh. Those who believed beheld a glory "as of the only Son from the Father" (v. 14). "Grace and truth came through Jesus Christ" (vs. 16–17). "No one has ever seen God; the only begotten one, God who is in the bosom of the Father, has made him known" (v. 18).[17] This verse stresses the unique revelation of God through Jesus Christ; it is unique because of the uniqueness of the relationship between "the only begotten" and God. In verse 14 this is explained in terms of divine glory: "the Word became flesh"; verses 1–3 explain that there has been a unique relationship between "the Word" (active at the creation of the world) and God right from the beginning. The Word was God at the beginning, after becoming flesh, *and* after the return of the Son to the Father. Thomas is right when, at the end of the Gospel, he addresses Jesus as "my Lord and my God" (20:28). Yet, despite the clear reference to preexistence and the ontological implications of all that is said in 1:1–18, the emphasis is on the functional identity of Son and Father, and not for a single moment is the reader allowed to forget that the Word / the Son is identical with *and yet subordinate to* the Father.

Three additional aspects of the Christology of the Fourth Gospel require our attention before we turn to the letters of John.

First, we note the use of "Lord," in the vocative, addressed to Jesus, but also in the nominative, as in the Gospel of Luke. See John 6:23, "After the Lord had given thanks"; 11:2, "Mary who anointed the Lord with ointment"; and especially 20:2, 13, 18, 20; 21:7 and 12 in connection with the risen Lord (cf. Luke 24:34). We have already noted Thomas's confession "my Lord and my God" in 20:28, in which John brings out the full implications of the use of this title in his Gospel.[18]

Second, although the structure of the narrative focuses the reader's attention on the crucifixion, as in the other Gospels, relatively little is said about the significance of Jesus' death. We have already noted in passing the reference to the cross in the expression "to be lifted up" (John 3:14; 8:28; 12:32, 34). The good shepherd lays down his life for the sheep (10:11); Jesus does so of his own accord (10:15–18). Here and in 11:50–52 (cf. 18:14), dealing with Jesus' death "for the nation," the preposition *hyper* is used, which we have already encountered in pre-Pauline formulas. In chapters 10 and 11 the Gospel emphasizes that Jesus did not die for Israel alone, but for God's children all over the world.[19] We may add here 6:51 (reminiscent of eucharistic terminology), "and the bread which I shall give for the life of the world is my flesh"; and 17:19, "for their sake I consecrate myself." In 15:13, "Greater love has no man than this, that a man lay down his life for his friends" (cf. 1 John 3:16) draws out the ethical implications for those who follow Jesus (see 13:37–38). So also 12:25–26 after 12:24, where Jesus' death is compared to that of a grain of wheat that dies in order to bear much fruit. Finally, we have to mention 1:29 (cf. v. 36), where John the Baptist calls Jesus "the Lamb of God, who takes away the sin of the world." Neither here nor in 1 John 3:5 is the background of the image explained. In view of 19:36[20] a reference to the Paschal lamb is possible. Alternatively, we may find here just another variant on the early Christian theme of the sacrificial death of Jesus which removes sin(s) (see 1 Peter 1:19; Rev. 5:6, 12; cf. Heb. 9:12, 14), and that no specification is intended.

Third and last, it has often been noted that the Fourth Gospel hardly speaks about Jesus' *parousia.* All emphasis lies on the fact that the decision about life and death is made in the encounter with the Son—see John 3:16–21, 36; 5:19–27, 30 (and 1:9–13 in the Prologue). The Son gives life and judges (condemns) in the name of the Father (5:24). The next verse, 5:25, introduced with the words "the hour is coming and now is" (cf. 4:23), indicates that a certain prolepsis is meant here, an authentic "already." The same view on life and resurrection is found in the story of Lazarus (11:23–26 in particular). "Life" is a present and continuous reality; nevertheless, John has a number of futurist utterances, sometimes connected with utterances in the present tense (5:28; 6:39f., 44, 51, 54; 12:48). He envisages a consummation in the future. Hence the exhortations in the farewell discourses, connected with promises of a future union of the believers with the Son and the Father in glory (17:24–26; 14:1–3). In all this the Fourth Gospel concentrates its attention on the fate of the community of believers that possesses "life" and looks forward to the final and definitive "being with the Lord." (See also, in the letters of Paul, 1 Thess. 4:17; 5:10; Rom. 6:8; 2 Cor. 5:8; Phil. 1:22.) The world that rejects Jesus has no life and no future. We do not hear of a (re)appearance of Jesus on earth in a way recognizable to all.

The Christology of 1 and 2 John

In 1 and 2 John we find a later stage of Johannine Christology, developed in opposition to the views of a rival Johannine group that has separated from the one for which the "we" of 1 John 1–4 and the elder of 2 John write. The main areas of dispute between the two groups were clearly Christology, ethics, eschatology, and pneumatology, and it can be argued that both parties had reason to claim that they gave a correct interpretation of the views current in Johannine circles—which we now find in the Gospel.

As far as Christology is concerned, it seems that the opponents did not pay enough attention to the statement "the Word became flesh" in John 1:14, but emphasized the following: "[he] dwelt among us, full of grace and truth; we have beheld his glory, glory as of the only Son from the Father."[21] In any case, it is no longer sufficient to confess "Jesus is the Christ"; it is necessary to say unequivocally: "Jesus Christ has come in the flesh" (1 John 4:2; cf. v. 3; see 2 John 7). He who denies that the man Jesus is the Christ (that is how we should interpret 1 John 2:22a) denies at the same time the unity of Son and Father, an essential point in Johannine Christology. We have to give heed to what was preached from the beginning if we want to abide in the Son and the Father. The authors stress that the eternal life which was with the Father has been made manifest to them; they have heard it, seen it, touched it with their hands. On this experience the fellowship with Son and Father is based—and only through fellowship of the readers with the authors of the letter can that fellowship be maintained (1 John 1:1–4).

If one stresses that the Son, Jesus Christ, was a real human being, one should also pay attention to the fact that he died a human death and that he died in order that those who believe in him may live. This is expressed in a number of passages. In 1 John 5:6 it is asserted that Jesus Christ ("the Son of God," v. 5) "came by water and blood,

... not with the water only but with the water and the blood." Jesus' baptism and his death are both essential elements in his humanity. There are for the believers three witnesses: "the Spirit, the water, and the blood" (5:7–8), that is: baptism and the Holy Supper/Eucharist besides (or: embedded in) the overall witness of the Spirit in the community of believers.

Referring to claims of ethical perfection by the secessionists (reflected in 1 John 1:6–10; 2:3–9), the authors of 1 John confess that God is light, and stress that believers should walk in that light. This is, however, only possible because "the blood of Jesus his Son cleanses us from all sin" (1:7), and because God is faithful and just so as to forgive our sins and cleanse us of all unrighteousness (1:9).[22] This leads up to the final statement, "If any one does sin, we have an advocate with the Father, Jesus Christ the righteous; and he is the expiation for our sins, and not for ours only but also for the sins of the whole world" (2:1–2). Several motifs are brought together here. First, Jesus Christ is the one who intercedes for us with God—a notion found in Rom. 8:34 and occupying a central place in Hebrews (e.g., 7:25; 9:24). He is our advocate; 1 John uses here the word *paraklētos,* which in John 13–17 is used of the Holy Spirit. Second, Jesus is (note the present tense, indicating continuity!) "the expiation for our sins." "For our sins" (with the Greek preposition *peri*) is already found in a number of ancient formulas concerning Jesus' death, as we know. The word *hilasmos* ("expiation") is found only here and in 1 John 4:10. The corresponding verb is used in Heb. 2:17, a related noun is used for the "mercy seat" on the Ark in the tabernacle and the Solomonic temple (Heb. 9:5; cf. Rom. 3:25). The word used in our passage denotes the act that removes the obstacles in the relationship between God and his people or the sacrifice which has this effect (e.g., Ezek. 44:27). In Heb. 2:17 Christ makes expiation for the sins of his people; here, he *is* expiation; in 1 John 4:10 God sends his Son to be the expiation of our sins. In chapter 11 we shall see that this and related terms are also used in connection with martyrdom in Israel.

It is interesting to see that in 1 John 2:2 the expiation is "for our sins" as well as "for the sins of the whole world." In view of the repeated use of "us" and "you" in ancient formulas, the first expression is perfectly understandable. It also fits in with the Johannine emphasis on the inner circle of the believers which is also very prominent in the letters. The additional phrase reminds us of John 3:16 and related passages (John 1:29; 4:42; 12:47) speaking about God's love for the world (which becomes effective only in those who accept it).

There is one further aspect in the Christology of 1 John requiring our attention. The letter not only dwells on what has been achieved by the Son's appearance in the flesh, but also on what will come about at his (second) appearance in the future—see 3:2, "Beloved, we are God's children now; it does not yet appear what we shall be, but we know that when he appears we shall be like him, for we shall see him as he is" (cf. 2:28). In 4:17 the authors add, "we may have confidence for the day of judgment." In the section that describes the secession of the authors' opponents, the "not yet" aspect is brought out very clearly: "Children, it is the last hour" (2:18); then, referring to the expectation of the coming of "the Antichrist" (which is evidently known to the readers), the authors add that this Antichrist now reveals himself in a group of "antichrists" (2:18; 4:3; 2 John 7), deceivers (2 John 7), false prophets (4:1). The word "Antichrist" occurs here for the first time. Neither the word nor the figure of an eschatological antagonist of Jesus Christ is found in the Gospel. The closest equivalent is the "man of lawlessness" in 2 Thess. 2. There is also the "beast rising out of the sea" in Rev. 13, which is backed up by a second Beast (13:11–18), the great deceiver (compare Rev. 13:13–14 with 2 Thess. 2:8–9). The authors of 1 John are the first ones to use a distinctly Christian term: the final opponent of Jesus the Christ is the Antichrist, that is, the one who opposes the Christ and tries to take his place. When he speaks and acts, all looks deceptively real and genuine!

PART III
Terms and Concepts Applied in the Response to Jesus

The preceding chapters have shown how Jesus' first followers used a great number of terms, ideas, and patterns of thought to express what they believed about him and about his unique place and function in God's dealings with Israel and humanity. They borrowed them from the world in which they lived, and in particular from the Jewish tradition in which they had been brought up. They viewed Jesus in the light of the scriptures and tried to explain his preaching, his deeds, and in particular his suffering, death, and resurrection with the help of certain scriptural passages. Those among the first generation of Christians who came from a non-Jewish background (though mostly from circles of sympathizers connected with the synagogues) were rapidly introduced to terms and arguments derived from the scriptures which their fellow Christians had come to regard as indispensable for an adequate understanding of Jesus.

Right from the start there was a great variety in Christological terms, concepts, and ways of thinking. As Christianity spread around the northeastern part of the Mediterranean, this variety became even richer. The language that the converts used to express what they believed they had received in Jesus became more complex as time went on. In all cases words and ideas also used by others were adopted and adapted to formulate convictions about Jesus and to characterize the various aspects of what he had brought about.

In this chapter an attempt will be made to elucidate the use of a number of terms and concepts by the early Christians with regard to Jesus by pointing out the ways in which those terms were employed by their contemporaries. As was made clear in the Introduction, comparative study of religious concepts and ideas is a very complicated affair. There were no fixed terms to be used as convenient labels because religious concepts and arguments were always intrinsically geared to the specific situations they wanted to address. In adducing parallels we always have to take their literary and historical contexts into account. And because the number of literary sources dating from the period between 100 B.C. and A.D. 100 is limited and our knowledge of Judaism during that period is far from complete, the picture that emerges is sketchy at best.

Within the scope of the present study it is impossible to deal with all aspects of Christology. We shall concentrate on its earliest stages and discuss the relevant material under three headings: first, we shall deal with "Jesus as herald of a New Age," as a prophetic figure, as Christ/Messiah, Son of God and Son of man. Second, we shall discuss the various views on Jesus' death (as that of a messenger from God, a suffering righteous person, a martyr) and his vindication (resurrection, exaltation). Here we shall also speak about the designation "Lord" and about the use of Ps. 110:1 in early Christianity—a typical example of early Christian interpretation of scripture. Third, we shall examine the concept of "the envoy sent from above," implying in many cases preexistence, descent and ascent, and the concept of Wisdom as divine messenger and as mediator at creation.

10
Jesus as Herald of a New Age

From the earliest strands in the Gospel tradition as transmitted in the Gospel of Mark and Q onward, Jesus is portrayed as a preacher, teacher, healer, and exorcist. He is a prophetic figure, and outsiders compare him with John the Baptist, Elijah, or one of the prophets of old (Mark 6:14–16; 8:27–28). But he is greater than John, who himself is more than a prophet (Luke 7:24–28, par. Matt. 11:7–11; cf. Mark 11:27–33 and parallels). He preaches the good news to the poor (Luke 7:18–23; par. Matt. 11:2–6) and promises them a share in the kingdom of God (Luke 6:20; par. Matt. 5:3). Mark 1:14–15 summarizes this good news as follows: "The time is fulfilled, and the kingdom of God is at hand; repent, and believe in the gospel." Jesus is herald of a New Age and inaugurates it. God's sovereign rule is about to become reality, and Jesus' mission—in words and deeds—is an integral part of the realization of the kingdom.

For Mark and Q Jesus' message and mission find their origin in the unique relationship with God. His knowledge and his power to act have been given to him exclusively by the Father (Luke 10:21–22; par. Matt. 11:25–27). Jesus is God's Son (Mark 1:9–11 and parallels) and, as Mark and the other evangelists emphasize, he is the Messiah / the Christ (e.g., Mark 8:29). He frequently refers to himself as the Son of man.

Do Jewish sources around the beginning of the common era speak about prophetic figures comparable to Jesus, and, in particular, about prophets who claim to announce or to bring about a decisive change in the conditions of Israel or of humanity in general? Can we elucidate the use of Messiah, Son of God, and Son of man in Christian literature by comparing it with parallels in Jewish sources? These questions will be dealt with briefly in this section. First, however, something will have to be said about the use of the terms "to bring the good news" *(euaggelizesthai)* and "good news" *(euaggelion)* in connection with "the kingdom of God," which is typical of the early Christian picture of Jesus' activity and is also used to characterize the mission of his disciples.

"To Bring the Good News" and "The Kingdom of God"

There is little doubt that the use of the verb *euaggelizesthai* goes back to the early Christian interpretation of Isa. 40–66, and that the noun *euaggelion* received its special meaning from this verb. We find the verb and its Hebrew/Aramaic equivalents used in Jewish sources with a comparable meaning.[1] There are, however, very few direct parallels, and nowhere does the term play such a central role as in early Christianity. Among the fragments found in Qumran there is the fragment on Melchizedek (11QMelch) that refers to Isa. 52:7 and 61:1 and identifies "he who brings good tidings" with one "anointed by the Spirit" (see especially line 18). The Isaiah passages are two from among a number quoted by the author to elucidate Melchizedek's role at the end of days. Next we have *Pss. Sol.* 11:1 which (again echoing Isa. 52:7 and related texts) says, "Proclaim in Jerusalem the voice of him who brings good tidings, that the God of Israel has shown mercy in his visitation of them." The noun *euaggelion* and its Hebrew/Aramaic equivalents are not found very often in Jewish sources. It is, however, also used in the plural in the context of emperor worship to denote the tidings about important events in the lives of the emperors. This may explain, at least partly, its popularity in early Christianity.[2]

In Isa. 52:7 the good news is concerned with peace, salvation, and God's reign. The idea that God reigns and that his sovereign rule will one day overcome all resistance is current in the Old Testament and in Judaism.[3] God's servants have to take his commandments seriously; if they do, they will have a share in the new dispensation in which God's rule is fully realized.

The actual term "kingdom/reign of God" occurs far less often than the notion of God's sovereignty. To mention a few examples: *Pss. Sol.* 17 is a hymn from about the middle of the first century B.C. which begins and ends with a praise of God's kingship: "Lord, you yourself are our king for ever and ever" (17:1; cf. 17:46; also 2:30; 5:18, 19). "The kingdom of our God is for ever over the nations in judgment" (v. 4); this will become evident when, after the present unworthy kings will have been expelled, a true king, a son of David, will be sent by God to rule over Israel, to conquer all oppression and to remove all pollution and unrighteousness (vs. 21–44). Even the nations will come from the ends of the earth to see God's glory (v. 32):

And he (will be) a righteous king over them, instructed by God;
and there is no unrighteousness among them in his days.
For all are holy, and their king an anointed (of the) Lord.

This ideal Davidic ruler is, of course, completely dependent on God. In fact, "The Lord himself is his king, the hope of him who is strong through hope in God" (v. 34). Secondly, the Eighteen Benedictions may be mentioned. We do not know the exact wording of this daily prayer in the time of Jesus, but it is very likely that also at that period Jews prayed what is found in Benediction 11 of the (shorter) Palestinian recension: "Bring back our judges as in the beginning, and our counselors as at the outset. And be king over us, Thou alone. Blessed art Thou, Lord, who lovest righteousness," followed in Benediction 14 by a request for God's mercy over Israel, his people, over Jerusalem, his city, and over "the Kingdom of the house of David, Thine [Thy righteous] anointed," and by the blessing, "Blessed art Thou, Lord, God of David, who buildest Jerusalem."

We should realize that strict, observant Palestinian Jews who prayed this with all their heart lived in a land that since Pompey's intervention in Jewish affairs in 63 B.C. was ruled by a client king ultimately responsible to the Romans, or by a Roman governor. Many of the Jews found some sort of compromise, protesting only when the Roman emperor or his subordinates infringed upon the essentials of the Jewish faith and on the worship in the Jerusalem temple. Judas the Galilean, however, whom Josephus introduces as a teacher *(sophistēs)* and the leader of "the fourth of the philosophies," which in all other respects agreed with the opinions of the Pharisees, was firmly convinced "that God alone is leader and master" *(Ant.* 18.23). Consequently, he reproached his fellow countrymen "for consenting to pay tribute to the Romans and tolerating mortal masters, after having God for their Lord" *(J.W.* 2.118).[4] Judas (aided by a Pharisee named Saddok) made his radical stand at the occasion of the registration of property organized by the Roman special envoy Quirinius in A.D. 6 after the removal of Herod's son Archelaus *(Ant.* 18.3–9). Josephus does not mention any acts of violence or revolution, but nevertheless accuses him of spreading unrest through the nation and planting the seeds of troubles that were to lead to the war between the Jews and the Romans in A.D. 66–70. Elsewhere, Josephus himself, describing the work of Moses, stresses that the lawmaker of Israel was not attracted by monarchy, oligarchy, or rule of the masses, but "gave his constitution the form of what—if a forced expression be permitted—may be termed a 'theocracy' *(theokratia),* placing all sovereignty and authority in the hands of God" *(Against Apion* 2.164–165). For Josephus, acknowledging God's authority did not exclude cooperation with the Romans, when radical elements during the Jewish rebellion against Roman rule gained control. An interesting speech by Herod the Great is recorded by Josephus in *Ant.* 15.382–387. In an attempt to win the support of the people for his great plan to reconstruct the Jerusalem temple, this staunch supporter of the Roman Empire in the Eastern Mediterranean also claims divine support for his rule: "But since, by the will of God, I am now ruler and there continues to be a long period of peace and an abundance of wealth and great revenues, and—what is of most importance—the Romans, who are, so to speak, the masters of the world, are my loyal friends, I will try to remedy the oversight caused by the necessity and subjection of that earlier time, and by this act of piety make full return to God for the gift of his kingdom" (387). To acknowledge God's sovereignty over Israel, and to define the relation between the powers that be and God was a necessity for Herod as well as for Judas the Galilean—or for Josephus, for that matter.

Early Christian expectations concerning the full realization of God's sovereign rule on earth have to be viewed in the context of such contemporaneous Jewish conceptions. In our sources[5] the emphasis is on radical obedience to the summons issued by Jesus, and on complete trust in what is offered and promised by God through him. The urgency of the appeal is underscored by what is already happening—for instance when Jesus casts out demons or when the disciples are sent out by him to heal people. The imminent full realization of the kingdom of God will be a dynamic event changing the entire world. It will mean the end of the rule of all human authority and of all demonic forces of evil. Those who pay heed to Jesus' words should realize that obedience to God takes absolute precedence over obedience to Caesar. Yet Jesus' answer to the question whether it is lawful to pay taxes to Caesar, "Render to Caesar the things that are Caesar's, and to God the things that are God's" (Mark 12:13–17 and parallels), will not have satisfied the followers of Judas the Galilean. It is also clear that Jesus is not a "king of the Jews" in any earthly, political sense, nor will he be when the kingdom of God comes "with power" (Mark 9:1).[6] At a later stage, Matthew stresses that the kingdom of God will be taken away from the Jewish leaders and given to "a nation producing the fruits of it" (Matt. 21:43), that is, people who "seek first his kingdom and his righteousness" (6:33). Luke describes how Jesus' disciples expect Jesus to bring about a turn in Israel's destiny (Luke 19:11; 24:19–21; Acts 1:6), but are told to wait and to allow themselves to be led by the power of the Spirit.

Jewish Charismatics

In the Gospels Jesus as a prophetic figure is a man not only impressive as a preacher and teacher but also "mighty in deed." This receives special emphasis in Luke, where Jesus is compared with Elijah and Elisha, well known for their miracles and healing (Luke 4:14–30; 7:16), and where the disciples on the road to Emmaus describe him as "a prophet mighty in deed and word before God and all the people" (24:19), bringing out what is characteristic of Jesus in the reports found in all the Gospels. It is interesting to compare this picture of Jesus with that of Jewish charismatics of the period. In his book *Jesus the Jew,* [7] G. Vermes has rightly devoted a separate chapter to "Jesus and Charismatic Judaism," in which he pays special attention to two pious charismatics, Honi the Circle-Drawer (called Onias the Righteous by Josephus) and Hanina ben Dosa. The first lived in the time of the quarrels between Hyrcanus II and Aristobulus II just before Pompey's intervention in Judean affairs. Josephus describes him as "a righteous man and dear to God," who "had once in a rainless period prayed to God to end the drought, and God had heard his prayer and sent rain." The connection with Elijah bringing drought and rain (1 Kings 17:1; 18:41–46; cf. James 5:17) is obvious. Refusing to utter a curse against Aristobulus and his fellow rebels, Honi is stoned to death by "villains among the Jews" (no doubt belonging to the party of Hyrcanus; *Ant.* 14.22–25). The stories about Honi the Circle-Drawer in rabbinic sources are more critical of him. In his prayers his behavior toward God is outspoken if not impertinent. When it does not rain after his first prayer, he draws a circle around himself and refuses to leave it until the rain comes.[8] It is interesting that he regards himself as "a son of the house" *(ben bayit)* before God, and that even the leading Pharisee Simeon ben Shetah, though critical of him, recognizes his special relationship with God. "What can I do with you, since even though you importune God, he does what you wish in the same way that a father does whatever his importuning son asks him?"[9]

Hanina ben Dosa, who probably lived in the period just before A.D. 70, is portrayed as a healer and a miracle worker.[10] In *M. Berakot* 5:5 he is said to have known when his prayer was efficacious. If his prayer was fluent in his mouth (inspired by God) the sick person was favored. In an additional story found in *B. Berakot* 34b we are told that Hanina applied that rule when he prayed in behalf of a son of the famous Rabban Gamaliel, healing him from a distance. When, later on, they checked the time, it was evident that the son was healed exactly at the moment Hanina said his prayer. (Compare John 4:46–54.) It is interesting to note that Hanina, in this story, refuses to be called a prophet or a prophet's son. Nevertheless in a following story, in which he heals a son of another well-known Pharisaic leader, Yoḥanan ben Zakkai, he is portrayed as praying with his head between his knees, in imitation of Elijah (1 Kings 18:41). Not surprisingly, among the many stories about him there is one about his ability to stop rain and make it start again.[11] In *M. Soṭa* 9:15 we read, "When Rabbi Ḥanina ben Dosa died, the men of deed ceased." This powerful charismatic lives in such an intimate union with God that the Heavenly Voice is said to have called him "my son" every day.[12] G. Vermes adds an anecdote told of Ḥanan, grandson of Ḥoni and equally a charismatic rainmaker, who calls God "Abba,"[13] as Jesus did in Gethsemane.[14]

Jewish Prophets[15]

Rabbinic sources give no information about prophets; the rabbis are of the opinion that "since the death of the last prophets, Haggai, Zechariah and Malachi, the holy spirit ceased from Israel, but they received messages by means of a heavenly voice."[16] This heavenly voice, as Vermes reminds us, "was allowed no authority in matters relating to *halakhah* [= binding rules for human conduct], a discipline which was to be constructed, not on new revelation but on tradition and reason."[17] It could, however, testify to a person's holiness and his special relationship with God, as in the case of Ḥanina, just mentioned.[18] Prophetic revelation, clearly considered vastly superior, was thought to return only at the end of times (cf. Joel 2:28–32; Ezek. 37:1–14).

Needless to say, this view of scribes and Pharisees was only a theoretical construction. Charismatics and prophets were active in the centuries between the return from exile and the destruction of Jerusalem. Josephus mentions a number of these people, although he is by no means an unbiased reporter.[19] He views himself as one who was privileged to announce the things that were to come. This is brought out clearly in *J. W.* 3.350–354, where he describes his deliberations before surrendering to the Romans, and in 3.399–408, where he introduces himself to the future emperor Vespasian as "a messenger of greater destinies" and as one sent on this errand by God (cf. 4.622–629). But nowhere does Josephus refer to himself as a prophet; yet it is clear that he claims to have judged the events of his days correctly and to have predicted what was to come in a reliable way; he is convinced that his decisions, including to surrender to the Romans and to assist the Roman commanders in their fight against the rebels, had been inspired by God.[20] He is very much opposed to "the numerous prophets . . . suborned by the tyrants to delude the people" till the last, and he mentions especially a false prophet responsible for the death of six thousand refugees in a portico of an outer court of the temple because he "had on that day proclaimed to the people in the city that God commanded them to go up to the temple court, to receive the tokens of their deliverance" (*J. W.* 6.283–287; see also 288).

Yet in the years before the destruction of the temple God had issued a number of warnings which Josephus enumerates in *J. W.* 6.288–315. Among them was a warning of a certain Jesus, son of Ananias, a rude peasant who, four years before the war, at the Feast of Tabernacles, uttered a lament against Jerusalem in the temple.[21] Nobody was able to silence him, and he continued wailing for seven years and five months, until a Roman missile killed him during the siege (*J. W.* 6.300–309).

Among the prophets in the period under discussion Josephus mentions a number of Essenes. A certain Judas predicts the murder of Antigonus by the bodyguard of his brother Aristobulus I (103 B.C.; *J. W.* 1.78–80; *Ant.* 13.311–313). Menahem announces to Herod in his boyhood that one day he will be king of the Jews (*Ant.* 15.371–378). Josephus tells this story in order to explain why Herod honored the Essenes and even exempted them from taking an oath of loyalty (*Ant.* 15.371 and 378f.). A third Essene, Simon, interprets a dream of Herod's son Archelaus as an announcement of his imminent downfall (*J. W.* 2.112–113; *Ant.* 17.345–348).

In his description of the Essenes in *J. W.* 2.120–167 Josephus tells us: "There are some among them who profess to foretell the future, being versed from their early years in holy books, various forms of purification and apophthegms of prophets; and seldom, if ever, do they err in their predictions" (2.159). Their predictions are directly connected with their interpretation of Holy Scripture.[22] This is corroborated by one of the scrolls found in Qumran, the Commentary on Habakkuk. In 1QpHab 2:7–10 the Teacher of Righteousness is spoken of as "the Priest in [whose heart] God set [understanding] that he might interpret all the words of His servants the Prophets, through whom he foretold all that would happen to His people and [His land]." In 7:1–8 the commentary adds that God told Habakkuk to write down that which would happen to the final generation, but did not tell him when time would come to an end. It is the Teacher of Righteousness "to whom God made known all the mysteries of the words of His servants the Prophets. . . . The final age will be prolonged and will exceed all that the Prophets have said."[23]

We should add here that the Community Rule of Qumran announces the coming of a prophet in the future. The so-called "primitive concepts" will remain valid "until there shall come the Prophet and the Messiahs of Aaron and Israel" (1QS 9:11). The fragmentary text 4Q *Testimonia* combines the passages Deut. 5:28–29 plus 18: 18–19 (the prophet like Moses; cf. Acts 3:22; 7:37; and John 1:21; 4:19; 6:14; 7:40; 9:17) with Num. 24:15–17 ("A star shall come forth out of Jacob . . .") and Deut. 33:8–11 (an oracle on Levi). As in 1 Macc. 4:46 and 14:41, the future prophet is expected to give further explanation and final guidance.[24]

Of prophets among the Pharisees we hear very little. Josephus mentions a certain Samaias who rebukes Hyrcanus II and the Sanhedrin for their lack of courage to condemn the young Herod for his atrocities, and predicts Herod's future glory (*Ant.* 14.172–176). Elsewhere, he ascribes this rebuke and prophecy to the Pharisee Pollio— who with his pupil Samaias was honored by Herod, despite their continuously independent and critical attitude (*Ant.* 15.3–4, 370). Later, in *Ant.* 17.41–45, Josephus describes how the Pharisees exercise great influence on the women of Herod's court. At one occasion they predict that Herod's throne would be taken from him to be given to his brother Pheroras.[25]

The last prophet to be named here is John the Baptist, who not only figures prominently in all four Gospels, but is also mentioned by Josephus in *Ant.* 18.116–119. Josephus stresses John's appeal to the Jews to lead a righteous life. Because of his influence on the people who flock to him in crowds, he is killed by Herod Antipas. In the Gospels he is an eschatological prophet—who announces the coming judgment and summons the Jewish people to repentance. Mark 9:12–13 implies and Matt. 17:11–13 (cf. Matt. 11:14; Luke 1:17) says explicitly that he is Elijah returned to earth, in accordance with Mal. 4:5–6 (and Sir. 48:10). In this way John became in Christian eyes the forerunner of their master,[26] who, although outsiders compared him with John and identified him with Elijah, was superior to the one who at one time had baptized him.

Popular Prophetic Movements

In their *Bandits, Prophets, and Messiahs,* Horsley and Hanson pay special attention to prophets who acted as leaders of popular movements in the Palestine of the first century A.D. They rightly distinguish these people, and the groups that formed around them, from the bandit leaders and their bands who operated in those turbulent times, and from the royal pretenders who were active in the time after the death of Herod the Great and again during the Jewish war against Rome. Prophets of this type are interesting for the purpose of our inquiry, not only because they are mentioned in Acts,[27] or because the Christians are warned against them in the Synoptic

Apocalypse (Mark 13:22 and par., "False Christs and false prophets will arise and show signs and wonders, to lead astray, if possible, the elect"),[28] but above all because these prophets and their followers are convinced that they are about to participate in an act of divine liberation.

Josephus, who for obvious reasons had little sympathy for these prophets, calls them "deceivers and impostors, under the pretense of divine inspiration fostering revolutionary changes." He adds: "They persuaded the multitude to act like madmen, and led them out into the desert under the belief that God would there give them tokens of deliverance" (*J. W.* 2.259–260; *Ant.* 20.168). The Roman governor Felix (A.D. 52–60) does not take any risk and suppresses their actions, which he regards as preliminary to insurrection. Yet the incident that follows (see *J. W.* 2.261–263 and *Ant.* 20.169–172) does not point in the direction of armed rebellion. A certain man from Egypt, who called himself a prophet, asked the large multitude of people to follow him through the wilderness to the Mount of Olives. He predicted that "at his command Jerusalem's walls would fall down, through which he promised to provide them an entrance into the city" (*Ant.* 20.170). The prophet expected a miracle like that performed by Joshua at Jericho long ago during the entry into Canaan (Josh. 6).[29]

There is the interesting report about Theudas in the time when Fadus was governor (A.D. 44–46). He stated that he was a prophet, and persuaded a great number of people to follow him to the Jordan River. He promised "that at his command the river would be parted and would provide them an easy passage" (*Ant.* 20.97–99). Did he intend to imitate Joshua's action in Josh. 3, but then to lead the people in the opposite direction, to be purified in the wilderness and to be prepared for a new conquest of the promised land? Or was this to be a new exodus from oppression and a new entry at the same time?[30] In any case, although the Roman governor used military force to suppress the movement, there is little evidence that Theudas and his like planned rebellion. The fact, however, that these prophetic leaders could find so many followers, shows that many in the Palestine of the first century found themselves in a desperate situation and that longing for decisive change was intense.[31]

Royal Pretenders

Describing the period of great unrest after Herod's death, Josephus mentions three leaders of rebellious groups who seem to have aspired to kingship (*Ant.* 17.271–285; cf. *J. W.* 2.50–65). Needless to say, he does not sympathize with them. In 285 he concludes his report with the statement, "And so Judaea was filled with brigandage. Anyone might make himself king as the head of a band of rebels whom he fell in with, and then would press on to the destruction of the community."[32] The first to be mentioned is Judas, son of the brigand chief Ezekias,[33] who operates from Sepphoris (near Nazareth!) in Galilee, who raids the royal palace, captures stores of arms, and plunders all property he can lay his hands on. Josephus criticizes "his ambition for royal rank" (272). The next one is Simon, a servant of King Herod who sets fire to Herod's palace at Jericho and numerous other royal residences. Of him Josephus says, "He was bold enough to place the diadem on his head, and having got together a body of men, he was himself also proclaimed king by them in their madness, and he rated himself worthy of this beyond anything else" (272–274). The third is Athronges, an obscure shepherd but remarkable for his stature and strength, who operates with his four brothers, each commanding an armed band of his own. Josephus tells us, "That man had the temerity to aspire to the kingship" (278) and "This man kept his power for a long while, for he had the title of king and nothing to prevent him from doing as he wished" (281).

These royal pretenders were men of humble origin and obviously natural leaders, able to attract and to lead large bands of people in country districts. Horsley and Hanson have rightly emphasized that "they stormed the royal palaces at Sepphoris and Jericho, not only as symbols of the hated Herodian rule or to obtain weapons, but to recover property that had been seized by Herodian officials and stored in the royal palaces."[34] These three men were leaders of popular uprisings directed against the royalist gentry; Varus, the Roman legate in Syria, had to use a large military force to suppress these revolts.

Horsley and Hanson[35] do not hesitate to speak of popular *messianic* movements, assuming that Judas, Simon, and Athronges and their followers were inspired by popular memories and expectations concerning David, who, after all, had in his younger days been a successful leader of a sizable band of brigands (1 Sam. 21–30), before being installed as king in Jerusalem and becoming the founder of the Davidic dynasty. This is an attractive theory, but unfortunately difficult to substantiate from literary sources: we have only Josephus' very one-sided presentation of the facts.

We may mention, finally, two leaders during the Jewish War, to whom Josephus ascribes royal aspirations. The first is Menahem, son of Judas the Galilean, who in 66 breaks into Herod's armory at Masada, and marches to Jerusalem "like a veritable king," to become leader of the insurrection (*J. W.* 3.433–434). He is murdered when "arrayed in royal robes and attended by his suite of armed fanatics" he goes up to the temple to pay his devotions (*J. W.* 3.441–448). Much more influential was Simon bar Giora, who eventually became the principal Jewish commander in Jerusalem. He is the one who is kept under guard after being captured, and who marches in Vespasian's and Titus' triumphal procession in Rome before being executed (*J. W.* 7.36 and 153–155). Josephus, who understandably pays much attention to Simon's activities, records that "his was no longer an army of mere serfs and brigands, but one including numerous citizen recruits, subservient to his command as to a king" (*J. W.* 4.510). When he enters the city to expel the Zealots he is "acclaimed by the people as their saviour and protector" (*J. W.* 4.475). We may add that he gives himself up to the Romans in a very spectacular way: dressed in a white tunic with a purple mantle, he arises out of the ground at the very spot where the temple had once stood (*J. W.* 7.29). It is not quite clear what this symbolic action was meant to convey, but possibly Simon not only wanted to indicate that he was a high-ranking officer but also claimed to be the king of the Jews.[36] Whether Menahem and Simon had messianic pretensions or were regarded as royal messiahs by their followers remains unclear; Josephus simply does not allow us to draw firm conclusions. This historian admits, however, that messianic expectations played a role in the Jewish War, when, after recording a number of divine warnings in the days preceding the fall of city and temple (*J. W.* 6.288–315),[37] he refers to "an ambiguous oracle . . . found in their sacred scriptures, to the effect that at that time one from their country would become ruler of the world." The Jews think of someone of their own race; to Josephus, however, it is clear that "the oracle . . . in reality signified the sovereignty of Vespasian, who was proclaimed Emperor on Jewish soil" (312–313).[38]

Josephus' reports on the leaders of prophetic movements and on the royal pretenders make clear how easily the message about Jesus Christ could be misunderstood by outsiders and insiders alike. After all, he was reported to have been arrested as a "bandit" (Mark 14:48) and to have been crucified between two "bandits" (Mark 15:27). He was a prophetic figure with a group of disciples who had attracted crowds in Galilee, was known for his sharp and incisive summons to a radical obedience to God, and announced the imminent arrival of God's kingdom. Claims that this man was the Messiah called for a careful presentation of his activity in Galilee, his trial and death in Jerusalem. Especially his preaching about the kingdom of God and his own role in the realization of that kingdom ("King of Israel") had to be defined precisely over against the promises of prophetic leaders and the claims of the royal pretenders in the period between 4 B.C. and A.D. 70.

Jesus the Messiah

As we have seen in the section "Jewish Prophets," our literary sources say very little about the expectation of a future prophet. There are also surprisingly few references to a future "anointed one." And yet, contrary to the designation "the prophet," the term *Christos* (Greek for "anointed" = Hebrew *mešiah*, from which we get "Messiah") became so important in early Christianity that in the letters of Paul it is already virtually interchangeable with the name Jesus. There is only one Christ, the Christ who died and rose again, Jesus.[39]

In the Old Testament the terms "anointed" and "anointing" are first of all used in connection with the kings of Israel. Saul, David, and Davidic kings[40] are called "the Lord's anointed." Secondly, in a few places in Leviticus (4:3, 5, 16; 6:15 [22]) we find the term "the anointed (high) priest." Thirdly, the terms are used in connection with prophets in 1 Kings 19:16; Isa. 61:1; Ps. 105:15. This Old Testament usage is reflected in the literary sources of our period.

The priestly sect of Qumran, as we have seen, expects "the anointed ones of Aaron and Israel" (1QS 9:11).[41] The royal anointed one of Israel is clearly subordinate to the high priest (see the first appendix to the Community Rule, 1QSa 2:14, 20, and compare lines 11–12). He belongs to the family of David, as is clear from 4Q *Patriarchal Blessings* 3, where "the Messiah of Righteousness" stands parallel to "the Branch of David."[42] Also important is the Blessing for the Prince of the Congregation (1QSb 5:20–29), where the ideal king is called upon to establish the kingdom of his people forever, but where the term "anointed" is not used.[43] The Qumran scrolls also preserve one instance of an anointed prophet, as we have already noticed. 11Q *Melchizedek*, line 18, speaks of "the anointed by the Spirit" in a context referring to Isa. 52:7 and 61:1.[44]

Psalms of Solomon 17, as we have seen, describes the future reign of an ideal Davidic king whose military and political successes are recorded. Yet the deliverance of Israel is only a means toward the triumph of God's righteousness and power as manifested in his law. Verse 37, referring to Isa. 11:1–5, tells that "God has made him (the king) strong with holy Spirit, and wise in the counsel of understanding with strength and righteousness." In verse 32, almost in passing, he is called "an anointed (of the) Lord." This term is a qualification rather than a title.[45]

The complex heavenly figure who is central in the Parables of Enoch[46] is twice called "his Messiah/anointed": once in 48:10 with a clear reference to Ps. 2:2 in the phrase, "for they have denied the Lord of the Spirits and his Messiah," and once in 52:4, where the emphasis is equally on the reign of "his Messiah." Also *4 Ezra* and *Syr. Baruch,* two apocalypses dating from the end of the first or the beginning of the second century A.D., reflect the expectation of a royal figure—this time one reigning only during a limited period. In *4 Ezra* 12:32 he is called "the Messiah whom the Most High has kept back until the end."[47] *Syriac Baruch* speaks about "my Messiah," "my servant, the Messiah," and "the Messiah" (in 39:7; 40:1; 72:2; 70:9; and 29:3; 30:1, respectively). Finally, the fourteenth of the Eighteen Benedictions (Palestinian recension) looks forward to "the kingdom of David, Thine Anointed."

Early Christian use of the term *Christos* does not show any acquaintance with the notion of an anointed (high) priest. The notion of "an anointed one by the Spirit" does not occur before Luke (see Luke 4:16–18 and Acts 10:36). In most cases there is a link with kingship and with the designation "Son of David" (for instance, Mark 12:35–37 and parallels; 14:55–56 and parallels; Matt. 1–2; Luke 1:32; 2:11; 23:2). This is quite understandable in the case of statements about Jesus' future kingly rule; but how did this designation come to be connected with Jesus as preacher, teacher, and exorcist? Here it is important to note that scripture and tradition presented a picture of King David as a prophet and an exorcist. Two examples may demonstrate this: In *Antiquities* 6.166–168 (commenting on 1 Sam. 16:14–23), Josephus tells us, "The Deity abandoned Saul and passed over to David, who, when the divine Spirit had removed to him, began to prophesy" (cf. 1 Sam. 10:6, 10, 12; 16:13; 2 Sam. 23:1–7; Mark 12:36; Acts 2:30; 1:16; 4:25), and he continues with a description of David's exorcisms. Next, there is a fragment called "David's Compositions" found in the Psalms Scroll discovered in the eleventh cave at Qumran. It lists 3,600 psalms and no less than 450 songs, four of which were "songs for making music over the stricken" (line 10), and concludes with the words, "All these he spoke through prophecy which was given him from before the Most High."[48] That Jesus was a true Son of David, an Anointed One of the Lord, not only would be revealed in the future but was already evident in his words and actions in the time he preached in Galilee and Jerusalem.

Jesus the Son of God[49]

In Mark the designation *Son of God* is found a few times in connection with *Christos.* We mention here 8:38 (where it is presupposed in the term "in the glory of the Father") after 8:27 and 14: 55–65 (see also 12:35–37). In both cases it is used of Jesus as the future king. Also in the ancient formula preserved by Paul in Rom.

1:3–4 the one who is designated Son of God in power is descended from David (cf. 1 Thess. 1:9–10). This use of "Son of God" is intelligible against the background of 2 Sam. 7:12–14; Pss. 2:7; 89:3f., 26f.; 1 Chron. 17:13; 22:10; 28:6. In fact, Heb. 1:5 quotes Ps. 2:7 and 2 Sam. 7:14 together in connection with Jesus (cf. Luke 1:32–33); and Heb. 5:5 as well as Acts 13:33 refer to Ps. 2:7 alone (cf. the quotation from Ps. 2:1–2 in Acts 4:25–26). We may compare here the Qumran fragment 4Q *Florilegium* 1:7–11, which quotes from 2 Sam. 7:11–14, applying the words "I will be his father, and he shall be my son" to the "Branch of David" whom we have already encountered while discussing the title "Messiah." Recently, J. A. Fitzmyer[50] has drawn attention to another fragment, 4QpsDan^a (=4Q246), that speaks of a descendant of an enthroned king who "shall be hailed (as) the Son of God, and they shall call him Son of the Most High." The kingdom of the enemies shall last only "until there arises the people of God, and everyone rests from the sword." Further details are lacking because of the fragmentary state of the evidence; Fitzmyer presupposes an apocalyptic setting and points to a number of interesting parallels with Luke 1:32–35.

The early Christian use of the term was also influenced by other traditions. We have already pointed to Wisd. of Sol. 2:12–20; 5:1–7, where the exemplary righteous man is called "Son of God"—a picture that probably influenced the passion story in Mark 15:29–32 (and esp. Matt. 27:39–44) and 15:39 (Matt. 27:54; Luke 23:47). This may be connected with the notion found in Mishnah and Talmud that there is a special father-son relationship between pious charismatics and God.[51]

In the Q text Luke 10:21–22 (par. Matt. 11:25–27), Jesus claims a unique relationship with God as that of the Son par excellence with the Father; he alone is able to impart true knowledge to his followers. This agrees with the proclamation of God at Jesus' baptism and the special endowment with the Spirit in Mark 1:9–11; Matt. 3:13–17; Luke 3:21–22, and with the divine proclamation in the transfiguration story (Mark 9:2–10; Matt. 17:1–9; Luke 9:28–36). Jesus is the obedient Son of God in the story of the temptation (Matt. 4:1–11; Luke 4:1–13), on whom Satan has no hold. He is stronger than Satan and his demons, who acknowledge him for what he is, and on a few occasions call him "Son of God / Son of the Most High" (Mark 3:11; 5:7). Jesus is portrayed as addressing God as "Abba, Father" when he prays at Gethsemane (Mark 14:36; cf. Matt. 26:39; Luke 22:42). This indicates a particular intimacy with God. The Jesus portrayed by Q and Mark is the perfect righteous one obedient to the utmost (Mark 14:36 par.), led by the Spirit, more powerful than the forces of Satan, initiated by his Father into all there is to know.[52]

Many scholars think that this portrait was true to life. The earliest attestation of the use of "Abba" in prayer is Gal. 4:6, a text which along with Rom. 8:15 reflects a tradition of prayer in Greek-speaking Christian communities—very probably an echo of the tradition about a prayer uttered by Jesus himself—later recorded in Mark 14:36.[53] Also the other "Son" texts mentioned may reflect Jesus' own sense of sonship in relation to God the Father.

Galatians 4:6 is found in a passage that applies an early pattern of thought according to which God sent his Son on a unique mission, also found in Mark 12:1–9 and John 3:16f., and later developed into the very subtle disquisition on the relationship between the Father and the Son which may be said to form the heart of Johannine Christology. Already in the early pattern the term "Son" is used to denote a unique envoy of God. Now, as J. D. G. Dunn has pointed out,[54] the wise man is called God's son, but is not "sent" by God. Human messengers are sent by God but are not called "sons of God." Angels are sometimes called "sons of God," but then always collectively.[55] The best illustration is, perhaps, the special position of the "son of the house" as plenipotentiary in the Jewish laws of agency. This is brought out fully in John 3:35 and 13:3, but the idea of the son as representative par excellence may already have been present at the earliest stage.[56]

The early Christians lived in a Hellenistic world in which heroes, kings, philosophers, and other outstanding people were regarded as sons of [a] god or as divine men, and Hellenistic-Jewish authors of the period reflect these ideas when they write about the servants of the Lord of Israel mentioned in the Bible. When the term "Son of God" was used for Jesus it may therefore have held a wealth of connotations for individual Christians. It is probable, however, that the notions of Messiah / Son of David / Son of God, and wise and righteous man / perfectly obedient servant of God / pious charismatic / son of God, were constitutive for the earliest stages of the Christian use of the term.

Jesus the Son of Man

The Greek phrase *ho huios tou anthrōpou* occurs in the Gospels and Acts 7:56, where it is always found in utterances of Jesus himself (with the exception of John 12:34 and Acts 7:56). One should note the consistent use of the article: Jesus speaks about *the* Son of man.[57] The expression "Son of man" itself in Hebrew and Aramaic means nothing but "man"—as in Ps. 8:5 (4E), "What is man that thou art mindful of him, and the son of man that thou dost care for him?" (cf. Heb. 2:6–8, where the expression is not used as a title for Jesus).

It means simply "man" in the book of Ezekiel, where God addresses the prophet frequently as "son of man." Likewise in Dan. 7:13–14, where after four great beasts a human figure appears:

And behold, with the clouds of heaven
there came one like a son of man,
and he came to the Ancient of Days
and was presented before him.
And to him was given dominion
and glory and kingdom,
that all peoples, nations, and languages
should serve him;
his dominion is an everlasting dominion,
which shall not pass away,
and his kingdom one
that shall not be destroyed.

This passage is quoted here in full, not only because the expression "one like a son of man" recurs in Rev. 1:13 and 14:14, clearly influenced by Dan. 7:13, but also because Mark 8:38; 13:26; and 14:62 show acquaintance with it. However, the Gospels have the expression *the* Son of man as a self-designation of Jesus, whereas in Dan. 7 the human figure in the vision is said to represent "the saints of the Most High," who receive the kingdom after having been oppressed by the last ("little") horn of the fourth beast, which stands for the last king of the fourth empire (vs. 18–27). We should also note that in Dan. 7:13 the one like a son of man comes to the Ancient of Days with the clouds of heaven, while in Mark the clouds bring the heavenly Son of man back to the earth.

The "one like a son of man" of Dan. 7:13–14 has certainly influenced the picture of the complex heavenly figure in the so-called Parables of Enoch (*1 Enoch* 37–71). In 46:1 we read, "And there I saw one who had a head of days, and his head (was) white like wool; and with him (there was) another, whose face had the appearance of a man, and his face (was) full of grace, like one of the holy angels."[58] Enoch asks about that Son of man, and receives instruction from an accompanying angel about his functions in God's dealings with mankind and with his people. The figure in question has a number of titles, but seems to be called Son of man only where Dan. 7:13–14 is referred to or where further qualifications are added. In *1 Enoch* 71:14 the Head of Days says to Enoch: "You are the Son of man who was born to righteousness. . . ." The Parables of Enoch are important because they show that the Danielic expression was in fact applied to a single figure. They do not show that "the Son of man" was used as a fixed title. Moreover, the Parables are only found in Ethiopic; no Greek or Aramaic fragments are extant (as is the case with most other sections of the composite work *1 Enoch*). Consequently, their date is uncertain. Nowadays scholars tend to date them toward the end of the first century A.D.[59]

Around the same time another apocalypse was written, *4 Ezra,* whose author saw "a human figure rising from the depths, and as I watched, this man came flying with the clouds of heaven" (13:3). The picture is clearly influenced by Dan. 7 (where the beasts come up out of the sea, and the one like a son of man flies with the clouds of heaven), but "Son of man" is not used as a title. The central figure is later on referred to as "the man" (vs. 5, 6, 8, 12); in the subsequent interpretation of the vision he is called "my son" (vs. 32, 37).

To conclude: We have evidence that Dan. 7 influenced Jewish hopes concerning a future deliverer at the end of the first century A.D. We have no evidence that "the Son of man" was known as a title for such a figure, then or earlier. Interestingly, the self-designation of Jesus is also never taken up by Jesus' disciples or his opponents. Nobody confesses him as "the Son of man," or takes him to task for claiming to be "the Son of man." Yet when Mark and Q let Jesus use this term as a self-designation it must have had a special force and meaning for them. It must have been present in the sayings tradition on which they drew, and at a very early moment in Christian history the Greek term must have been introduced as a standard translation of a Semitic expression.

The most likely explanation of this state of affairs is that Jesus did in fact use the expression as a self-designation. Later Christians have exercised some freedom while transmitting these sayings orally and in writing; in a number of cases the unusual solemn expression may have crept in where it was not originally used. But the phrase would never have been added if it had not been known that it had been used very early, even by Jesus himself.

Much has been written lately about the possible meaning of the Aramaic expression *bar (e)nash(a)* in the Palestinian Aramaic of Jesus' time.[60] Was it only used in general statements in which the speaker could sometimes include himself? Could it be used as an exclusive self-reference? Or did it also denote a class of persons with whom the speaker identified himself ("a man like myself")? It is clear that at the stages of the transmission of the sayings of Jesus represented by Mark and Q the term is used as an exclusive self-reference that nevertheless does not unequivocally disclose the identity of the speaker.

For Mark there is a link with Dan. 7:13–14. Jesus claims to be the Son of man to whom will be given "a kingdom that shall not be destroyed." His authority will be revealed in the future, when he will bring together those who belong to him (Mark 13:26f.). It is already evident now, as he forgives sins—and thereby exercises a divine prerogative (2:1–12)—and as he acts as Lord over the Sabbath (2:23–28). The passages speaking about his suffering and resurrection (8:31; 9:31; 10:33–34) may be seen in connection with the suffering and vindication of the saints of the Most High represented by the "one like a son of man" in Dan. 7:21–28. We should note that the statements about Jesus' suffering and his vindication which will become evident at the *parousia* in Mark 8:27–10:52 have direct consequences for his disciples as followers of Jesus, and that the passages about the future activities of the Son of man directly involve those who have rejected it or have proved unfaithful (8:38–9:1; 13:26f.; 14:62).[61]

The picture presented by Q is less explicit, but here too the Son of man acts with authority, is not accepted by the people of his generation, but will be vindicated. Those who have remained watchful and will be prepared for the sudden arrival of the Son of man will share in his glory.

We cannot enter here into a discussion on the further use of the term in Matthew, Luke, and John. Outside the Gospels it is used only in Acts 7:56 (to be connected with Luke 12:8–9 [Q]). It was clearly an unsuitable term to denote Jesus' authority for a non-Jewish audience.[62] Nor can we go back in time and distinguish between those "Son of man" sayings that go back to Jesus himself and those that were added later—let alone try to determine their exact Aramaic wording. Much is bound to remain uncertain; yet there seems to be no reason to deny that Jesus himself did claim a particular authority, there and then and in the future; thought of himself in terms of suffering and vindication; and expressed this in the term *"the* Son of man"—covertly referring to the destiny of the "one like a son of man" in Daniel. There it is a general term applied to people in a special position, eminently suited to denote one who wants to be God's obedient servant par excellence, living in a perfect union with him, and (at the same time) indicative of the implications for those who have got involved with him—those who have deliberately chosen to follow in his footsteps.

11
Jesus' Death, Resurrection, and Exaltation

Jesus' early followers, who firmly believed in him as herald and inaugurator of the New Age and were eagerly looking forward to the day when God's sovereign rule would be manifested on earth, were unwaveringly convinced that their master, who had died on the cross, had been vindicated by God. His death was not the end of his mission and did not disprove his message. To quote the ancient formulas in Paul's earliest letter again: Christians serve "a living and true God" and "wait for his Son from heaven, whom he raised from the dead, Jesus who delivers us from the wrath to come" (1 Thess. 1:9–10). Further: "Since we believe that Jesus died and rose again, even so, through Jesus, God will bring with him those who have fallen asleep" (4:14).

The belief in Jesus' resurrection, his life with God, his share in God's sovereign rule over the world, now and in the (near) future, is essential for the Christian faith. "If Christ has not been raised, then our preaching is in vain and your faith is in vain," Paul writes to the Corinthians (1 Cor. 15:14). Convinced that Jesus lives, one has to explain the fact of his death and to attach a meaning to it. The ancient formula preserved in 1 Cor. 15:3–5 declares that Christ died for our sins (and was raised on the third day) "in accordance with the scriptures." This may be just a general statement to the effect that all happened in accordance with God's will laid down in the scriptures, but it called for further reflection on specific passages in the scriptures. The same applies to Mark's statements "the Son of man *must* suffer many things . . ." (Mark 8:31, emphasis added), and "the Son of man goes as it is written of him" (14:21).

In the present chapter we shall trace a number of important aspects of early Christian reflection on Jesus' death and subsequent vindication by God in their relation to certain passages of scripture and to contemporary Jewish and Hellenistic ideas. In doing so, we have to bear in mind that the followers of Jesus, meditating on texts and traditions concerning the suffering, death, and vindication of servants of God and righteous persons in past and present, wanted to explain the death and the triumph over death of a *unique* servant of God, whom they confessed as the Son of God par excellence, the Messiah, the Son of man. In their eyes Jesus had appeared at the turn of the times, to announce and to inaugurate God's sovereign rule on earth. That a person occupying such a central position in God's final intervention, and standing in such a unique relationship to him, was killed and died such an ignominious death on the cross was unheard of and could only be explained with great difficulty. The message of the crucified Messiah was indeed "a stumbling block to Jews and folly to Gentiles." To recognize "the power of God and the wisdom of God" in this man required a firm faith and deep reflection, inspired by God's Spirit (1 Cor. 1:18–25; 2:6–16).

The Christian message concerning one who *has come* to announce and bring a decisive change in the life of Israel and, indeed, of all people, *and* who *will come again* when God's kingdom comes with power (Mark 9:1), is unparalleled. It takes into account the astounding fact that Jesus as herald of the New Age had been put to death, and it reflects the conviction that God had vindicated him. The belief in the Christ/Messiah who died and rose again enabled his followers to treat the coming in the past and the coming in the future as two aspects of the one supreme and final intervention of God. Jesus' mission cries out for its fulfillment, and this fulfillment is expected by the early Christians in the near future, just because the first decisive step has already been taken.

Jesus as Final Envoy of God, Rejected by Israel

In our discussion of 1 Thess. 2:14–16 and the Q texts Luke 11: 49–51 (par. Matt. 23:34–36) and Luke 13:34–35 (par. Matt. 23:37–39) in chapters 1 and 2, we have already noticed the existence of an early Christian portrait of Jesus as a messenger from God, standing in the succession of a whole series of divine messengers sent to call Israel to repentance and true obedience, who were rejected and killed. We saw that this early Christian conception, found in different strands of the tradition, links up with Jewish notions concerning the prophets in the context of a Deuteronomistic view of history.[1]

In the group of texts under discussion, the emphasis is on the responsibility of the leaders of Israel for Jesus' death; it is the climax in a long tradition of stubborn opposition to those who were sent by God to remind the people of their obligations toward him. What the Jews have done to Jesus' followers since his death is in line with their attitude to Jesus—see 1 Thess. 2:15–16; Matt. 23:24; Luke 6:22–23 (par. Matt. 5:11–12); Stephen is put to death as was his master (Acts 7:54–60). It is very clear that the point of no return has been reached. "The blood of all the prophets, shed from the foundation of the world . . . , shall be required of this generation" (Luke 11:50–51). "What will the owner of the vineyard do? He will come and destroy the tenants, and give the vineyard to others" (Mark 12:9). "God's wrath has come upon them for ever" (1 Thess. 2:16, RSV margin; cf. Matt. 23:32–33 and Luke 13:35; par. Matt. 23:38–39).

This model of interpretation explains Jesus' death as inevitable in view of Israel's history of continuous disobedience to God and his servants. It does not attach any particular meaning to Jesus' death, except that it is the death of God's final envoy to Israel at the turn of the ages. Moreover, the emphasis is not so much on the fate of the messenger but rather on the responsibility of the persecutors, and on the consequences of their opposition. It is also clear that there is a complete break between Jesus' followers who share his fate and Israel and its leaders.

The model does not speculate on what God did to Jesus after his death. After Mark 12:9 the evangelist speaks about it, but does so by quoting from Ps. 118:22–23: God has done a marvelous thing in that he made the stone which the builders rejected into the head of the corner! In Acts 7 Stephen is allowed to see "the Righteous One, whom you have now betrayed and murdered" as "the Son of man standing at the right hand of God" (vs. 52, 56). Early Christianity could not restrict itself to this explanation of Jesus' death; other aspects had to be taken into account. Especially the continuation of Jesus' relation to God and of his part in the history of salvation had to be expressed. In the section on possible ancient elements in Acts[2] we noted that the contrast pattern employed in the speeches in Acts (you killed him—but God raised him from the dead) combines a pre-Pauline resurrection formula with the explanation of Jesus' death expressed in the passages under discussion here. The latter clearly had to be supplemented with the former.

Jesus and the Tradition of God's Suffering Servants

Luke 6:22–23 (par. Matt. 5:11–12) reflects the conception just outlined. Those addressed are persecuted and reviled because of Jesus; their oppressors do to them what their fathers did to the prophets. But this statement is phrased as a beatitude, the last in the series of four that very probably marked the beginning of Jesus' teaching in Q. Those who are oppressed by the enemies are mentioned together with the poor who receive the kingdom of God, those who hunger but shall be satisfied, and those who weep but shall laugh

(Luke 6:20–23). These statements belong to a very rich and extremely varied group of passages in the Old Testament and early Jewish literature, according to which God in his righteousness comes to the rescue of his faithful servants who in distress, poverty, and oppression continue to expect everything from him.[3] In these passages the emphasis is on the oppressed rather than on the oppressors, and also on divine help and deliverance: in Luke 6:20–24 these are promised in connection with the coming of the kingdom of God, announced and inaugurated by Jesus, for whom and with whom his followers suffer.

In the Old Testament, many psalms give voice to the lament of pious people, falsely accused or oppressed by their enemies and calling to God for help. It is sometimes followed in the same psalm by a thanksgiving for God's intervention bringing about a turn in the fate of the sufferer. Alternatively, there are psalms that give thanks to God and look back on the distress in which he came to the rescue. Although the sufferer's lot is described in very poignant terms and compared to death, there is no doubt that in these psalms deliverance is thought to take place during the earthly life of the supplicant.[4] Only Pss. 49:16 (15E) and 73:24 may go a step further.

In the third Servant Song in Deutero-Isaiah (50:4–11), the one who suffers and is reviled is a prophetic figure (compare Isa. 50:6 with Mark 10:34; 14:65; 15:19). Also the picture of Jeremiah in the various passages of the book of Jeremiah is clearly influenced by that of the righteous sufferer found elsewhere (see, e.g., Jer. 11:18–12:6; 15:10–21; 17:14–18; 18:18–23; 20:7–18). Jeremiah's suffering, however, is not only due to his opponents, but is also caused by his distress over Jerusalem's plight (8:18–23). The Bible also gives some telling examples of God's help for the faithful in a number of stories about the persecution and exaltation of a righteous person. Among them are the story of Joseph and his brothers told in great detail in Gen. 37–50; that of Mordecai and Haman in the book of Esther, and the stories of the three young men in the fiery furnace in Dan. 3, and of Daniel himself in the lions' den in Dan. 6. In the last two cases the exemplary servants of God are ready to be martyred rather than to become unfaithful to their Lord in heaven. At the crucial moment angels sent by God come to the rescue, and the young men and Daniel escape unharmed. Nebuchadnezzar has to confess, "Blessed be the God of Shadrach, Meshach, and Abednego, who has sent his angel and delivered his servants, who trusted in him" (Dan. 3:28; cf. 6:20–22, 25–27).[5]

Many more elements are found in individual psalms and passages representing the tradition of the suffering righteous. In Psalm 69, verses 8 (7E) and 10 (9E) emphasize that the speaker is reviled because of his obedience to God (v. 9: "For zeal for thy house has consumed me,[6] and the insults of those who insult thee have fallen on me"). In the thanksgiving that concludes this psalm (vs. 31–37 [30–36E]), God is portrayed as one who gives heed to the oppressed, the poor, and those who are in bonds. Righteous people are likely to be in those conditions, just as sinners and unrighteous people often prosper. Psalm 34:18–20 (17–19E) assures its readers:

> When the righteous cry for help, the LORD hears,
>   and delivers them out of all their troubles.
> The LORD is near to the brokenhearted,
>   and saves the crushed in spirit.
> Many are the afflictions of the righteous;
>   but the LORD delivers them out of them all.[7]

The picture of the righteous given here is very like that found in the Beatitudes in the version of Luke and that of Matthew (5:3–11), or in *Syr. Baruch* 52:6–7: "Rejoice in the suffering you now endure: why concern yourselves about the downfall of your enemies? Make yourselves ready for what is reserved for you, and prepare yourselves for the reward laid up for you."[8]

In the book of Psalms, unlike in the New Testament and *Syr. Baruch,* no eschatological deliverance is envisaged. A number of scholars, however, have drawn attention to the fact that the author of Ps. 69:35–37 (34–36E) asks heaven and earth to join in the praise of God, and connects God's help for the poor and oppressed with his salvation for Zion and the rebuilding of the cities of Judah. Similarly, the thanksgiving in Ps. 22:23–32 (22–31E) ends with an outlook on worldwide salvation: "All the ends of the earth shall remember and turn to the LORD; and all the families of the nations shall worship before thee. For dominion belongs to the LORD, and he rules over the nations."

Now the cry "My God, my God, why hast thou forsaken me?" in Ps. 22:2 (1E) receives a very prominent place in Mark's (and Matthew's) description of Jesus' agony on the cross. It was even preserved in its Aramaic form (Mark 15:34; Matt. 27:46). There are many more (often implicit) references to Psalms 22 and 69 and other passages representing the various aspects of the tradition of the suffering righteous, and it is quite possible that even before Mark the story of Jesus' passion on the cross and of the events leading up to it was told in terms familiar to that tradition.[9] It is remarkable that the hymns of thanksgiving and praise which conclude Psalms 22 and 69 are not referred to in the passion story, however suitable they might have been for linking the story of Jesus' gruesome suffering and ignominious death with his own message of the kingdom now and in the future.

Of course, the use of Ps. 22:2 is intended to suggest divine deliverance.[10] However, in the Gospels as well as in the earliest traditional material available to us, God's intervention in behalf of Jesus *after* his suffering and death is expressed in terms of resurrection and exaltation. In Mark, Jesus' resurrection is announced in the three predictions of the passion and resurrection in 8:31; 9:31; and 10:32–34, and proclaimed by the young man in a white robe who meets the women at the empty tomb (16:6). Jesus' mission has not come to an end yet. His disciples will see him in Galilee (16:7) and, in fact, his opponents also will see him as "the Son of man seated at the right hand of Power, and coming with the clouds of heaven" (14:62). Not only those who believe in him but also those who rejected and persecuted him will see that he is really "God's Son in power" (to borrow a phrase from Rom. 1:4).

In a number of passages in Jewish literature God's salvation after death is viewed as resurrection.[11] Important in this connection is Dan. 12:1–3, to be read together with Dan. 11:29–35 and to be understood against the background of the fierce struggle in the time of the Maccabees. After a time of great trouble in which many will stumble even among "the wise who will make many understand" (Dan. 11:33; 12:3), God will bring about a turn in the life of Israel through Michael, "the great prince who has charge of your people" (12:1). Those who have endured the test (11:35) will be delivered. "Many of those who sleep in the dust of the earth shall awake, some to everlasting life, and some to shame and everlasting contempt" (12:2). In particular "those who are wise shall shine like the brightness of the firmament; and those who turn many to righteousness, like the stars for ever and ever" (12:3).

God's vindication of those who have proved faithful takes the form of resurrection at the time of his final intervention in the affairs of the world. A similar conception is found in other apocalyptic texts like *1 Enoch* 102–104 and *Syr. Baruch* 48:48–50 and 52:6–7 (mentioned above). The message of hope of Dan. 12:1–3 is expressed in other terms in the vision of Dan. 7 and the interpretation that follows it. Here, as we have seen,[12] the "one like a Son of man" who comes to the Ancient of Days in order to receive "dominion and glory of kingdom" stands for the saints of the Most High, oppressed by the last worldly power, but destined to receive the kingdom forever. Dan. 12 and Dan. 7 together form the background of the predictions of the passion and resurrection of *the* Son of man, Jesus, and of the emphasis on the (resurrected) Son of man as inaugurator of God's kingdom-in-power in Mark 14:62 (and 9:1).

In our brief discussion of the Markan story of the crucifixion we have already mentioned two further passages that shed light on it: Wisd. of Sol. 2:12–20 and 5:1–7.[13]

In the first passage, the opponents plan to condemn the righteous man to a shameful death, because he professes to have knowledge of God and calls himself a servant and son of God (Wisd. of Sol. 2:14, 18), and because he reproaches them for sins against the law (2:13). The righteous man's assurance that God, his Father, will deliver him from the hands of the adversaries (2:16–17) is put to the test. He is not put to shame, as 5:1–7 shows. There we meet the righteous man again, "numbered among the sons of God" (v. 5). Saved by God and exalted to glory, he confronts those who have afflicted him with great confidence, as a (silent) witness to God's help for those who are truly righteous. His opponents stand condemned—as they themselves have to admit (5:1–2 and following verses).

The possible reference to Wisd. of Sol. 2:17–20 in Mark 15:29–32 (more explicit in Matt. 27:39–44) and the use of "son of God" in verse 39 suggest that Mark (and perhaps earlier narrators of the passion story) were influenced by the conception of God's vindication of the righteous man found in the book of Wisdom. We may also point to the scene of Jesus' trial before the Sanhedrin in Mark 14:45–65. Jesus' opponents accuse him of blasphemy, yet it is he whom they will see vindicated by God at the final coming of the kingdom-in-power! Then, we have to understand, it will become clear to everyone who is really a righteous and true servant of God: the high priests, the elders and the scribes, staunch defenders of God's law, *or* the Jesus whom they have rejected. For Mark and his predecessors Jesus was, of course, not just a righteous man, however perfect and exemplary, and not just a son of God. He was *the* Son of God, the Messiah, and his coming in glory is that of *the* Son of man.

Jesus, the Man Who Died for Others

So far we have not come across the notion of "dying for others" that is so prominent in early Christian statements about the death of Jesus.[14] In chapter 1 we found expressions such as "Christ died for us (for our sins)"; "who gave himself for us (our sins)"; and "the blood of the covenant poured out for many," varied and adapted according to the context in which they occur. Can they be explained against the background of contemporary notions of the death of (special) individuals in behalf of other people?

Many have pointed to Isa. 52:13–53:12, the fourth Servant Song in Deutero-Isaiah. That poem presents a great many textual and exegetical difficulties, but they need not be solved here. The passage may be classified among those portraying a suffering servant of God who is exalted.[15] It is not clear whether it is the righteous in Israel who are envisaged or a prophetic figure (or perhaps both), but it is evident that in 52:13–15 and in 53:10–12 God speaks about his servant who "shall prosper, he shall be exalted and lifted up,[16] and shall be very high," and "he shall see his offspring, he shall prolong his days." The servant is righteous and will make many righteous (53:11; see also v. 9). Many nations and kings are astonished at the sudden change in the servant's fate. In 53:1–10 a group introduced with "we" (those nations and kings, or the prophet and a group of pious Israelites?) describes at great length the servant's sufferings. Moreover, they confess their own sins: "All we like sheep have gone astray; we have turned every one to his own way," adding, "and the LORD has laid on him the iniquity of us all" (53:6). In several ways we are told that the sufferings unto death of the servant were for others (for "us," for "many")—see in particular verses 4–6; 10–12.

Isaiah 52:13–53:12 is the only "suffering righteous" passage that brings out this last element, and it seems not to have had much influence in Jewish circles. It has often been argued, for instance,[17] that Dan. 12:1–3 and Wisd. of Sol. 2:12–20; 5:1–7 were greatly influenced by this passage; if so, their authors did not take over the element of "suffering for others." Was it left to early Christianity to bring out the deep thoughts of Isaiah 53 in connection with the suffering and death of Jesus? Many have thought so, yet we have to tread lightly. There is no doubt that it occupies a central place in the story of Philip and the Ethiopian eunuch in Acts 8:26–40 and that it was used for the hymn incorporated in 1 Peter 2:21–25. But if we go back in time we may be less sure. The use of the designation "the servant of the Lord" in Matt. 12:18–21 and Acts 3:13, 26 does not necessarily point to the notion of the *suffering* servant of Isa. 53 (compare also Luke 2:32).[18] Stray quotations such as those of Isa. 52:15 in Rom. 15:21; of 53:1 in Rom. 10:16; or of 53:4 in Matt. 8:17 do not help us here very much. There is, however, the reference to the one who "was numbered with the transgressors" (Isa. 53:12) in a saying of Jesus found only in Luke 22:37, and it is possible that the use of "many" in Mark 10:45 and 14:26[19] was influenced by that in Isa. 53:11–12. These two Markan passages have often been compared in detail with Isa. 53, and influential scholars have tried to prove that they show how Jesus himself was deeply influenced by the concept of the Deutero-Isaianic suffering servant.[20] On close inspection, however, there is little unequivocal evidence for either a close connection between Isaiah 53 and the Markan passages or the theory of Jesus' inspiration by this aspect of Deutero-Isaiah's teaching. More likely is the influence of the Greek translation of 53:12 on the use of the verb "to deliver up" *(paradidonai)* in ancient formulas, and elsewhere, in connection with Jesus' death. In the Deutero-Isaiah passage in the Greek we find "his soul was delivered up to death" and "because of their sins he was delivered up" (so also Rom. 4:25). Isaiah 53:4 makes clear that it was God who "delivered him up for our sins" (cf. Rom. 8:32).

A fuller picture of what "to die for others" signifies is found in 2 and 4 Maccabees, which describe the deaths of the old man Eleazar and of seven brothers and their mother and comment upon them (in the case of 4 Maccabees even very extensively).[21] It can be demonstrated that these descriptions of martyrs giving their lives for their people and their country are greatly influenced by Greek, Hellenistic, and Roman ideas.[22] On the strength of this, it has been argued that we are confronted here with Hellenistic-Jewish ideas that can only have had an effect upon Hellenistic Christians at a later stage of the history of the church; the first Palestinian Christians would not have thought along these lines, and even a formula like "Christ died for us" would not have originated in their circles.

This approach is definitely one-sided, or even wrong. Not only does it give a picture of early Christianity that cannot be maintained, but it also mistakenly assumes that efforts to interpret incisive events in Jewish history—like the death of many innocent and righteous Israelites in the times of the Maccabees—with the help of Hellenistic conceptions, could not be thoroughly Jewish.[23]

For the present purpose I concentrate on a number of points in 2 and 4 Maccabees that help us to understand Christian interpretations of Jesus' death and resurrection. In 2 Macc. 6:27–28 and 7:9, 37 the martyrs make it very clear that they die for God's laws. As obedient servants of God they bring about a turn in the fate of their people, caused by the sins of the Israelites, particularly those of a number of leading figures in Jerusalem.

How God's wrath turned to mercy is explained in the redactional passage in 2 Macc. 6:12–17 and in a number of dying declarations of the seven brothers in chapter 7. In 6:12–17 the author of 2 Maccabees urges his readers not to be depressed by all the calamities he relates. They are punishments designed not to destroy but to discipline Israel. The other nations are left to themselves "until they have reached the full measure of their sins."[24] Israel is punished immediately, for God does not forsake his people and does not allow them to heap sin upon sin.

The martyrs Eleazar and the seven brothers share in the sins and the punishments of the people (2 Macc. 7:18, 32). The youngest brother declares, however, "If our living Lord is angry for a little while, to rebuke and discipline us, he will again be reconciled[25] with his own servants" (7:33). Through the suffering and death of these exemplary Israelites, who are in solidarity with Israel as the people of God, God's wrath comes to an end; henceforth he will show his care for Israel in mercy. The last of the martyred brothers in his final words appeals "to God to show mercy soon to our nation . . . and through me and my brothers to bring to an end the wrath of the Almighty which has justly fallen on our whole nation" (7:37–38).[26]

God tempers or ends his wrath by forgiving sins. For the latter activity the Greek Bible uses a verb akin to the word translated as "to show mercy" in 2 Macc. 7:37. A related composite verb[27] is used in Ex. 32:30 in connection with Moses' intercession ("perhaps I can make atonement for your sin"), and regarding Phinehas' punishment of sinners in Num. 25:11–13 ("made atonement for the people of Israel"—parallel to "have turned back my wrath from the people of Israel"). Moses' intercession for the people and his willingness to share their fate, Phinehas' punitive action in his zeal for the Lord, and the death of the Maccabean martyrs are instrumental in inducing God to end his wrath and to punish Israel no longer. Second Maccabees 6:18–7:41, read against this background, makes clear what it means when someone dies for (the sins of) others. Presupposed are a complete solidarity with the community to which a person belongs, and a covenant relationship between God and this community, for better and for worse. In the cases just mentioned, that community is Israel; in early Christianity the "for all" and "for us" include all, Jews and Gentiles, who put their trust in Jesus and live in communion with him.[28]

One other important aspect of 2 Macc. 7 deserves our attention. The mother and her seven sons firmly believe in the resurrection. They are convinced that "the King of the universe will raise us up to an everlasting renewal of life" (7:9; cf. vs. 11, 14, 23, 29, 36). God the creator will, in his mercy, give everlasting life. Various terms are used, and the conception behind them is not entirely clear. Very likely the author envisaged an eternal existence in a new body in heaven. For the martyrs there will be resurrection to life, but not for the tyrant.[29] In their faithfulness to God leading to their death at the hands of the enemy, they will be vindicated.[30] Nowhere in 2 Maccabees do we find the conception of a resurrection at the end of time.

Second Maccabees was probably written sometime during the reign of John Hyrcanus (135–104 B.C.). Fourth Maccabees, dependent on 2 Maccabees, is considerably younger, around A.D. 100 at the earliest, so that for our purpose we have to use the evidence from this writing with caution. It relates the examples of the martyrdoms of Eleazar and the seven brothers in order to demonstrate that "devout reason is absolute master of the passions" (1:1),[31] employing philosophical language. Eleazar, and the seven brothers and their mother, "died for virtue's sake" (1:8) in their obedience to the law. In 9:1 the seven brothers cry: "Why do you delay, tyrant? We are prepared to die rather than transgress the commandments of our fathers."[32]

The effect of their martyrdom on the country and the people of Israel is expressed in several ways. In 4 Macc. 6:27–29 Eleazar, on the point of expiring, prays to God: "You know, God, that though I could have saved myself I am dying in these fiery torments for the sake of the Law. Be merciful to our people and let our punishment be a satisfaction in their behalf. Make my blood their purification[33] and take my life as a ransom[34] for theirs." God's mercy for Israel (cf. 2 Macc. 7:37) recurs in 4 Macc. 9:24 and 12:17 together with his punishment of the tyrant. The idea of "purification" is also found in 1:11 and especially in 17:21–22, where in the course of a retrospective statement it is said: "And the tyrant was punished and our land purified, since they became, as it were, a ransom for the sin of our nation. Through the blood of these righteous ones and through the propitiation[35] of their death the divine providence rescued Israel, which had been shamefully treated."

As does 2 Maccabees, 4 Maccabees stresses the crucial importance of the death of the martyrs for the great change that has taken place in the history of the nation. The terms employed to express the vicarious nature and the atoning effect of these deaths are much more developed than those in the earlier document. Yet in the overall picture of the book more emphasis is laid on the exemplary nature of their devotion and on the divine reward granted to them and to all true children of Abraham. Abraham himself is mentioned as an example of bravery and fear of God (15:28; 16:20). Isaac is praised for his endurance (13:13; cf. 7:14); he did not flinch when Abraham took a knife to sacrifice him (16:20–21; cf. 18:11).[36] Also Daniel and the three young men in the oven are praised for their obedience to the law and their brave conduct (13:9; 16:3, 21; 18:12).

God's suffering servants (martyrs and near-martyrs!) will have eternal life. The brothers "knew full well themselves that those who die for the sake of God live unto God, as do Abraham and Isaac and Jacob and all the patriarchs" (4 Macc. 16:25; cf. 7:18–19; 13:17). So the final verse, 18:23, gives the picture of "the sons of Abraham, together with their mother, who won the victor's prize . . . gathered together in the choir of their fathers, having received pure and deathless souls from God, to whom be glory for ever and ever. Amen."

Returning to the writings of the New Testament for a moment, we note that in the discussion of Jesus with the Sadducees on the resurrection of the dead recorded in Mark 12:18–27 (par. Matt. 22:23–33; Luke 20:27–40), God's self-revelation to Moses at the burning bush as "the God of Abraham, and the God of Isaac, and the God of Jacob" is taken as a proof of the fact that "he is not God of the dead, but of the living." Luke 20:38 explains: "for all live to him" (cf. 4 Macc. 16:25). In Luke 13:28–29 (par. Matt. 8:11–12 [Q]) the three patriarchs participate (Luke: "and all the prophets") in the eschatological banquet in the kingdom of God. Those who have rejected Jesus will not be admitted; they will watch many others from east and west flock in. In the Lukan parable of the rich man and Lazarus, the poor beggar reclines in the bosom of Abraham immediately after death (16:23), just as Jesus promises one of the two crucified with him: "today you will be with me in Paradise" (23:43). We may compare this with Paul's desire "to depart and be with Christ" after death in Phil. 1:23.[37]

Finally, the emphasis on new life granted by God to his (suffering) servants in 2 and 4 Maccabees explains why in Luke-Acts special attention is paid to Jesus' glory and exaltation in the period between his death on the cross and his *parousia*—which, of course, continues to receive due attention. (See Luke 22:69; 23:43; 24:26 as well as 24:46; and Acts 2:33; 3:13; 5:31; 7:56.)

Jesus, the Lord

In calling Jesus "Lord" his followers acknowledged his authority over their lives, individually and collectively. A lord *(kyrios)* administers his property and commands his servants (or slaves, *douloi*), who are expected to do what he wants. Such is the picture we find in many New Testament parables, in accordance with ordinary life in Palestine and elsewhere in the Hellenistic world. Christians are servants of their Lord. Paul calls himself "a servant of Jesus Christ, called to be an apostle" (Rom. 1:1; Gal. 1:10; Phil. 1:1; cf. James 1:1), and specifies: "For what we preach is not ourselves, but Jesus Christ as Lord, with ourselves as your servants for Jesus' sake" (2 Cor. 4:5).

In our discussion of a number of passages in 1 Corinthians and elsewhere in chapter 1 we found that the title "Lord" was originally especially used in a liturgical context. People acclaimed Jesus as Lord (1 Cor. 12:3) led by the Spirit; they confessed with their lips "Jesus is Lord" because in their heart they believed "that God raised him from the dead" (Rom. 10:9). It is the living Jesus Christ, vindicated by God, invested with authority, actively present in the Spirit among his servants, who is worshiped and obeyed as Lord. His *parousia* is expected: "Our Lord, come!" the congregation prays, using an ancient Aramaic formula (1 Cor. 16:22). Of course, Jesus' Lordship did not start with his resurrection/exaltation. At the Lord's Supper the community commemorates the Lord's death "until he comes," on the authority of the Lord himself (1 Cor. 11:17–21), whose sayings are also elsewhere referred to as authoritative "words of the Lord." But the significance of his words and the effects of his death "for us/you" are acknowledged because of the firm conviction that the authority of this man Jesus was borne out in his resurrection.[38] That is the reason why the designation "Lord" is best discussed in the present context.

If we ask whether *kyrios* had any special connotations beyond the general one of authority, we may point to two passages already briefly mentioned in chapter 1. In 1 Cor. 8:5–6 Paul, probably using an ancient formula, mentions many "so-called gods in heaven or on earth—as indeed there are many gods and many lords," over against whom the Christians confess one God, the Father, and one Lord Jesus Christ. "Lord" is indeed often used in Hellenistic texts[39] to denote the authority of gods, particularly of Hellenized oriental deities. The term is also employed for Hellenistic kings, and for Roman emperors,[40] who in the course of the first century of our era were more and more worshiped as gods, certainly in the Eastern part of the empire. Domitian, as is well known, called himself "Lord and God"—a designation totally unacceptable to Christians in Asia Minor whose experiences are reflected in the book of Revelation. The conflict between obedience to the one God and the one Lord Jesus Christ and loyalty to the emperor is a central theme in the acts of the Christian martyrs in the period until the reign of the emperor Constantine. Tertullian speaks for many when he states: "I could certainly call the emperor 'lord' but only in the generally accepted sense, and only when I would not be compelled to call him 'lord' instead of God."[41]

The Hellenistic use of the term "lord" will certainly have influenced early Christian usage. In Hellenistic surroundings it was, no doubt, a more suitable term to denote the authority of the One who determined Christian life and thought than "Christ" or "Son of man." But it is questionable whether the mission to the Gentiles was the principal, let alone the only, factor in introducing the term.[42] The pre-Pauline hymn Phil. 2:6–11 culminates in verse 11 in the confession "Jesus Christ is Lord." "Lord" is "the name which is above every name" mentioned in verse 9, the name of the God of Israel. As already noted, there is a clear reference to Isa. 45:23, belonging to a passage that emphasizes that there is no God but the God of Israel. The exalted Jesus, the Lord, is worthy of the same adoration as Yahweh, the God of Israel himself, although he remains subordinate to God the Father ("to the glory of God the Father," Phil. 2:11). As in 1 Cor. 8:5–6, it is clear that his Lordship is not restricted to the Christian community, but extends over the entire creation. All beings ("in heaven and on earth and under the earth," Phil. 2:10) should acknowledge his authority.

From very early, Christians called Jesus "Lord" just as they called the God of Israel "Lord," and they felt free to apply texts from scripture referring to the Lord (= Yahweh) to the Lord Jesus. Previously, we called attention to the use of the expression "those who call upon the name of the Lord" for Christians, which is clearly derived from Joel 2:32.[43] More examples of such a use of scripture passages in the early Christian writings could be mentioned here.

The great manuscripts of the Greek translation of the Old Testament dating from the fourth and fifth centuries A.D., on which our editions of the Septuagint are based, indeed translate *kyrios* where the Hebrew text has the divine name *Yahweh* that ought not to be pronounced. In the standardized Masoretic text of the Hebrew scriptures the consonants of the divine name are supplied with the vowels of *'adonay* (translated by "the LORD" in the English versions). Now it has been rightly remarked that in earlier manuscripts written for Greek-speaking Jews in pre-Christian times the divine name was not translated in this way, but was inserted in (ancient) Hebrew characters or transcribed in some other way. The question remains, however: What did Greek-speaking Jews say when they read the scriptures aloud, in the synagogue or in private? Hellenistic Jewish authors do use the word *kyrios* to denote God, and recent Qumran finds have substantiated that Aramaic- and Hebrew-speaking Jews in the time around the beginning of the common era also could refer to God as "Lord."[44] It is this Jewish usage that was taken over by early Christians when they spoke about the only God, *and* about the exalted Jesus whose unique authority they wanted to express.

Jesus' Status After His Death, and Psalm 110:1

The LORD says to my lord:
"Sit at my right hand,
till I make your enemies your footstool."

Psalm 110:1 is one of the passages in the Jewish scriptures most quoted or alluded to in early Christian writings.[45] In all cases the verse as a whole or significant phrases from it are used to express certain aspects of Jesus' status after death. Comparing the various references to this psalm verse, the reader is astonished at the creativity and flexibility of early Christian interpretation of scripture. It was certainly not so that Jesus' resurrection, vindication, sitting at God's right hand, or *parousia* were deduced from this passage. On the other hand, it would be an understatement to say that certain beliefs about Jesus were merely illustrated by scriptural texts like the present one, interpreted creatively. Once certain Christological convictions and conceptions had originated in the context of reflection on scriptural and traditional views on God's dealings with Israel and mankind through intermediaries, particular passages from scripture were read with new eyes and received a special meaning. Some of those, like Ps. 110:1, could be used in different circumstances to bring out different aspects of Jesus' status and activity and clearly continued to inspire early Christian believers. It is worthwhile to have a brief look at the places in the New Testament where Ps. 110:1 is quoted or alluded to. Analysis of the interpretation of this passage may give us at least some idea of the way other texts from scripture were read and influenced early Christian thinking.[46]

The full verse "The LORD says to my lord: 'Sit at my right hand, till I make your enemies your footstool' " is quoted in Mark 12:36 (par. Matt. 22:44; Luke 20:42–43) and in Acts 2:34–35. Applied to Jesus, it shows how, after his exaltation, he occupies a position of honor beside God, without calling into question the glory and sovereignty of God himself. The quotation stems from a psalm of David, and the "my lord" addressed is no doubt a royal figure. That is why in Mark 12:36 the verse can be used to qualify the common assumption that the Messiah is the Son of David. Jesus is certainly more: Mark 14:62 (par. Matt. 26:64) portrays his future glory as "Son of man seated at the right hand of Power, and coming with the clouds of heaven" in a context in which it is clear that he is the Messiah, the Son of God. The emphasis is on his *parousia* and on the coming judgment. His sitting at God's right hand, mentioned in Ps. 110:1, is directly connected with what will happen in the immediate future.[47]

In Luke 20:42–43 the *parousia* is not mentioned, and in keeping with the overall approach in Luke-Acts the activity of the exalted Jesus as Lord receives attention for its own sake.[48] This is evident in Acts 2:34–35, where Ps. 110:1 occurs in a complex argumentation in a speech by Peter. After demonstrating that David predicted that his descendant Jesus would be raised from the dead, Jesus' exaltation at the right hand of God (*and* his pouring out the Holy Spirit) is connected with the verse under discussion (cf. Acts 5:31–32). Significantly, the speech ends with the statement, "Let all the house of Israel therefore know assuredly that God has made him both Lord and Christ, this Jesus whom you crucified."[49] Only here in the New Testament writings is Jesus' Lordship brought into relation with Ps. 110:1.[50]

In 1 Cor. 15:24–28 the emphasis is on Ps. 110:1b, connected with Ps. 8:6, "thou hast given him dominion over the works of thy hands;

thou hast put all things under his feet."[51] At the end, Christ "delivers the kingdom to God the Father after destroying every rule and every authority and power. For he must reign until he has put all his enemies under his feet." The emphasis is on the final victory, but it is clear that Christ already before that exerts his rule. This present dominion is brought out clearly in 1 Peter 3:22, where it is stated that Christ "has gone into heaven and is at the right hand of God, with angels, authorities, and powers subject to him." It does not come as a surprise that this aspect receives due emphasis in the cosmic Christology of Colossians and Ephesians (Col. 3:1; 2:10, 15; Eph. 1:20–23; 2:5–6). Here, the corporate Christological thinking includes the notion that Christians have not only been raised up with Christ but have also been made to sit "with him in the heavenly places in Christ Jesus" (Eph. 2:6; cf. Col. 3:1). Similarly, but then connected with the future and not with the present, in Rev. 3:21: "He who conquers, I will grant him to sit with me on my throne, as I myself conquered and sat down with my Father on his throne."

The epistle to the Hebrews presents a special case. On the one hand, as we have seen, the quotations and allusions to Ps. 110:1 underscore that Jesus, the Son of God, is more powerful than all his adversaries, who will someday be annihilated forever (see Heb. 1:3, 13; 8:1; 10:12–13; 12:2; cf. Ps. 8:7 in 2:5–9). But this Son is also the high priest who intercedes for those who put their trust in him (7:24). This notion is also found in Rom. 8:34: "Christ Jesus, . . . who is at the right hand of God, who indeed intercedes for us." The author underlines the special position of Jesus as high priest by calling him "a (high) priest for ever after the order of Melchizedek" (Heb. 5:6, 10; 6:20; ch. 7). In his heavenly position, but also in his suffering and death on earth, this high priest who offered up himself once and for all, thus securing eternal redemption, is infinitely superior to the earlier Levitical priests of the old dispensation. The author of this epistle was familiar with the notions of Jesus as Son of God, of Jesus as high priest, and of Jesus' sacrifice in behalf of others; the combination of the first verse of Psalm 110 with the fourth, and the theological disquisitions on the implications of Jesus being a priest after the order of Melchizedek, is clearly of his own invention.

12
Jesus Christ and God Before Jesus' Mission on Earth

Our analysis of the terms and concepts applied by Christians in their response to Jesus has concentrated so far on the interpretations of Jesus' mission in word and deed and on those of his death and subsequent vindication by God. The latter, in turn, led to reflection on his present exalted status and to continued speculation upon his imminent *parousia* to realize God's sovereign rule on earth. These different aspects of early Christology are directly connected. If one is to believe that Jesus came as God's final envoy with a unique authority at a point of no return, one has to be convinced of his continued close relationship with God after his ignominious death on the cross, leading to the inauguration of God's kingdom on earth one day in the immediate future. Beliefs and hopes centering around Jesus' earthly mission led to, and were in turn enriched by, reflections on his resurrection and exaltation. If Jesus' disciples had not been certain that he lived in God's presence and continued to guide his followers on earth, their trust in Jesus as God's supreme and final representative and their expectation of the speedy arrival of God's kingdom in power would not have survived their bewilderment and disappointment at the crucifixion of the master whom they followed.

The early Christian writings employ such terms as resurrection, exaltation, lifting up, ascension, return to the Father, sitting at the right hand, to indicate that Jesus as Lord continues to carry out his mission. With a comparable variety of terms and images they speak about the final stage of that mission, his return to earth in order to inaugurate God's kingdom. They are, in general, not concerned to explain in what state Jesus exists in heaven, in what form he appeared to his disciples,[1] and how one should envisage his encounter with the faithful at the *parousia* and their "being with the Lord" (1 Thess. 4:17) forever afterward. Early Christians expressed their beliefs and convictions by means of terms, images, and analogies derived from the traditions and culture in which they lived. They used a variety of terms to express the various aspects of the "facts," the "reality" they wanted to convey. They did not present a consistent overall picture giving all aspects, clearly connected and neatly balanced. Nor do we find any interest in questions of "essence" or "modes of existence" of Jesus Christ (or God, for that matter) like those raised by Greek theologians of later centuries, influenced by contemporary philosophical discussions.

The same applies to speculations about what is usually called Jesus' preexistence. As we have seen in chapter 1, at a very early stage people raised the question whether the special relationship between Jesus and God, so evident during his mission on earth and so clearly demonstrated in what followed after his death, existed already before his earthly life began. Those who believe that God sent his Son on a very special mission when the time had fully come (Gal. 4:4) are bound to reflect on the nature of the connection between the Sender and his envoy as Father and Son before the latter's mission started. And if a congregation worships Jesus Christ as Lord, to the glory of God the Father, and is convinced that it does so together with numerous beings in heaven, on earth, and under the earth (Phil. 2:10–11), it is likely to wonder whether there was any special bond between the now-exalted Lord and God the Father before Jesus Christ humbled himself and obediently died his death on the cross.

In the present section we shall explore this matter a little further under two headings. First we shall pay attention to the notion of Jesus as the unique envoy sent from "above"; next we shall deal with the various ways in which Jesus is spoken of in terms connected with God's personified Wisdom or God's Word. It will become evident that there is some overlap between the two topics.

Jesus as the Unique Envoy Sent from Above

We have to start here with the ancient Christian expression "God sent his Son in order that . . ." found in Gal. 4:4–6; Rom. 8:3–4; Mark 12:1–9; John 3:16–17; and 1 John 4:9.[2] The emphasis is on the eschatological character of Jesus' mission and his special relationship to God: he is *the* Son of God. Whether this special relationship to God is thought of in terms of existing with God as a heavenly being before the start of the mission on earth becomes clear only on examination of the specific contexts in which this pattern of thought is used. In the parable in Mark 12:1–9 the relation of the owner of the vineyard to his beloved son who is his heir is totally different from that to the many servants he sent before. The son is his final envoy, and the fact that he is killed leads the owner to take drastic and definitive measures. The parable does not allow us to draw any conclusion as to the mode of existence of Jesus in the time before he was sent by God. But the situation is different in the two passages in the letters of Paul.[3] The fact that in Gal. 4 Paul emphasizes that the Son was "born of woman, born under the law," and that he released the believers from their bondage to the elemental spirits of the universe, strongly suggests that the Son was in God's presence in a form other than human before being sent. The term "in the likeness of sinful flesh" in Rom. 8:3 also implies an earlier existence without sin, in the Spirit (see the discourse on "flesh" and "spirit" that follows). It is clear, however, that Paul does not indulge in speculations about this earlier form of existence; his attention centers on the unique status of the Son which enabled him to fulfill his mission to deliver people from the oppressing forces of evil. In the case of John 3:16–17 and 1 John 4:9 the pattern of thought under discussion is embedded in a very elaborate and consistent "Christology of mission."[4] In the Fourth Gospel, as we have seen, we find the picture of the Son operating in complete unity with the Father, sent by him and returning to him. There is no description of the Son's "journey" from God in heaven to "the world" and back again to a renewed sharing in God's glory. Yet this Gospel cannot dispense with spatial imagery. Jesus is not simply "a teacher come from God," as Nicodemus calls him (John 3:2). He is God's only Son sent into the world to save all who believe in him (3:16–21); yes, he is the one "who comes from above" and "bears witness to what he has seen and heard" (3:31–36). Again, there is no speculation on Jesus' modes of existence at the various stages; yet it is impossible to speak about the origin of Jesus' mission without taking into account the origin of the one whom God sent.[5]

Are there parallel conceptions in earlier texts that help us to explain why not only the Johannine Christians but also, before them, Paul and his contemporaries regarded it as important to stress the special relationship that existed between God and Jesus prior to his actual mission on earth? We should note that the Old Testament and early Jewish literature know a number of heavenly messengers.[6] We usually speak about "angels" to distinguish them from human envoys, but we should bear in mind that the Hebrew and Greek words used to indicate them mean simply "messenger." In the Old Testament the "angel of the Lord" is sent by God to speak and act on his behalf, and in fact his words and actions cannot be distinguished from those of God himself. In Exodus 3 the angel of the Lord appears to Moses at the burning bush (v. 2) and (through him) the Lord speaks directly to Moses. When in verse 8 it is said, "and I have come down to deliver them (= the people) out of the hand of the Egyptians," this may apply to the angel as well as to the Lord himself. To mention yet another example: in Judg. 13 the angel of the Lord appears to Manoah and his wife to announce the birth of Samson. Manoah's wife refers to the angel as "a man of God" whose "countenance was like the countenance of God, very terrible" (v. 6; cf. v. 8). This messenger appears in a human form, with a message of joy and salvation, but he is clearly more than human. In fact he does not eat of Manoah's food, but orders it to be offered to God and ascends in the flame of the altar (vs. 15–20).[7] In the book of Tobit God sends Raphael to heal Tobit and Sarah, the daughter of Raguel, who marries Tobias, Tobit's son. As Azarias, the son of one of Tobit's relatives, he accompanies Tobias on his journey. Only at the end of the story does the guardian angel reveal himself as "one of the seven holy angels who present the prayers of the saints and enter into the presence of the glory of the Holy One" (12:15). God sent him to heal and give assistance (v. 14). Raphael declares that he is now "ascending to him who sent me" (v. 20); the author makes him explain that "all these days I merely appeared to you and did not eat and drink, but you were seeing a vision" (v. 19). Again, God's messenger and representative is clearly a figure sent by God "from above" appearing as a human being.

These examples are given here to show how the concept of God sending representatives and envoys could include the mission of heavenly messengers and their descent and ascent. Nowhere, however, in the earliest Christian documents is Jesus Christ called "angel,"[8] nor is there, in texts speaking about Jesus' mission, any speculation on a transition from a heavenly to a human existence. Only in 1 and 2 John do we find a dispute on the matter, between two Johannine groups. The author(s) stress Jesus' coming "in the flesh" over against opponents who lay so much emphasis on the Son's divine origin that they can no longer imagine him as a true human being dying a human death on the cross.

In a number of Old Testament passages we find the notion that God sends his word (Ps. 107:20; 147:15, 18; Isa. 9:8; 55:10–11).[9] This word effects what God wants. In Isa. 55:10–11 the author compares God's word with the rain and snow that bring water and fertility to the earth, and continues:

> So shall my word be that goes forth from my mouth;
> it shall not return to me empty,
> but it shall accomplish that which I purpose,
> and prosper in the thing for which I sent it.

Here in a daring image God's word is pictured as a messenger going the way expected of him. This near-personification of God's word explains the way in which a number of passages in Wisdom literature speak about (God's) Wisdom as an entity separate from God. We shall come back to this in the next subsection but should note here that sometimes Wisdom is also spoken of as "being sent." In connection with the sending formula scholars[10] have often pointed to Wisd. of Sol. 9:10 and 17–18, where Solomon prays for wisdom and asks, among other things,

> Send her [i.e., Wisdom] forth from the holy heavens,
> and from the throne of thy glory send her,
> that she may be with me and toil,
> and that I may learn what is pleasing to thee.

And he adds,

> Who has learned thy counsel, unless thou hast given wisdom
> and sent thy holy Spirit from on high?
> And thus the paths of those on earth were set right,
> and men were taught what pleases thee,
> and were saved by wisdom.

The use of "sending" parallel to "giving" (as in John 3:16–17); the emphasis on the purpose of the mission (the granting of knowledge, salvation) and the parallel between giving wisdom and sending the Spirit (as in Gal. 4:4–6) have led to the theory that the sending formula should be explained against the background of ancient Jewish speculations on Wisdom. An extra argument is that in the passages to be discussed in the next subsection, the influence of ideas about Wisdom as God's helper at creation is evident too.

Perhaps, however, the picture is slightly more complicated.[11] In Wisd. of Sol. 9:17 we have just found a close link between Wisdom and Holy Spirit;[12] in 9:1–2 Wisdom and Word are equated. In 18: 15–16 the angel of death who on the Lord's behalf kills the firstborn of the Egyptians is described in the following words:

> Thy all-powerful word leaped from heaven, from the royal throne,
> into the midst of the land that was doomed,
> a stern warrior carrying the sharp sword of thy authentic command . . .

But in 10:15–16, forming part of a long section describing Wisdom's guidance and protection of the righteous in the history of Israel, it is Wisdom who through Moses delivers Israel from Egypt:

> A holy people and blameless race
> she [i.e., Wisdom] delivered from a nation of oppressors.
> She entered the soul of a servant of the Lord,
> and withstood dread kings with wonders and signs.

In the Wisdom of Solomon God's redeeming activity is spoken of in personal terms; the revealer/redeemer figure is variously identified as Wisdom, Word, angel, and Holy Spirit. The merger of traditions and concepts is even more pronounced in the writings of Philo, who uses the rich variety of images provided by the Old Testament and Alexandrian-Jewish tradition before him in an allegorical fashion. In connection with the sending formula found in the New Testament, for instance, attention has been drawn to *On Agriculture* 51, where Philo links the Word, the first-born *Son,* and the angel of the Lord; he does so in a passage describing God's care for his entire creation and all living creatures in it, quoting as a proof text Ex. 23:20 in the Greek version: "Behold I am, *I send* my angel before you to guard you on the way."

We may conclude that the sending formula and its various applications in early Christian writings presuppose a variety of images of activities of God represented as "intermediaries" carrying out God's intervention in human affairs. This time, of course, all emphasis is on God's final intervention through Jesus Christ.

Jesus as Wisdom and Word of God[13]

In a number of passages in Wisdom literature, personified Wisdom is pictured as dwelling and operating on earth. In Prov. 1:20–33 and in the well-known chapter Proverbs 8, Wisdom takes her stand where people gather or pass by and exhorts them all to pay attention to what she has to offer; in 9:1–6, the passage directly following, she has built a house and invites people to take part in the meal she has prepared. In Sir. 24 we find a similar invitation (vs. 19–20). Here, Wisdom is said to dwell in Israel, in the beloved city Jerusalem, and in the holy tabernacle in Zion (vs. 8–12).[14] We should note that in verse 23 Wisdom is explicitly identified with the law: "All this is the book of the covenant of the Most High God, the law which Moses commanded us." In Sir. 51:23–30 (the closing verses of the book) we read a final exhortation, put in the mouth of personified Wisdom. Baruch 3:29–4:4 stresses again that God found Wisdom and gave her to Israel, in the form of "the book of the commandments of God, and the law that endures for ever" (4:1).

As we have already noted, these passages help us to understand a number of sayings in Q and the way they were redacted in Matthew. In Luke 7:35 John the Baptist and Jesus are among the "children of Wisdom." In Luke 11:49–51 Wisdom is portrayed as sending out apostles and prophets, and in Luke 13:34–35 Jesus speaks as a representative of Wisdom announcing the imminent destruction of Jerusalem, which refuses to accept the messengers inviting people to take shelter under Wisdom's wings. In Luke 10:21–22 Jesus speaks as the Son who stands in a unique relationship to the Father, as the wise and righteous man par excellence, to whom *all* knowledge has been given. For Q Jesus is the ideal and final representative of Wisdom, in fact one who can most adequately be described as "the Son" operating in close communion with God, but it stops short of identifying Jesus with Wisdom. This identification is found, however, albeit implicitly, in Matt. 11:19; 23:34; and in particular Matt. 11:28–30, a Matthean addition to Matt. 11:25–27 (par. Luke 10:21–22). Here Jesus invites people to come to him and share in his rest, using words reminiscent of Sir. 51:23–27.

In Proverbs, Sirach, and Wisdom of Solomon, Wisdom is portrayed as being with God from the beginning. In Prov. 8:22–31 Wisdom describes herself as created before the beginning of the earth. While the world was being created, Wisdom was beside God "like a master workman." The meaning of the Hebrew word in question is not certain—an alternative rendering is "a little child"[15]—but the rendering in the Greek Old Testament favors the first translation. We may compare Wisd. of Sol. 8:4, 6, where Wisdom is called "an associate of his works" and "a fashioner of what exists." In Sir. 24 God is said to have created Wisdom "from eternity, in the beginning"; Wisdom adds "for eternity I shall not cease to exist" (v. 9; cf. Sir. 1:1–10). She is described as a companion of God in heaven (vs. 1–4), but plays no role at the creation of the world. In Wisd. of Sol. 9, Wisdom "sits by [God's] throne" (vs. 4, 10). It is from there that she will be sent to assist the king in judging his people justly and in teaching man to do what pleases God. Wisdom was present when God made the world (v. 9) and she was instrumental in the formation of humanity. Verses 1–2 address God:

> who hast made all things by thy word,
> and by thy wisdom hast formed man.

The imagery used in these and similar passages (again, also in the works of Philo) explains how in 1 Cor. 8:6 Jesus can be called the one Lord "through whom are all things and through whom we exist."[16] He is the mediator at the creation (a role ascribed to Wisdom) as well as the (final) agent of salvation (in line with Wisdom's efforts to guide men on the path to salvation and her invitations to share in her blessings). In the same way Col. 1:15–20 can be explained against the background of Wisdom speculation. The cosmic implications of Christ's work as Savior and Redeemer, which are brought out so clearly in the letter to the Colossians, find support in the statement that "in him all things were created, in heaven and on earth, visible and invisible, whether thrones or dominions or principalities or authorities" (Col. 1:16). The power manifested in Jesus Christ's death (effecting reconciliation) and in his exaltation is the same as the power that brought the world into being, with all it contains.

Colossians 1:15 calls the beloved Son (v. 13) "the image of the invisible God." This recalls Wisd. of Sol. 7:26, which speaks of Wisdom as

> a reflection of eternal light,
> a spotless mirror of the working of God,
> and an image of his goodness.

The Greek word translated "reflection" returns in Heb. 1:2–3, where it is said of the Son through whom God created the world and who upholds the universe by his word of power: "He reflects the glory of God" (v. 3)—here we can again compare Wisd. of Sol. 7:25: "and a pure emanation of the glory of the Almighty."

The few examples given here (to which many others could be added) illustrate how notions and images concerned with personified Wisdom were instrumental in relating God's final saving action in Jesus Christ to his plan and purpose when creating the universe, and to his perpetual care for the earth and its inhabitants.

It is difficult to characterize the Jewish way of speaking about Wisdom in the passages mentioned in this and the preceding section, and equally difficult to give an adequate assessment of the related Christological statements. Are we confronted with vivid personifications serving to express God's active involvement with his world and his people without compromising his transcendence,[17] which can be used alongside "ordinary" expressions concerning Wisdom as a quality or an attribute of God? Should we say, with James Dunn, that for (Hellenistic-) Jewish authors "Wisdom never really became more than a convenient way of speaking about God acting in creation, revelation and salvation"?[18] Perhaps we should, but at the same time we have to realize that to the authors this way of speaking presented itself as more adequate than other language about God. The literature of Israel preserved in the Old Testament has always used stories to make clear who God is, what he wants, and how he acts. Narrative can convey certain truths about God better than discourse. In the same fashion stories are told about God's heavenly entourage, consisting of angels with different qualities and functions, and about intermediaries personifying attributes and activities of God. Mythological representations current in the religious thought of the surrounding world also, no doubt, regularly influenced Israel's religious leaders, just as at a later stage philosophical ideas of Platonic and Stoic provenance inspired Philo to use all these images allegorically.

In short, in a great number of cases "reflective mythology" presented itself as the most adequate means of expression. Elisabeth Schüssler Fiorenza, who has reintroduced the term, defines it as "a form of theology appropriating mythical language, material and patterns from different myths." She adds that it "is not interested in reproducing the myth itself or the mythic elements as they stand, but rather in taking up and adapting the various mythical elements to its own theological goal and theoretical concerns."[19] In the Jewish and early Christian passages under discussion mythological language is not used to describe physical and metaphysical entities and phenomena and their interaction, but, indeed, to define and describe God's activity in creation, revelation, and salvation. For this reason the person and work of Jesus Christ, too, are described in terms derived from mythological reflection on the role of intermediaries in the interaction between the God of Israel and the world, his people, and humanity as a whole.

Reflective mythology lies also behind a characterization like the one found in 2 Cor. 8:9: "For you know the grace of our Lord Jesus Christ, that though he was rich, yet for your sake he became poor, so that by his poverty you might become rich." It is also very evident in the well-known Christological hymn Phil. 2:6–11 already discussed briefly in chapter 6. Here we may stress that in these verses we find an extension of a humiliation-exaltation pattern like that found in Isa. 52:13–53:11 so as to include Jesus Christ's preexistence "in the form of God" and his exaltation to the highest place in heaven. The emphasis is on the fact that the one who was in the form of God chose to be a humble servant, to be obedient unto the death on the cross, and was highly exalted by God. Closer examination of the terminology used shows that hymnic language does not allow for metaphysical or systematic theological conclusions.

We end this subsection with some remarks on the Prologue of the Gospel of John, in the eyes of many the most systematic exposition of the question of the preexistence of Jesus Christ, including a clear statement about the incarnation. The central figure in this Prologue is "the Word"; again we are able to adduce many parallels from the Old Testament, Hellenistic-Jewish authors (in particular Philo), and earlier writings in the New Testament to illustrate the various aspects of the Word and its activity highlighted in John 1:1–8. We should note that the Word was in the beginning (John 1:1)—like Wisdom in Prov. 8 and Sir. 24—but that nothing is said about it being *created* first. The emphasis is on the fact that "all things were made through him, and without him was not anything made that was made" (1:3). It does not come as a surprise that "the Word was with God" (this is said twice), nor that "the Word was God" (vs. 1–2).

In the latter case the article before "God" that is used in the expression "with God" is omitted, and this is significant. A similar distinction is found in Philo.[20] The author of this Prologue clearly wants to identify "the Word" and God as closely as possible without infringing the belief in the One God.

"The Word" is then pictured as bringer of light and life. In fact he is identified with the Light shining in the darkness, rejected by men, yet giving new life ("power to become children of God") to those who accept him (John 1:4–13). One may differ about the extent to which the story of Jesus Christ told later in the Gospel influenced the description of the way of the Word (Light) in the world. In view of the introduction of John the Baptist in the Prologue in verses 6–8 and the obvious reference to Jesus Christ in verse 8 ("He was not the light, but came to bear witness to the light"; cf. 1:20; 5:35; 8:12), it is probable that Jesus Christ is on the scene from verse 9 onward. But undoubtedly the central statement concerning him is verse 14:

> And the Word became flesh and dwelt among us,
> > full of grace and truth;
> we have beheld his glory,
> > glory as of the only Son from the Father.

Here the Christology of the Word is combined with that of the Son in his relationship to the Father, which occupies a central place in the Fourth Gospel. There is no doubt that the author wants to make clear that the Son dwelt as a human being among human beings. Yet the "glory" typical for his preexistence as well as for his "postexistence" (17:24) remained visible for those who accepted him as God's final envoy to the world.

What is stated here certainly goes beyond anything we have encountered so far. But are we really allowed or even required to say that the way of speaking in the Prologue can no longer be characterized as "reflective mythology"? In the thorough seventh chapter of his *Christology in the Making,* entitled "The Word of God," James Dunn strongly emphasizes the differences between the Fourth Gospel and earlier writings in this respect. "Here we have an explicit statement of *incarnation,* the first and indeed only such statement in the New Testament," he says, and "the identification of Christ with the word of God in a deliberately metaphysical way (John 1.14) must be regarded as marking a new stage in Christian thinking." Though he continues, "We must as always beware of oversystematizing such expansions or deepening of thought," he does seem to overstate his case.[21]

The word "became" in John 1:14 remains ambiguous insofar as it does not provide any metaphysical clarification with regard to the relation between the Word as God, existing in the glory as of the only Son from the Father, and the Word as true human being.[22] The conflict between the Johannine groups reflected in the first and second letters of John would not have broken out if the Christology of the Johannine Christians had been clear on this point. The opponents in the letters have no doubt stressed what is expressed in verse 14b at the expense of verse 14a, and over against this the author(s) of 1 and 2 John emphasize verse 14a. Yet in 1 John 1:1–4 the authors of that letter go even less far than the author of the Prologue of the Gospel when they write, "We . . . proclaim to you the eternal life which was with the Father and was made manifest to us" (v. 2).[23]

We are left with the conclusion that even in the relatively advanced Christology of Johannine Christianity the nature of the appearance on earth of the Son who was with the Father from the beginning was not determined in philosophical, metaphysical terms, but by means of words and images used in current "reflective mythology." The interpretation of John 1:1–18 was of central importance for Christian thought about Jesus Christ and his relation to the Father in the following centuries. Philosophically trained theologians differed widely in their conclusions, and we may argue that the great dogmas of the Trinity and the two natures of Christ circumscribe the central mystery rather than define it.

PART IV
The Very Beginning

13
The One with Whom
It All Began

The Earliest Response to Jesus

This book is concerned with the earliest response to Jesus by those who put their trust in him and assigned to him a central role in God's dealings with Israel and all humanity. Sources at our disposal are Christian sources, reflecting various forms and various stages of belief in Jesus' continuing importance for people in their relation to God and to one another. They were all written long after Jesus' death on the cross and reflect the firm conviction of early Christianity that God had vindicated his obedient servant Jesus, had raised him from death and exalted him. There are good reasons to suppose a rather extended period of oral transmission of traditions concerning Jesus' teaching and his actions addressing situations in the groups of followers of Jesus Christ in the land of Israel and elsewhere.

When we look at our oldest written sources, the letters of Paul, and at the even older formulas he quotes, it may seem that these early witnesses are not really concerned with Jesus' life and teaching: they concentrate on his death and resurrection and the meaning of these events for those who believe in him. Yet there are references to Jesus' life and teaching in Paul's letters, and we may rightly ask whether Paul could really speak about Jesus' death "for us" in a hortatory context without having and presupposing knowledge of the one who gave his life.

Speaking about the Gospel of Mark we found that at the time of writing it had become imperative to combine the message *(euaggelion)* about Jesus Christ with the narrative of the Passion and the events leading up to it. Especially reflection on Jesus' death on the cross and the controversies and conflicts leading to the crucifixion must have been indispensable already at a very early stage. The message of the death and resurrection of Jesus Christ called for further explanation. Who was it who was crucified and whom God made conquer death? There should of necessity be continuity between what he stood for during his lifetime and what those who believed in him professed and practiced in the period after his exaltation. It had to be clear that accepting a crucified Messiah did not mean putting one's hope in a well-meaning but deluded martyr. Finally, it was necessary to explain that confessing Jesus as the Christ/Messiah did not have political implications in the stormy days preceding and during the war of the Jews against the Romans.

Studying Q, a collection consisting mainly of words of Jesus, we found that these sayings were collected and handed down by people who regarded themselves as disciples of Jesus called to preach the good news of the Kingdom of God and to perform the "mighty deeds" accompanying it. Here, too, continuity between Jesus' ministry and that of his followers after his death is presupposed. Although Q does not include traditions about Jesus' death and resurrection, it is clear that those who handed down the Q material believed that God had vindicated Jesus' work and message and were convinced that Jesus would come again to bring about the full realization of the kingdom of God.

A living tradition brings with it continuity *and* continual change. In part II we saw both continuation and development in Matthew, Luke, Paul, and later writers. Traditional material that is regarded as meaningful and relevant in later situations is, for that reason, transmitted, but the process of transmission leads to adaptation to the needs of the new situation. Authoritative traditions are treated with respect and handed down with care, but precisely because they continue to be of utmost importance, their transmission entails more than mere repetition.

The same dialectic between preservation and adaptation was active even earlier, when those traditions that Paul, Mark, and Q used and transformed were first being shaped. Between Jesus' own mission and the period in which the oldest Christological statements were formulated, memory struggled with discovery. All along, Jesus' followers wanted to make clear what Jesus had stood for and what had happened to him, and in telling their story they had the desire to remain true to Jesus. The question remains, however, to what extent historical inquiry, applying modern standards and using the methods described in the Introduction, can still reconstruct what Jesus himself believed about his relation to God and his role in God's dealings with Israel and humanity.

In modern investigation it has been argued that one cannot be too cautious and should start with applying the so-called "criterion of dissimilarity."[1] A saying of Jesus (in the oldest form we can reach) may be regarded as authentic if it can be shown to be dissimilar to characteristic emphases both of ancient Judaism and of early Christianity. This clearly is a minimum rule, emphasizing continual change at the expense of continuity and attaching too little weight to the many convictions Jesus and his Jewish contemporaries had in common, and to the many Jewish notions and images used by Jesus to express his own particular views.[2] This one-sided approach is only partly offset by applying a second criterion, "the criterion of coherence," by means of which material from the earliest stages in the tradition is regarded as authentic if it can be shown to cohere with material accepted on the basis of the criterion of dissimilarity. We should allow for the possibility that the variety of response to Jesus found in the earliest sources reflects, at least to some extent, the various ways in which Jesus spoke about his own role in God's plan for Israel and the world. A third criterion is that of "multiple attestation": if material is transmitted along different lines, e.g., in Mark and in Q (and in some cases in Paul too), it may be accepted as authentic. This really broadens our view, although application of this criterion has its restrictions too. It is useful for discovering a number of motifs underlying Jesus' words and actions, but will only very rarely enable us to establish the historicity of a particular story, especially of particular details or the exact wording of Jesus' sayings. And for obvious reasons application of this criterion can only tell us about traditions for which there is multiple attestation. There is no reason why some of those sayings which have come down to us via only one of our sources may not be authentic.

In the present short chapter we shall restrict ourselves to what we may say with some certainty about Jesus' own "Christology" when we argue "backward," starting from the traditions reflecting the earliest Christian response to Jesus that we have been able to trace. Much will remain uncertain, and our picture will necessarily be incomplete and to some extent subjective. But it is worth a try; and in any case we *have* to speak about Jesus' own teaching, including his teaching about himself, if we want to do justice to the early Christian message about him.

Jesus and the Kingdom of God

Application of the criterion of multiple attestation leads us back to the two last sections of chapter 3, devoted to common early Christological material in Q and Mark, and in Q, Mark, and Paul respectively. The question has to be asked: To what extent do corresponding views of Jesus in Mark and Q (and, in a number of cases, Paul) reflect Jesus' own teaching regarding himself? In answering this question we shall take into account the information about contemporary Jewish conceptions, persons, and movements brought together in chapter 10.

Our sources agree on the point of Jesus' close connection with John the Baptist, the eschatological prophet who announces the coming judgment and summons the Jewish people to repentance. Outsiders think of Jesus as such a prophet, too, comparing him with John or with Elijah (with whom certain Christian traditions identify John). Jesus himself is said to have spoken about John as "more than a prophet" and at the same time to have characterized his own mission as not only the announcement but also the inauguration of God's kingdom. "Go and tell John what you have seen and heard: the blind receive their sight, the lame walk, lepers are cleansed, and the deaf hear, the dead are raised up, the poor have good news preached to them" (Luke 7:22; par. Matt. 11:5), he is said to have replied to John's disciples. Together with the Beatitudes in Luke 6:20–23, this agrees with Mark's summary of Jesus' preaching of the gospel of God: "The time is fulfilled, and the kingdom of God is at hand; repent, and believe in the gospel" (Mark 1:15).

In many passages the dynamic presence of the kingdom of God in the words and deeds of Jesus receives emphasis. What happens through him and around him cannot but lead to the full realization of God's sovereign rule on earth, expected to take place in the near future on God's initiative. Scholars have given different answers to the question whether in Jesus' own preaching the future or the present aspects of the kingdom were central. In view of the unanimity of our sources in mentioning both aspects we have to assume that he spoke about the kingdom as a dynamic entity, both present and yet to be fully realized, and—very important—that he acted on that conviction.[3]

There can hardly be any doubt that Jesus was a forceful preacher and an impressive teacher, one who spoke with singular authority, challenging people to take radical decisions, calling a small band to accompany him for better and for worse, and to preach the message of the kingdom to Israel ("the twelve," related to "the twelve tribes"). It is also reasonably certain that Jesus' message was especially addressed to the poor, the underprivileged, and the outcasts in Jewish society, and that his radical challenge was coupled with a radical promise—see again the Beatitudes both in their Lukan (Luke 6:20–23) and their Matthean form (Matt. 5:2–12), linking up with Jesus' answer to John's disciples just mentioned, and with material preserved and highlighted in the Gospel of Luke.

Jesus' preaching and teaching are matched by his healings and his casting out of demons. We need not establish what happened exactly in each individual case to conclude that for his immediate followers these mighty deeds were signs of the beginning victory of the kingdom of God over the forces of evil, and proofs of Jesus' particular authority. I see no reason why Jesus himself should not have viewed his healings and exorcism, just like his sharing meals with publicans and sinners for which he was criticized, as the natural complement of his proclamation of the kingdom, that is, as "word in action."

Jesus spoke and acted with a special authority, and understandably people wondered who he was. We find their reactions recorded in the Gospel material. The question is whether we have reliable information as to what he himself said in the matter. It can be argued that the Gospel material incorporated in the Gospel of Mark had at its pre-Markan stage an implicit rather than an explicit Christology, just like the material collected in Q. In chapter 10 we have also tried to show that those who wanted to explicate Jesus' central role in the eschatological process, now and in the future, by means of a "title" had to define first in what sense they wanted to use that particular designation. Titles could not simply be attached to people as convenient, unequivocal labels!

In this connection it is of utmost importance that in our sources Jesus is said to have used "Son of man" as a self-designation. It is found in connection with Jesus' present authority on earth and with his future glory at the time God's kingdom will come with power. In Mark it is also employed in texts announcing the coming death of Jesus and his vindication by God afterward. The picture in Q is less explicit, but the basic elements are the same: authority on earth, opposition and rejection and, finally, vindication. In the section "Jesus the Son of Man" in chapter 10 we have argued that this use of the term can best be explained as the outcome of a particular interpretation of Daniel 7, where "one like a son of man" represents a group of "saints of the Most High" which has to suffer but will be glorified. In view of the unanimity of our sources with regard to the exclusive use of this term by Jesus himself, and its unsuitability for explaining Jesus' authority to a non-Jewish audience (so that it was given up later), it seems very likely that Jesus, in fact, used the term to denote his role in God's decisive intervention on earth. If the impression created by Mark and Q in any way resembles the historical situation, the term was used in such a way that a certain incognito could be preserved. "Son of man" is a veiled designation, yet not without a clear pretension. Comparison with the occurrences of the term in contemporary Jewish sources shows that it did not function as a title.

If we now turn to the earliest use of the designation "Son of God" we find a comparable situation. In the section devoted to "Jesus the Son of God" in chapter 10 we have argued that the use of "Son of

God" for Jesus as the future king (as early as Rom. 1:3–4), as the perfect wise man in a singular relationship to God, or as the final unique representative sent by the Father in heaven, may go back to Jesus' use of the term "Abba, Father" in prayer. We have every reason to assume that he lived in an intimate relationship with God, and that he called God his Father. He encouraged his followers also to address God as Father in prayer (the Lord's Prayer), and even the Aramaic term survived in Greek-speaking Christian groups. It is evident that a particular sense of sonship lay at the heart of Jesus' calling. The extent to which he regarded his relationship with God as unique or exclusive as compared to the relation between other children of God and their heavenly Father cannot be determined anymore. There are no indications that Jesus used the term "Son of God" as a special title.

But what about the designation "Messiah" (Christ)? It is not found in Q, and occurs only a few times in Mark, albeit in crucial sections of that Gospel, but it is found in the early creedal statement "Christ died for (us, you)" and in the double formula speaking about Christ's death and resurrection. In the writings of Paul the term "Christ" occurs very frequently, though seldom with the specific connotation of "Messiah"; in many cases "Jesus Christ" functions as a double name. Does this constant and almost automatic use of "Christ" in the earliest communities tell us anything of its use by Jesus (or others) in the time of his mission in Galilee and Jerusalem? In order to give an answer to that question we shall have to look into the circumstances around Jesus' death and the controversies leading up to it.

Jesus' Death on the Cross

Did Jesus foresee and predict that he would be put to death by the authorities of Jerusalem? The three predictions of his death and resurrection in Mark 8:31; 9:31; and 10:33–34 (taken over by Matthew and Luke) form part of Mark's Christological teaching preparing the readers for a right understanding of the events recorded in Mark 14–16. Particularly in the case of the third, most detailed, prediction we may speak of a prediction after the event. Yet Jesus was well aware of the fate of John the Baptist, and it is not in the least unlikely that he himself characterized the opposition on the part of leading people in Israel against John's message and his own as in line with the negative response to God's prophets recorded in many passages in the scriptures. In other words, Q passages like Luke 11:49–51 (par. Matt. 23:34–36) and Luke 13:34–35 (par. Matt. 23:37–39) may express what Jesus in fact felt and said.

In view of the great importance in contemporary Jewish thought of the idea of God's help for the righteous who have to suffer we may not exclude the possibility that Jesus, too, trusting that God would come to his aid in the suffering that lay ahead, expressed this trust in terms like those used in Mark 9:31 (the most summary prediction): "The Son of man will be delivered into the hands of men, and they will kill him; and when he is killed, after three days he will rise." The use of the designation "Son of man" in the Markan predictions is in itself significant. If Jesus used this self-designation with an implicit reference to Daniel 7 (as we have argued), he must have had the suffering of God's righteous and their subsequent glorification in mind when he thought of his own future.

It is more difficult to make out whether Jesus viewed his death as a death for others. In the oldest Gospel material there are Jesus' statements in Mark 10:45 and 14:24 to be considered. The first, however, clearly links up with other traditional expressions found in the Pauline and deutero-Pauline letters;[4] its wording may have been influenced by early Christian thought on the subject. And 14:24 is part of an account of the last supper clearly stamped by later liturgical practice.[5] On the other hand it may be argued that the notion that Jesus died for us/you was so central at a very early stage of Christian reflection that it must have been prepared by Jesus' own teaching on the matter. In view of the important role that Jesus' death and resurrection understandably played in all thinking about Jesus in the circles of the "Jesus movement" in the years after Golgotha it is impossible to determine with certainty in what respects there existed continuity or discontinuity between early Christians teaching on this crucial subject and Jesus' own views.

Still, are we not to assume that Jesus was crucified as "Messiah," and must we not suppose, then, that he allowed himself to be called thus? It is clear that we cannot accept Mark's picture of the course of events at face value. But can we, perhaps, draw some conclusions from the fact that the designation "Christ" was at a very early stage connected specifically with Jesus' death, and with his resurrection? This case has been argued in an exemplary fashion by N. A. Dahl in his influential article "The Crucified Messiah."[6] Dahl rightly stresses that from the very first, faith in Jesus as the resurrected one was faith in him as the Messiah/Christ. But his resurrection in itself did not make him Messiah. Dahl's conclusion is correct: "If he was crucified as an alleged Messiah, then—but only then—does faith in his resurrection necessarily become faith in the resurrection of the crucified Messiah."[7]

Dahl conjectures that Jesus' attitude to Jewish law and custom, his relation to the poor and outcasts, and especially his public appearance in the temple, could appear to be a revolt against the established religious and political order, and could lead the authorities to take steps against him. If not his own messianic claims, then at least the messianic hopes of his followers made him a dangerous man. Mark's account of the trial before the Sanhedrin in 14:55–65 too clearly serves Mark's own Christological purpose to be a useful historical source. In chapter 15, however, the inscription on the cross "The King of the Jews" (15:26) Dahl accepts as historical. He does so perhaps a bit too easily,[8] but we have to admit that the fact that Jesus was crucified by the Romans presupposes that they regarded him as politically dangerous. They put him out of the way, but probably did not consider his band of followers important enough to take steps against them. It is very likely that (as Dahl says) Jesus was accused before Pilate on the ground that he made a royal-messianic claim. "If so one may further infer that Jesus, confronted with that charge that he thought himself to be the Messiah, accepted the accuracy of the charge by his silence, if not in any other way." In fact, "Jesus could not deny the charge that he was the Messiah without putting in question the final eschatological validity of his message." And by not denying, he accepted the cross, willingly: "His willingness to suffer is implicit in Jesus' behavior and attitude throughout his preaching."[9]

Dahl and many other scholars hesitate to assume that Jesus claimed to be the Messiah because of the traditional overtones of Davidic kingship connected with this designation. There is no evidence that Jesus had any political intentions or could justifiably be regarded as an insurrectionist. Efforts to turn him into a revolutionary and a rebel (whose dangerous ideas were concealed in the Synoptic Gospels because the early Christians were eager to live in peace with Rome) have to be rejected.[10] But, on the other hand, is it likely that Jesus admitted only reluctantly that he could be called "Messiah," because his opponents pressed him to take up ideas living in the minds of his most ardent followers? And is it really probable that *Christos* became the central title because the title "King of the Jews" received such prominence at the crucifixion?

I must admit that I find it difficult to assign such a decisive role to Jesus' opponents in this matter. Also here, it is impossible to speak with any certainty, for again we have no other source than Mark if we want to find arguments pointing in a different direction. This Gospel, as we have seen, uses the title *Christos* with "Son of God" in connection with Jesus' future kingship. It also makes Peter confess Jesus as the Messiah in 8:29 after he has witnessed Jesus' activity in Galilee. Mark, well aware of the central importance of the confession "Jesus is the Christ," must have regarded it as a suitable term to designate Jesus, whom he has described as a unique preacher, teacher, and exorcist. For Mark, Jesus is the Christ as charismatic spirit-inspired figure on earth and as king on God's behalf at the final establishment of his kingdom. There is a link here with the early formula in Rom. 1:3–4 describing Jesus as a descendant of David qualified to be a royal Son of God in power.

Now, in view of the fact that David was not only portrayed as a king, and thereby as a political figure, but also as a prophet, a singer of psalms, and an exorcist, it does not seem impossible that Jesus regarded himself as a true Son of David who could properly be called the Lord's anointed—not only in view of his future role when God's rule would reveal itself with power, but already in the present while the kingdom of God manifested itself in his words and actions. Needless to say, if Jesus did not in fact avoid the designation Messiah, he used it creatively, in his own way, and did not widely advertise it. After all, the collection of Jesus' sayings in Q does not use the term, and in the Gospel of Mark Jesus is reticent about it. In view of the central position of the designation in early Christian Christology, however, it remains likely that the term was not chosen by overenthusiastic admirers or by his opponents, but was regarded as suitable by Jesus himself.

Epilogue

The early Christian response to Jesus shows a bewildering diversity right from the beginning. Scores of concepts and terms of different provenance were tried out in various ways to give expression to the conviction that in Jesus God had spoken a final word to Israel and humanity and had brought about a decisive turn in the history of the world. Nevertheless, there are some constant elements. In one way or another it had to be made clear that Jesus' mission marked the beginning of a dynamic process of renewal that would soon find its fulfillment when God's sovereign rule would encompass the entire creation. Early Christians lived in the tension between the "already" and the "not yet," between what had already changed and what was still outstanding. In the tribulations they had to endure they looked out for what had been promised, trusting in Jesus who had undergone suffering himself and who, as they believed, had been vindicated by God and would soon be revealed as a central figure in a new dispensation. Jesus was and remained the unique intermediary between God and humanity. It was the task of his followers to spell out the implications of this truth in words and action, and to proclaim the good news to all men and women who cared to listen.

Those who responded to Jesus during his life and in the first decades after his crucifixion all wanted to remain true to what they had heard and seen themselves, or to the Jesus tradition handed down to them, and to be faithful to the basic convictions of the communities of Jesus' followers. They sought eagerly in the scriptures and in the religious traditions inspired by the scriptures for terms which would do justice to the unique reality of Jesus. But they were different people living in very different circumstances, scattered over a number of small communities around the Eastern part of the Mediterranean, and they were confronted with different theoretical and practical problems. Their response to Jesus tried to provide an answer to essential questions of heart and mind.

Everywhere we find an abundant variety of expression. Terms and concepts are used alongside one another. They are complementary rather than mutually exclusive, because they answer different needs and address different aspects of the situation. Christology is, indeed, always Christology in context. Of course there are differences in emphasis and efforts to give a coherent picture of Jesus in which certain aspects of his mission predominate. But never is a particular element stressed in such a way that it makes other elements superfluous. In cases of conflict—as for instance those reflected in Paul's letter to the Galatians and in the letter to the Colossians—early Christian authors do not hesitate to exclude certain convictions or practices which others thought to be compatible or even called for by allegiance to Jesus Christ. Yet the human situation to be addressed was so variegated and the tradition about Jesus was clearly so rich that simple, single answers could never do justice to those who asked the questions; they would not be true to Jesus either.

All along, too, we are confronted with continuation and development. With some effort we are able to distinguish between subsequent stages in early Christological thinking. But much will remain uncertain, because those responsible for the oral and written transmission of what we have before us in the earliest Christian documents were not concerned with the distinctions that are indispensable for the type of historical reconstruction we are interested in. For them, as for the author of Hebrews, Jesus Christ was "the same yesterday and today and for ever" (Heb. 13:8). This sameness called for continuity in tradition and for variety in expression in different circumstances.

We have restricted ourselves to an analysis of the earliest stages in the response to Jesus in the circles of his followers. Much more could have been said about the Christology of the later writings collected in the New Testament, and a fascinating story could be told about the Christology in the writings of the so-called Apostolic Fathers, the Apologists, the Gnostics, and people belonging to other Christian groups in the second century. And even so we would have described only the very first stages in the history of Christological doctrine.

The process of Christological reflection continues up till the present day. And, in fact, many of those interested in the earliest stages of the Christian response to Jesus are so keen because they are in search of inspiration and guidance in their efforts to demonstrate the relevance of the message about Jesus for their present-day circumstances. This book, too, would probably not have been written had its author not been fascinated by the person of Jesus and the variegated response he evoked among his earliest followers, and had he not been convinced that orientation toward Jesus Christ is urgently needed if one is to address the vexing problems of our modern world.

Yet it is evident that a historical investigation like the present one cannot offer explicit guidelines for modern Christological thinking. At the most it may suggest that modern Christology, too, should respect the variety in response to Jesus from the earliest stages onward. It should resist tendencies toward harmonization, or reduction to one model; it is very likely that even today a variety of approaches, complementing and correcting each other, is called for. It should avoid applying distinctions between orthodoxy and heresy formulated by the Great Ecumenical Councils or in the time of the Reformation to either the earliest period of Christianity or to attempts to express the relevance of Jesus Christ for our time. The rich tradition in hand will always withstand efforts at systematization; "reflective mythology" can never be reduced to systematic theology. There will always remain a tension between the kaleidoscopic variety of concepts and images employed in the early Christian communities and terms that are relevant to a modern audience. On the one hand, modern theologians will have to take into account that our thinking (and our way of life!) bear the stamp of the decisive developments in Western society since the Renaissance and the Enlightenment. On the other hand, we need people who are able to reflect imaginatively, to create new images, tell modern parables, or compose new poems and hymns in order to bring out the relevance of the ancient traditions about Jesus for the present day. In his *The Language of the Gospel* A. N. Wilder,[1] after reminding his readers that there are three patterns of speech which renew themselves throughout the whole New Testament period—the dialogue, the story and the poem— concludes: "The word of God found its appropriate vehicles both in the sense of images and forms. Within limits one can say that to this very day and always Christianity will most characteristically communicate itself at least in these three modes: the drama, the narrative, the poem—just as it will always be bound in some degree to its primordial symbols, no matter how much the world may change."[2]

Notes

Introduction

1. These terms are borrowed from W. A. Meeks; see the title of chapter 6 in his *The First Urban Christians*. (The full facts of publication for this work, and for others cited in the Notes, are given in the Bibliography.)

2. For the history of the NT canon and of the writings contained in it, see the standard textbooks on "Introduction to the New Testament."

3. There may be other ancient material in the traditions incorporated by Matthew and Luke alone (indicated by the letters M and L respectively). One should note further "stray" Gospel material found in a variety of sources and listed at the end of the individual sections in the Greek Synopses of K. Aland and Huck and Greeven. It has to be studied in close connection with the related material in the canonical Gospels.

4. See, e.g., R. E. Brown's excellent survey in his *The Community of the Beloved Disciple*.

5. See F. Hahn, *The Titles of Jesus in Christology;* R. H. Fuller, *The Foundations of New Testament Christology;* and, earlier, O. Cullmann, *The Christology of the New Testament*.

6. In N. A. Dahl's Presidential Address to the 1978 meeting of the *Studiorum Novi Testamenti Societas* at Paris, to be published in a revised form in a future new edition of his *The Crucified Messiah and Other Essays*. Professor Dahl kindly put the text of his lecture at my disposal.

7. See M. Hengel, "Christology and New Testament Chronology" and also "Between Jesus and Paul."

8. E. Schweizer, in his *Jesus,* operates with great caution. After a chapter on the earthly Jesus he distinguishes a number of Christological approaches: the expectation of the one who will return to earth soon (very early, mainly in Palestinian Christianity); the belief in Jesus as the exalted one *and* the one who came from heaven (later, in Hellenistic-Jewish and Hellenistic circles); the emphasis on Jesus as the one crucified for the world (Paul, in reaction to Hellenistic Christianity); renewed attention to the earthly Jesus (the Gospels). Schweizer stresses that all these approaches were present *in nuce* at the earliest stage of post-Easter faith and can even be found in Jesus'

own teaching. He also refuses to connect a particular approach exclusively with one type of Christianity or a particular period. Yet he does not avoid the suggestion of a development in Christology from one period to another. We shall have to ask whether in this respect he does not go beyond the evidence.

9. See my *Jesus: Inspiring and Disturbing Presence,* especially chapter 3, "The Inquiry After the Man Jesus of Nazareth," 38–55.

10. Jesus' resurrection as such is not an object of historical investigation, but the modern interpreter will have to take seriously the unanimous opinion of early Christian sources that Jesus' disciples felt called to preach the gospel because they firmly believed that the crucified Jesus had conquered death and that he had appeared to some of his followers and had commissioned them.

11. See W. A. Beardslee, *Literary Criticism of the New Testament.*

12. For a survey of opinions see F. J. Matera, *The Kingship of Jesus,* 1–5. For an example of very detailed reconstruction, see R. Pesch's essay "Die vormarkinische Passionsgeschichte" in his *Das Markus-evangelium,* II, 1–27.

13. For an introduction see E. V. McKnight, *What Is Form Criticism?* For a more extensive survey see F. Hahn, ed., *Zur Formgeschichte des Evangeliums,* which includes a good evaluative article by the editor called "Die Formgeschichte des Evangeliums. Voraussetzungen, Ausbau und Tragweite," 427–477.

14. I use here the clear exposition in E. Lohse's *The Formation of the New Testament,* 32–33.

15. See M. Hengel, *Judaism and Hellenism* and *Jews, Greeks, and Barbarians.*

16. See my "The Earliest Christian Use of *Christos,* " in particular section 3, "The Use of the Term 'Anointed' in Contemporaneous Jewish Sources"; and chapter 10 below.

1. Early Christology in the Letters of Paul

1. For a more detailed treatment of this passage see E. Best, *1 and 2 Thessalonians,* 81–87. Scholars have called this passage a "missionary formula," a "creedal formula," or even a "baptismal hymn."

2. See, e.g., Tacitus, *Histories* 5.5, "toward all aliens they feel only hate and enmity." For a full list of such characterizations see M. Dibelius, *An die Thessalonicher,* 34–36.

3. We cannot deal with this difficult verse (1 Thess. 2:16) here. In the OT tradition mentioned by O. H. Steck (see note 4 below) Israel's relation to God is characterized by a succession of sin–punishment–repentance–new beginning, after which the whole sequence may start all over again. Paul stresses that for those who continue to obstruct God's intentions the definitive end has come. Paul and his readers reckon with the coming of Jesus on the clouds in the near future (see 1 Thess. 4:13–18, discussed below). Scholars have often wondered why Paul speaks so negatively about the Jews and their future punishment by God. It is difficult to reconcile 1 Thess.

2:14–16 with Paul's later, more considered views on Israel's future in Rom. 9–11. It has been argued that verses 13–16 were wholly or partly interpolated by some later editor of the Pauline epistles. For lack of evidence in the manuscripts, this solution remains conjectural. It may be that Paul simply followed here a traditional view current among Jewish followers of Jesus without thinking out all its implications.

4. In his *Israel und das gewaltsame Geschick der Propheten,* O. H. Steck has analyzed this type of passage in the Old Testament, Jewish literature, and the New Testament. He speaks of "deuteronomistic" passages about the prophets functioning in the context of the "deuteronomistic" view of history.

5. For a survey of possible explanations, see E. Best, *1 and 2 Thessalonians,* 189–194.

6. Important work on these formulas has been done by W. Kramer, *Christ, Lord, Son of God,* especially §§2–8. Another useful study is that by K. Wengst, *Christologische Formeln und Lieder des Urchristentums.*

7. *dia* instead of *hyper.*

8. The emphasis on Christ's death on the cross is typically Pauline. See 1 Cor. 1:17, 18, 23; 2:2, 8; 2 Cor. 13:4; Gal. 3:13; 5:11, 24; 6:12–14; Phil. 2:8; 3:18.

9. Greek *epathen,* in Greek manuscripts sometimes confused with *apethanen* ("died"). In fact it is not clear which reading is to be preferred in 1 Peter 3:18; see the note in RSV on this verse.

10. *peri* instead of *hyper.*

11. Compare 2 Tim. 2:11–12 and 1 Peter 3:18 (RSV margin), "For Christ also suffered for sins once for all, the righteous for the unrighteous, that he might bring us to God, being put to death in the flesh but made alive in the spirit."

12. Compare 1 Cor. 1:1; 2 Cor. 1:1 (and Eph. 1:1; Col. 1:1; 1 Tim. 1:1; 2 Tim. 1:1). Slightly different are Rom. 1:1 ("servant of Jesus Christ, called to be an apostle"); and Philemon 1 ("a prisoner for Christ Jesus"); compare Titus 1:1 ("a servant of God and an apostle of Jesus Christ").

13. See W. Kramer, *Christ, Lord, Son of God,* §§25–26; K. Wengst, *Christologische Formeln,* §3.

14. *didonai* instead of *paradidonai.*

15. Again, a different Greek preposition: *anti* instead of *hyper.*

16. See W. Kramer, *Christ, Lord, Son of God,* §§9–12. In §13 he adds a short chapter on the expression "apostle of Christ," which he regards as Pauline.

17. In 1 Cor. 10:1–13, where Paul draws a parallel between the people of Israel and the Christian church, he says that the Israelites were all "baptized into Moses in the cloud and in the sea," clearly presupposing that his readers realize that they have been "baptized into Christ"; 1 Cor. 10:14–22, which concludes that "we who are many are one body" on the grounds of participation in the blood and body of Christ at the Lord's Supper, will be briefly discussed below.

18. See the important section on "Baptism: Ritual of Initiation" in W. A. Meeks, *The First Urban Christians,* 150–157, and his "The Image of the

Androgyne." On Gal. 3:26–28, see the interesting comments by H. D. Betz
in his *Galatians,* 181–201.

19. See W. Kramer, *Christ, Lord, Son of God,* §33.

20. The RSV translation of the difficult word *stoicheia* in Gal. 4:3. Betz
describes them as "not simply material substance, but demonic entities of
cosmic proportions and astral powers which were hostile towards man"
(*Galatians,* 205).

21. In view of Gal. 3:28 Paul must use the word "sons" inclusively; in
Rom. 8:12–30 he uses "sons" (vs. 14, 19) and "children" (vs. 16, 17, 21)
side by side.

22. Compare Jesus' prayer in Mark 14:36 and the opening words of the
Lord's Prayer (Matt. 6:9; Luke 11:2). One should note that Paul (as well
as Mark) preserves the Aramaic term, probably because he knew it was used
in early Christian prayers also by non-Jews.

23. See J. D. G. Dunn, *Christology in the Making,* 39: "It underlines the
heavenly origin of his *commissioning* but not of the one commissioned." In
my view this applies only to the formula used by Paul, not to the way he
uses it (contra Dunn, 38–45).

24. First Corinthians is exploited with great expertise by authors writing
about the social context of early Christianity—see G. Theissen, *The Social
Setting of Pauline Christianity;* W. A. Meeks, *The First Urban Christians;*
J. Murphy-O'Connor, *St. Paul's Corinth.*

25. On the abuses at the Christian meals and the possible social conditions behind them, see W. A. Meeks, *The First Urban Christians,* 67–70,
157–162. Meeks adopts Theissen's reconstruction of the situation, with a
few criticisms.

26. W. A. Meeks, *The First Urban Christians,* 158.

27. Paul contrasts the exclamation "Jesus be cursed," which cannot
possibly be inspired by the Spirit of God, with "Jesus is Lord," which can
only be confessed by someone who is led by the Spirit. The first exclamation
is only mentioned as the absolute opposite to the true confession. For other
interpretations of 1 Cor. 12:3 see, e.g., C. K. Barrett, *1 Corinthians,* 279–
281.

28. See also "the words of the Lord" discussed on p. 36.

29. In Acts 2:38 and 10:48 we find the expression "to be baptized in the
name of Jesus Christ." For a survey of the various expressions with or
without "the name of" connected with baptism, see L. Hartman, "Baptism
'Into the Name of Jesus' and Early Christology," and "Into the Name of
Jesus." According to Hartman, "into the name of Jesus was above all a
definition, a phrase which mentioned the fundamental reference of Christian baptism which distinguished it from other rites" ("Into the Name of
Jesus," 400).

30. Colossians suggests that at a later time "dying and rising with Christ"
was connected with "enthronement in heaven"; see 1:12–13 followed by the
hymn Col. 1:15–20; 2:12–13, 20; 3:1–4. (Compare Eph. 1:3; 2:4–7; 2 Tim.
2:11–12; and Rev. 1:6; 5:10; 20:6.) But as Paul's very critical remark in 1
Cor. 4:8 shows, the Corinthians may already have known such a notion in
the context of the celebration of baptism. They may have emphasized the

presence of salvation disproportionately, forgetting that the final realization of God's sovereignty on earth was still outstanding (cf. also 1 Thess. 4:15–17).

31. See, again, W. A. Meeks, *The First Urban Christians,* 69–70, 97–100.

32. For Hellenistic-Jewish texts, see K. Wengst, *Christologische Formeln,* §12. Compare also Werner Kramer, *Christ, Lord, Son of God,* §22.

33. Commentaries on 1 Cor. 8:4–6 quote many parallels. C. K. Barrett, *1 Corinthians,* 193, singles out M. Aurelius 4.23: "From thee (Nature) are all things, in thee are all things, to thee are all things." There are related Hellenistic-Jewish statements.

34. On this and other interpretations, see C. K. Barrett, *1 Corinthians,* 396–398.

35. See W. Kramer, *Christ, Lord, Son of God,* §45. One should, however, note that Paul also uses the Old Testament expression "the day of the Lord"—see 1 Cor. 5:5; 1 Thess. 5:2 (cf. 1 Cor. 1:8; 2 Cor. 1:14) besides "the coming of the Lord" (1 Thess. 4:15 and cf. 1 Thess. 2:19; 3:13; 5:23).

36. On this difficult (and controversial) passage see further C. K. Barrett, *Romans,* 18–21, and C. E. B. Cranfield, *Romans,* I, 57–64.

37. So W. A. Meeks, *The First Urban Christians,* 144–146.

38. In M. Hengel, "Hymns and Christology."

39. "To put it briefly, the hymn to Christ served as a living medium for the progressive development of christological thinking. It begins with the messianic psalms and ends with the prologue to John" (M. Hengel, "Hymns and Christology," 95).

2. The Gospel Material in Mark

1. Mark uses the verb *ēgerthē,* a form of *egeirō* traditionally used for the resurrection in single and double formulas. In the announcement of the passion and the resurrection in 8:31; 9:31; 10:34 he uses forms of *anistanai.* In 16:6–7, as in 14:28, he may have wanted to stress God's action in Jesus' resurrection.

2. Nestle-Aland, *Novum Testamentum Graece,* 25th edition (1963), omits the words, but the 26th edition (1979) and K. Aland et al., eds., *The Greek New Testament* (United Bible Societies, 1979), give them between square brackets.

3. On the developments in the use of *euaggelion* in early Christianity one may consult a number of interesting contributions in the volume edited by P. Stuhlmacher, *Das Evangelium und die Evangelien,* esp. P. Stuhlmacher, "Zum Thema: Das Evangelium und die Evangelien," 1–26, and "Das paulinische Evangelium," 157–182; and R. Guelich, "The Gospel Genre," 183–220. On the genre of the Gospels and the Gospels as ancient biography, see D. E. Aune, *The New Testament in Its Literary Environment,* chapters 1 and 2.

4. On this, see G. Friedrich, art. *euaggelizomai,* etc., especially 708–710; and P. Stuhlmacher, *Das paulinische Evangelium,* I: *Vorgeschichte,* to be supplemented now by his contributions to *Das Evangelium und die Evangelien* mentioned in note 3.

5. For "the time is fulfilled," see Gal. 4:4, discussed above.

6. In three out of the four instances where Matthew uses the word *euaggelion,* he has the expression "the gospel of the kingdom" (4:23; 9:35; 24:14; the exception is found in 26:13). Mark does not use the verb *euaggelizesthai.* Matthew has it only in Matt. 11:5. Luke avoids the noun (but see Acts 15:7; 20:24) but uses the verb. John has neither noun nor verb.

7. On the "Gospel genre" see the contribution by R. Guelich to *Das Evangelium und die Evangelien* mentioned in note 3. See also *Didache* 15:3f.; 2 Clement 8:5; Justin, *Apology* 66:3; Irenaeus, *Against Heresies* 3.11. 10(7). The expression "the gospel according to John" is found as superscription in Pap. 66 (c. A.D. 200).

8. See esp. 200–213 in Guelich's article, mentioned in the previous note, and G. N. Stanton, *Jesus of Nazareth in New Testament Preaching,* 67–85.

9. In Acts 15:7, at the meeting of apostles and elders with Paul and Barnabas in Jerusalem, Peter reminds his brothers of the Cornelius episode with the words: "in the early days God made choice among you, that by my mouth the Gentiles should hear the word of the gospel *(euaggelion)* and believe."

10. I may refer here to two earlier articles of mine: "The Use of HO CHRISTOS in the Passion Narratives," in J. Dupont, ed., *Jésus aux origines de la christologie,* and "The Earliest Christian Use of *Christos.*"

11. Compare also Mark 1:14 (of John the Baptist); 14:41; 15:1, 10, 15. The word is also used for Judas' betrayal in 3:19; 14:10, 11, 18, 21, 42, 44.

12. To denote the latter, a form of the verb *anistanai* is used; Mark also writes "after three days," not "on the third day" (the usual expression, adopted by Matthew and Luke in the parallel passages).

13. The only exception is Acts 7:56, where the dying Stephen uses it.

14. Jesus' authority to forgive sins, and his authority over the Sabbath, respectively.

15. This point is rightly stressed by J. D. Kingsbury in his interesting book *The Christology of Mark's Gospel,* 157–173.

16. Mark does not bring out the implications of the use of Isa. 40:3 in 1:2, and the words "The Lord has need of it" in 11:3 do not receive any Christological emphasis.

17. The accusations of the Sanhedrin before Pilate are nowhere expressly formulated. Neither does Mark tell his readers during which insurgence (15:7) Barabbas was arrested. They are also expected to know who Alexander and Rufus are (v. 21).

18. The word *lēstēs* used here in Greek should not be translated "robber," but "bandit." From the Roman point of view, there was little or no difference between highway bandits and groups of freedom fighters.

19. On those, see also the brief section 3.5 in my article "The Earliest Christian Use of *Christos,*" which among other things refers to R. A. Horsley's article "Popular Messianic Movements Around the Time of Jesus." We should note also the political implications of the pericope, 12:13–17, where Jesus answers the question whether one should pay taxes to Caesar or not, with the words: "Render to Caesar the things that are Caesar's and to God the things that are God's." On these words, see my

Jesus: Inspiring and Disturbing Presence, chapter 9, "Jesus as Revolutionary," especially 142–145. There I concluded that "an exposition which connects this saying with Jesus' words about the imminent coming of God's Kingdom appears the most likely. God's kingship is confronted with the dominion of the emperor. There is no call for resistance to the emperor; he is destined to quit the field anyway!" (145).

20. On this, see, e.g., the section on "Scribes and Pharisees" in J. E. Stambaugh and D. L. Balch, *The New Testament in Its Social Environment,* 99–101.

21. See especially three studies of G. Theissen, assembled in his *Studien zur Soziologie des Urchristentums:* "Wanderradikalismus, Literatursoziologische Aspekte der Überlieferung von Worten Jesu im Urchristentum" (79–105); "Wir haben alles verlassen (Mc X, 28)" (106–141); and "Legitimation und Lebensunterhalt" (201–231). In English one may consult his more popular book *Sociology of Early Palestinian Christianity,* 8–30. Theissen stresses the difference between the wandering charismatics in the rural world of Palestine and the missionaries who, like Paul, went from town to town.

22. In Mark 10:28–31, Peter and the disciples who have given up their house and family life are promised not only eternal life in the age to come but also a substitute social family, albeit "with persecutions."

23. Jesus' word in Mark 6:4, "A prophet is not without honor, except in his own country, and among his own kin, and in his own house," is a common proverb and does not allow us to conclude that Jesus considered himself to be (only) a prophet.

24. Compare Mark 2:23–28 with a controversy on the rules for the sabbath ending with Jesus' word: "So the Son of man is lord even of the sabbath." See also Mark 7:1–23 with a conflict over the laws of purity. The Pharisees and the scribes are said to have left the commandment of God and to hold fast the tradition of men (7:8; see also vs. 6–7).

25. See J. D. Kingsbury, *The Christology of Mark's Gospel,* 86–88.

26. This is brought out convincingly by J. D. Kingsbury in chapters 1 and 2 of his *The Christology of Mark's Gospel.*

27. See G. N. Stanton, *Jesus of Nazareth in New Testament Preaching,* especially chapter 7, "The Gospel Traditions in the Early Church," 172–185. He adds: "How could one claim that Jesus was the one person in the whole of history who fulfilled Scripture in its widest and deepest sense, that Jesus was raised from the dead by God in a totally unexpected and unique way, and call for repentance and commitment to him without indicating who he was?" (177).

3. The Sayings of Jesus in Q

1. A. Polag, *Die Christologie der Logienquelle;* compare his *Fragmenta Q. Textheft zur Logienquelle.* Relatively little has been written on the subject. A valuable article is G. N. Stanton's "On the Christology of Q." Very influential has been H. E. Tödt's analysis of the Son of man sayings in Q in his *The Son of Man in the Synoptic Tradition.* One may also consult

P. Hoffmann, *Studien zur Theologie der Logienquelle,* and R. A. Edwards, *A Theology of Q: Eschatology, Prophecy, and Wisdom.*

2. In Luke 7:19 John sends his disciples "to the Lord." This title is found also in Luke 10:1; 11:39; 12:42; 17:5, 6, where Luke uses Q material. In none of these instances is the word found in Matthew, so that it can scarcely have figured in Q. In Luke 7:6 (par. Matt. 8:8) and 9:61 (par. Matt. 8:21) the word is used as a polite form of address, as in Mark 7:28.

3. For a detailed discussion of the various problems, see S. Schulz, *Q. Die Spruchquelle der Evangelisten,* 261–267. See also J. A. Fitzmyer, *Luke, X–XXIV,* 1114–1118.

4. Compare the reference to "the deeds of the Christ" in Matt. 11:2.

5. Just before Luke 7:31–35 Luke adds two verses (7:29–30) on the reaction of the people to Jesus' words: "all the people and the tax collectors justified God, having been baptized with the baptism of John." The Pharisees and the lawyers rejected the purpose of God for themselves. They were not baptized by John (cf. also Luke 3:7–9 [par. Matt. 3:7–10] and Luke 3:10–14).

6. For "finger of God" see Ex. 8:19. Matthew 12:28 changes "finger" to "Spirit."

7. See also Luke 9:60, "You, go and proclaim the kingdom of God" (cf. v. 62), belonging to a pericope on discipleship and following of Jesus in 9:57–62 (par. Matt. 8:19–22). Luke has here more sayings than Matthew, but they may all belong to Q.

8. Matt. 5:11: "on my account."

9. The Ninevites who listened to Jonah are joined by the queen of the South, who came from the ends of the earth to hear the Wisdom of Solomon. Together they will judge and condemn "this generation."

10. See also Sir. 1:15 (in Greek): "She made a nest among men as an everlasting foundation and among their descendants she will be trusted." See, however, also Ruth 2:12: "The LORD, the God of Israel, under whose wings you have come to take refuge"; the same image is found in the book of Psalms (17:8; 36:7; 57:1; 61:4; 63:7; 91:4). Compare Deut. 32:11 and Isa. 31:5.

11. I. H. Marshall, *The Gospel of Luke,* 434.

12. Perhaps in its latest form (so A. Polag).

13. See G. Fohrer in *TDNT* 8, 347–353.

14. Luke gives these instructions to disciples in the framework of a mission of the seventy(-two), after the mission of the twelve in 9:1–6 (par. Mark 6:6–13). Matthew combines the material from Mark and Q in chapter 10 (see also 9:37–38).

15. See also A. Polag, "Die theologische Mitte der Logienquelle."

16. On this, see also W. G. Kümmel, *Introduction to the New Testament,* 71–74.

17. Stanton, "On the Christology of Q," 42.

18. For a short introduction see, e.g., H. W. Attridge, "Gospel of Thomas," in *Harper's Bible Dictionary,* 355–356.

19. Translation by H. Koester and T. O. Lambdin, "The Gospel of Thomas."

20. See the good survey in the article by D. C. Allison, Jr., "The Pauline Epistles and the Synoptic Gospels." See also chapter 4, "Jesus in Paul's Preaching," in G. N. Stanton, *Jesus of Nazareth in New Testament Preaching*, 86–116.

21. This applies also to the other epistles in the New Testament. Compare, e.g., 1 John with the Fourth Gospel. There is also a clear discrepancy between the teachings of the apostles, evangelists, and Paul in Acts and the contents of the Gospel of Luke.

4. The Christology of Matthew

1. See also chapter 2, note 6. Compare the expression "the word of the kingdom" in Matt. 13:19. We should note that John the Baptist's message in 3:2 is the same as that of Jesus in 4:17. Compare 11:12, "From the days of John the Baptist until now the kingdom of heaven has suffered violence, and men of violence take it by force."

2. See J. D. Kingsbury in his *Matthew: Structure, Christology, Kingdom*, 32f.: "Matthew's august portrait of Jesus is . . . christologically based: the exalted Jesus addresses his community following Easter in the words of the earthly Jesus, and the earthly Jesus appears in the course of his ministry in the effulgence of the exalted Jesus."

3. It is also found in *Didache* 7.1, 3, alongside the single formula "baptized in the name of the Lord" in 9.5.

4. Here Matthew goes further than Q. The same is true in Matt. 11:19, where "Yet Wisdom is justified by her deeds" (RSV with capitalization of "wisdom") is parallel to "the deeds of the Christ" in 11:2. We should remember that in Matt. 23:34 "I" is substituted for "the Wisdom of God" found in Luke 11:49 (see chapter 3, p. 79).

5. See chapter 2, p. 65, and chapter 3, p. 76. J. D. Kingsbury, *Matthew*, 93–95, rightly argues that Matthew subsumes the title of "Servant" found in the passage from Isaiah under the broader category of Son of God; compare 12:18 with 3:17; 17:5 and 12:21 with 28:18–19.

6. Compare chapter 2, p. 62.

7. Note that also the name "Jesus" is explained: "for he will save his people from their sins" (Matt. 1:21).

8. See Matt. 8:2, 6, 8, 21, 25; 9:28; 14:28, 30; 15:22, 25, 27; 16:22; 17:4, 15; 20:30, 31, 33; 26:22. On the use of *Kyrios* in Matthew, see Kingsbury, *Matthew*, 103–113. In 27:63 it is simply used as a form of polite address.

9. So especially Kingsbury.

10. See Matt. 1:20, 22, 24; 2:13, 15, 19; 4:7, 10; 5:33; 9:38; 11:25; 21:9, 42; 22:37; 23:39; 27:10; 28:2, and compare the parable of the unforgiving servant in 18:23–35.

11. See chapter 2, p. 60. Also in 7:28, the "Yes, Lord" of the Syrophoenician woman may be used in a purely conventional fashion.

12. Kingsbury, *Matthew*, 143.

13. See W. D. Davies, *The Setting of the Sermon on the Mount*, 401–405, referring to the list of parallels between James and the Synoptics in J. B. Mayor, *The Epistle of James*, lxxxiv–lxxxvi.

14. F. Mussner, *Der Jakobusbrief,* 47–52; R. Hoppe, *Der theologische Hintergrund des Jakobusbriefes,* 119–145.

15. Whether "royal" in "the royal law" in James 2:8 means "the chief in rank" or (also) "belonging to the kingdom" remains disputed.

16. *Kyrios,* of course, also refers to God—so in James 5:10, 11, directly after 5:7–9. See also 5:17–18, where Elijah is mentioned as a righteous man under the old dispensation whose prayer had "great power in its effects" (v. 16).

5. The Christology of Luke-Acts

1. This clause, given in the margin of RSV, belongs to the original text.

2. The appearance to Paul forms a significant exception (Acts 9:1–29; 22:3–21; 26:9–23). This meeting with the Lord leads to Paul's conversion and to his activity as a new and important witness alongside the Jerusalem apostles.

3. See Luke's introduction to the parable of the pounds: "he proceeded to tell a parable, because he was near to Jerusalem, and because they supposed that the kingdom of God was to appear immediately" (Luke 19:11).

4. Note also Acts 1:5; 11:16, going back to Luke 3:16 and par.

5. Compare also Luke 1:19; 2:10 (where an angel is speaking), and 3:18, where the verb is used for the message of John the Baptist. See also below, p. 102.

6. See chapter 3, pp. 80–81.

7. The Greek term *archēgos* ("leader") returns as title for Jesus in Acts 5:31.

8. We find many expressions with "in the name of (the Lord, Jesus Christ, the Lord Jesus, etc.)"; see Acts 2:21, 38; 3:6 (16); 4:(7), 10, (12), (17), 18, 30; 5:(28), 40, (41); 8:12, 16; 9:15, 16, 27, 28; 10:43, 48; 15:14, 17, 26; 16:18; 19:5, 13, 17; 21:13; 22:16; 26:9. See also the remark made on p. 107 about the frequent use of "the Lord," "the Lord Jesus," and "the Lord Jesus Christ" in expressions denoting the content of the Christian faith.

9. A very good survey of Luke's Christology and soteriology is given by J. A. Fitzmyer in *Luke, I–IX,* 192–227. It should be read in the context of the entire section VII in the Introduction, which is called "A Sketch of Lukan Theology" (143–258).

10. We find it in the Markan pericopes of the blind man at Jericho (18:35–43) and of the discussion on the Messiah as Son of David (20:41–44).

11. Compare chapter 1, p. 38.

12. Compare also the teaching of Apollos in Ephesus in Acts 18:28.

13. For the use of *christos* in Acts 2:36 and 3:19–21, see below, pp. 110f.

14. The genealogy in Luke 3:23–37 makes Jesus a descendant of David (v. 31) and, finally, of God (v. 38).

15. See chapter 1, pp. 48f.

16. See chapter 4, note 5.

17. We may add that Acts 13:46–47 applies Isa. 49:6 to Paul (see p. 101)

and that Acts 26:16–18 alludes to Isa. 42:7, 16 also in connection with Paul's missionary charge.

18. Other elements connected with Elijah are found in Luke 7:11–17; 9:62; Jesus rejects an Elijah role in 9:52–54; and, of course, John the Baptist is depicted as *Elia redivivus* in Luke also (see, e.g., 1:17 and 7:27).

19. On the road to Emmaus the disciples call Jesus "a prophet mighty in deed and word before God and all the people" (Luke 24:19). This is a correct (cf., e.g., Acts 2:22) but incomplete and inadequate description, as the following discussion with the risen Jesus shows.

20. Also in 1 Cor. 15:4 the first appearance of Jesus is to Peter (here called "Cephas"). We may therefore have a pre-Lukan formula here. Whether this also used the title "the Lord" or whether this was inserted by Luke is difficult to say.

21. See also the *Kyrie* in the accounts of Paul's encounter with the Lord on the road to Damascus in Acts 9:5, 10, 13; 22:8, 10, 19; 26:15.

22. In Luke 22:48 and 24:7 the title "the Son of man" is used in connection with Jesus' suffering; 24:7 adds a reference to the resurrection; in fact it is a reminder of the predictions in 9:22, 44; 18:31–34, which correspond to those found in Mark (and Matthew)—see chapter 2, p. 58.

23. See chapter 3, p. 78. Compare Mark 8:38 (par. Luke 9:26), mentioned in chapter 2.

24. On this, see W. G. Kümmel, *Introduction to the New Testament,* 167–169.

25. Chapter 1, first section.

26. Ibid. For this point I am indebted to L. Schenke, "Die Kontrastformel Apg 4,10[b]." See also note 29 below.

27. See chapter 1, first section, and chapter 3, pp. 79–80. This point is brought out clearly by U. Wilckens in the third revised edition of his *Die Missionsreden der Apostelgeschichte,* 200–208. It does not come as a surprise that this tradition is taken up in speeches that aim at the conversion of Jews. They are reminded of what "they" (their fellows in Jerusalem, their fathers) did, and of how God vindicated Jesus and then urged them to repent and to accept Jesus as their Lord. For a different assessment of the relevant passages see the recent survey article by M. Rese, "Die Aussagen über Jesu Tod und Auferstehung in der Apostelgeschichte."

28. The longer text (Luke 22:19b–20), relegated to the margin in earlier editions of the RSV, is now generally considered to be the original.

29. Compare Acts 13:33, discussed on p. 105, and note that in 1:22; 4:2, 33 the apostles are said to be witnesses of the resurrection. See also Paul's message in 17:18, 31f. An explicit connection between this message and Pharisaic beliefs is established in 23:6–8; 24:21; 26:8.

30. For a recent survey, see, e.g., G. Schneider, *Die Apostelgeschichte,* I, 323–327.

31. The noun *apokatastasis* used in Acts 3:21 is directly connected with the verb *apokathistaneis,* translated "will you restore" (the kingdom of Israel) in 1:6. The verb is connected with Elijah in Mark 9:12 (par. Matt. 17:11): "Elijah does come first to restore all things" (cf. Mal. 3:22–23 in Greek = 4:5–6 in most English translations).

6. The Christology of Paul

1. See, especially, S. Kim, *The Origin of Paul's Gospel,* who overstates his case, however. Other important recent studies on Paul's theology are E. P. Sanders, *Paul and Palestinian Judaism,* together with his *Paul, the Law, and the Jewish People,* and J. C. Beker, *Paul the Apostle: The Triumph of God in Life and Thought.*

2. Deut. 21:22–23 speaks about exposure on a tree of a man put to death. The passage is applied to death by hanging from a tree also in 4Q pesher Nahum 3–4, I:7–8; and 11Q Temple Scroll 64:6–13.

3. We have no evidence for this other than that in Acts; see especially the (false) witness against Stephen, "This man never ceases to speak words against this holy place and the law; for we have heard him say that this Jesus of Nazareth will destroy this place, and will change the customs which Moses delivered to us" (6:13–14), and the speech by Stephen that follows in chapter 7.

4. For more details, see the studies by W. Kramer and K. Wengst mentioned in chapter 1, note 13, and, in particular, N. A. Dahl, "The Messiahship of Jesus in Paul." Besides Rom. 9:5 there may also be messianic connotations in the use of the term in Rom. 15:7; 1 Cor. 1:23; 10:4; 15:22; 2 Cor. 5:10; 11:2–3; Gal. 3:16; Phil. 1:15, 17; 3:7. See notes 11 and 12 in Dahl's essay.

5. Dahl, "The Messiahship of Jesus in Paul," 40.

6. See also the paradoxical sentence "They [i.e., the rulers of this age] . . . crucified the Lord of glory" in 1 Cor. 2:6.

7. Here and elsewhere, Paul brings out the implications of liturgical formulas, discussed in chapter 1.

8. Compare "Maranatha" in 1 Cor. 16:22, also discussed in chapter 1.

9. J. C. Beker, *Paul the Apostle,* 35.

10. Paul also uses the expression "in the Lord." On this, see, e.g., C. F. D. Moule, *The Origin of Christology,* 59: "Broadly speaking, Jesus tends to be spoken of as 'Christ' in the context of verbs in the indicative mood and of statements, while he tends to be spoken of as 'Lord' when it is a matter of exhortations or commands, in the subjunctive or the imperative. Roughly speaking, 'Christ' is associated with the *fait accompli* of God's saving *work,* and 'the Lord' with its implementation and its working out in human conduct." Moule emphasizes that there are obvious exceptions to this general rule.

11. On the relationship between the two types of language used by Paul in his soteriology see, e.g., E. P. Sanders, *Paul and Palestinian Judaism,* 433–523. The two central passages on baptism using "corporate" language are Gal. 3:26–28 and Rom. 6:1–11.

12. The Greek word *hilastērion,* which is used by Paul only here, is also used in Heb. 9:5 to refer to the "mercy seat" of the Ark of the Covenant. See also below, p. 150, on 1 John 2:2.

13. The word used here is related to a verb employed in the Greek Old Testament for the act of liberation by which God set Israel free from slavery in Egypt. Compare the hope of the people on the road to Emmaus that Jesus

would be "the one to redeem Israel" (Luke 24:21). There is also a link with the word *lytron* used in Mark 10:45 (and Matt. 20:28), "to give his life as a ransom for many" (cf. 1 Tim. 2:6 and see chapter 1, p. 40). "To redeem" is also used as a translation of the verb *exagorazein* in Gal. 3:13 (see p. 113) and 4:5 (see chapter 1, pp. 42f.). In the related *agorazein* found in 1 Cor. 6:20; 7:23 ("you were bought with a price"), the notion of payment comes out again. Nowhere, however, is it said to whom the price is to be paid. God keeps the initiative from the beginning to the end; he is the one to whom people owe their life in freedom. For another description of God's action in Christ in terms of Israel's liberation from slavery in Egypt, see 1 Cor. 5:7: "For Christ, our paschal lamb, has been sacrificed."

14. More should be said about this much-disputed passage. According to some scholars the complicated wording arises because Paul is commenting on an ancient formula consisting of Rom. 3:25, "Whom God put forward as an expiation by his blood. . . . This was to show God's righteousness, because in his forbearance he had passed over former sins," or even more. For detailed comments on these and other matters see C. E. B. Cranfield, *Romans,* I, 199–218, and U. Wilckens, *Der Brief an die Römer,* I, 182–202.

15. See also chapter 1, p. 38.

16. 2 Corinthians 5:16 stresses that those who live in communion with the one who died for their sake and was raised no longer regard people from a human point of view (literally: "according to the flesh"). This also applies to Christ: "Even though we once regarded Christ from a human point of view, we regard him thus no longer." There is no doubt an autobiographical element in this statement, but Paul extends it to other believers as well. Jesus' earthly life can only be properly assessed by people who live in communion with the living resurrected Lord.

17. The kingdom of Christ is here distinguished from the kingdom of God—as in some forms of Jewish apocalyptic hope (see, e.g., *4 Ezra* and *2 Baruch,* writings that are somewhat later than Paul). Paul does not specify when Christ's kingdom begins. The nearest parallel to the picture given here is found in Matt. 13:24–30, 36–43; see p. 95. In Rev. 20 Christ rules during a period of a thousand years after the *parousia* and before the final destruction of evil (see pp. 137f.).

18. Paul reacts here to Jewish speculations about the First Man; for details see the commentaries on this passage.

19. Note again the reference to the (future) kingdom of God in 1 Cor. 15:50, "flesh and blood cannot inherit the kingdom of God."

20. Compare Rom. 8:23, "adoption as sons, the redemption of our bodies," and 8:30, "whom he justified he also glorified"; one should read these verses in the context of the entire passage, 8:18–39.

21. The term "Savior" occurs only here in Paul's letters.

22. "The Lord who is the Spirit" takes up 2 Cor. 3:17, where "the Lord" from verse 16 (which quotes Ex. 34:34) is said to refer to the Spirit: "where the Spirit of the Lord is, there is freedom." C. K. Barrett, *2 Corinthians,* 123, comments: "It is in the realm of action (cf. 1 Cor. XV.45) rather than of person (or of substance, as Lietzmann says [in his commentary]) that the terms of *Lord* and *Spirit* are identified."

23. See also 2 Cor. 4:7–5:10, especially 4:10–11, "always carrying in the body the death of Jesus, so that the life of Jesus may also be manifested in our bodies. For while we live we are always being given up to death for Jesus' sake, so that the life of Jesus may be manifested in our mortal flesh." Paul connects this with the vicissitudes of his life as an apostle; see 4:8–9; 6:4–11. See also note 29.

24. Discussed at great length in S. Kim, *The Origin of Paul's Gospel,* especially chapter 6, 137–268.

25. See chapter 1, pp. 42f.

26. Not the manner of Jesus' birth but the fact that he was born of a human being is important.

27. Also, the fact that he released the believers from bondage to "the elemental spirits of the universe" (Gal. 4:3, 6–10) suggests that he had a status surpassing those.

28. For a survey of recent opinion on Phil. 2:6–11, see R. P. Martin, *Carmen Christi.*

29. There is a clear correspondence between the preachers of the gospel, Paul in particular, and Christ who is the center of it. Compare 1 Cor. 2:1–5; 4:6–13, and 2 Cor. 11:22–33; 12:9–10; 13:4. See also note 23.

30. For further passages speaking about the revelation of God's hidden mystery, see pp. 126f.

31. C. K. Barrett, *1 Corinthians,* 222–223, refers to Pseudo-Philo, *Biblical Antiquities* 10.7: "he brought forth a well of water to follow them," and Philo, *Allegorical Interpretation* 2.86: "for the flinty rock is the Wisdom of God which he marked off highest and chiefest of his powers, and from which he satisfied the thirsty souls that love God."

7. Documents of the Pauline School

1. A good survey of the exegetical problems of 2 Thess. 2:1–12 and of parallel notions in Jewish and early Christian sources is given by E. Best, *1 and 2 Thessalonians,* 273–310. There are also parallels with the Synoptic apocalypse in Mark 13 par.

2. For the situation addressed in Colossians, see W. G. Kümmel, *Introduction to the New Testament,* 338–340. Two essays in J. Jervell and W. A. Meeks, eds., *God's Christ and His People: Studies in Honour of Nils Alstrup Dahl,* proved very helpful: F. O. Francis, "The Christological Argument of Colossians," 192–208, and W. A. Meeks, "In One Body," 209–221.

3. For this view see, in particular, F. O. Francis, "The Christological Argument."

4. See also chapter 1, note 30. In Col. 3:11 we find a variant of the unification formula applied in Gal. 3:28 and 1 Cor. 12:13 (see chapter 1, pp. 41f.).

5. The code of domestic behavior in Col. 3:18–4:6 is comparable to those found in Eph. 5:22–6:9; 1 Peter 2:18–3:7. In these "household duty codes" early Christians brought together in a Christianized form rules of conduct commonly accepted in the Greco-Roman world; see J. E. Stambaugh and D. L. Balch, *The New Testament in Its Social Environment,* 123–124.

6. Opinions differ as to the original pre-Colossians (which does not mean early, pre-Pauline!) contents of the hymn. But then it may never have had one fixed form; see chapter 1, last section. On "Wisdom" elements in this hymn, see chapter 12, last section.

7. See also Col. 2:15, "He disarmed the principalities and powers and made a public example of them, triumphing over them in him," after verse 14, "having canceled the bond which stood against us with its legal demands; this he set aside, nailing it to the cross."

8. See also Eph. 1:7, "In him we have redemption through his blood, the forgiveness of our trespasses," parallel to Col. 1:14 and Eph. 2:5, "even when we were dead through our trespasses, [God] made us alive together with Christ," parallel to Col. 2:13.

9. For "mystery" terminology see also Eph. 1:9; 3:9; 5:32; 6:19. Here and in 3:9–10 we meet it together with the "hidden-revealed" pattern. The mystery in 3:4–6 is that the Gentiles are "fellow heirs, members of the same body, and partakers of the promise in Christ Jesus through the gospel."

10. See chapter 1, p. 40.

11. See J. P. Sampley, *"And the Two Shall Become One Flesh."*

12. See also 2 Thess. 2:8, where *epiphaneia* and *parousia* appear together.

13. See pp. 122f.

8. Other Letters and Revelation

1. The leading monograph on the Christology of Hebrews is W. R. G. Loader, *Sohn and Hohepriester.* The expositions in H. Feld, *Der Hebräerbrief,* 65–82, and H. J. de Jonge, "Traditie en exegese," proved very helpful.

2. As in 1 Cor. 15:23–28 (see p. 119; cf. Eph. 1:22), clauses from Ps. 8 are connected with Ps. 110:1 (found here in 1:13); neither there nor here does the designation "son of man" in Ps. 8:5 (4E) receive any attention.

3. See also *1 Clement* 36.1, which may be directly influenced by Hebrews ("Jesus Christ, the high priest of our offerings, the patron and helper of our weakness"); Ignatius, *To the Philadelphians* 9.1; Polycarp, *To the Philippians* 19.2; *Martyrdom of Polycarp* 14.3.

4. See chapter 1, first section.

5. Compare, earlier in the Hebrews, "when he had made purification for sins" (1:3); "to make expiation for the sins of the people" (2:17); "the source of eternal salvation to all who obey him" (5:9).

6. In Hebrews the relatively frequent expressions "for us/them" and "for (the) sins (of)" nearly all occur in connection with the various aspects of the work of Christ as high priest and his counterparts of the old dispensation.

7. The author of Hebrews reminds his readers of the fact that, according to Ex. 24:3–8, the first covenant was ratified by blood. He quotes Ex. 24:8, "This is the blood of the covenant which God commanded you," in Heb. 9:20 (cf. also 10:29; 12:24, and 13:20, "the blood of the eternal covenant"). In the background is, no doubt, the saying connected with the cup in the texts concerning the last supper.

8. This is a clear reference to the ratification of the covenant at Mount

Sinai (Ex. 24:3–8); compare Heb. 9:15–22.

9. The author of 1 Peter refers to Isa. 28:16; Ps. 118:22; and Isa. 8:14; compare Mark 12:10 and parallels (esp. Luke 20:17, 18); Rom. 9:33 and Eph. 2:20–22.

10. For "rejoicing in suffering" see, e.g., Matt. 5:11–12 (par. Luke 6:22–23); James 1:2, 12. "Suffering and glorification with Christ" presupposes the corporate notion found in Paul's letters and probably already used before him in connection with baptism. (In the passages on "new birth" in 1 Peter the readers are reminded of their baptism as a new beginning in life!) The expression "in Christ," familiar from Paul, is found in 1 Peter 3:16; 5:10, 14. These (and other) similarities should be explained by continuity in tradition rather than by literary dependence.

11. See, e.g., E. Best, "1 Peter and the Gospel Tradition."

12. I follow here the cautious judgment of L. Goppelt in his *Der erste Petrusbrief,* especially 121–127, 198–212, 239–264.

13. See p. 148 on John 1:29 (36).

14. See also the reference to Israel's sojourn in Egypt in Isa. 52:4.

15. See p. 122 on 1 Cor. 2:6–10; p. 126 on Col. 1:25–28; and pp. 126f. on Ephesians.

16. Also in Rom. 4:24 this forms the center of the Christian faith. On "and gave him glory" see, e.g., Luke 24:26; Acts 3:13.

17. See chapter 1, p. 37.

18. See chapter 5, pp. 104f.

19. Compare Rom. 6:11, 18, where Paul draws a conclusion from the fact that Christians have died (to sin) and received a new existence (to God) "in Christ," in baptism. Compare also 1 Peter 4:1–2.

20. For Christ as shepherd, see also 1 Peter 5:4.

21. See pp. 179–181. Compare Luke 22:37 quoting Isa. 53:12 and Acts 8:32f., where Philip applies Isa. 53:7–8 to Jesus. See also Heb. 9:28 with a reference to Isa. 53:12.

22. For "spirits" in the sense of "souls of deceased persons" see Heb. 12:23; Dan. 3:86a (LXX); and *1 Enoch* 22:3. In all these cases, however, a genitive follows. Those who favor this interpretation connect 1 Peter 3:19–20a with 4:6, "the gospel was preached even to the dead"; others think the latter clause refers to Christians who have already died.

23. "Spirits" very often denotes (good and evil) spiritual beings, angels and demons. For (variations of) the myth of the angels, see, e.g., *1 Enoch* 6–16; 21; 106:13–16; *Jubilees* 5:1–6; *Syr. Baruch* 56:12f.; *Testament of Naphthali* 3:5 (and *Testament of Reuben* 5:6f.); 1QapGen (Genesis Apocryphon) 2:1, 16. Compare also Jude 6: "And the angels that did not keep their own position but left their proper dwelling have been kept by him in eternal chains in the nether gloom until the judgment of the great day," taken up in 2 Peter 2:4–5.

24. The Greek verb *kēryssein* does not necessarily always have the meaning of the (Christian) message of *salvation* (see Luke 12:3; Rom. 2:21; Rev. 5:2). On Christ's exaltation and subjection of angels, see 1 Cor. 15:25–27; Col. 2:10–15; Eph. 1:20–22; and Heb. 2:5–9 (plus related texts in Hebrews; see first section of this chapter). Everywhere Christ's present supremacy

over other powers is emphasized; 1 Cor. 15:25–27 specifies that the final victory is still to come. One should note that Christ's ascension to heaven is mentioned explicitly, as in Acts 2:33–36 (cf. 5:31).

25. We do not find here, therefore, an early statement about Christ's "descent to hell" which would later become part of the so-called Apostles' Creed. On early Christian ideas about a journey of Christ to Hades, see L. Goppelt's commentary, 250–254.

26. In view of the parallel expressions, it seems likely that "our God" refers here to Jesus Christ. For a different conclusion in the case of Rom. 9:5 and Titus 2:13 see pp. 122f. and 129.

27. Compare 1 Thess. 5:2; Matt. 24:43 (par. Luke 12:39); Rev. 3:3; 16:15. The analysis of the description of the Day of the Lord in 2 Peter 3 cannot detain us here.

28. A good introduction to the problems of Revelation is given in W. G. Kümmel, *Introduction to the New Testament,* §34.

29. See, e.g., J. Lambrecht, "A Structuration of Revelation 4,1–22,5."

30. For a survey of the use of Christological titles and conceptions as well as of new images for Christ appearing in the visions, see, e.g., T. Holtz, *Die Christologie der Apokalypse des Johannes.*

31. Compare Deut. 10:17; Ps. 136:3; Dan. 2:47 (speaking of God).

32. See pp. 124f. on 2 Thess. 2:3–12 and p. 151 on 1 John 2:18.

33. On this very difficult passage, see my essay "The Use of the Expression *ho Christos* in the Apocalypse of John."

34. In the concluding passage, Rev. 22:6–21, Christ calls himself "the Alpha and the Omega, the first and the last, the beginning and the end" (v. 13, cf. 1:8, 17 and 21:6, where these designations are applied to God, and 2:8, where "the first and the last" is applied to the risen Lord). In 22:16 he says: "I am the root and the offspring of David [cf. 5:5, "the Lion of the tribe of Judah, the Root of David" and Isa. 11:1, 10], the bright morning star" (cf. 2:28 and Num. 24:17).

35. See the preceding note.

36. See p. 134 on 1 Peter 1:18 and p. 148 on John 1:29.

37. The same Greek verb is used in Rev. 14:3, 4 (see below, RSV "redeem"), 2 Peter 2:1, and already by Paul in 1 Cor. 6:20; 7:23; compare the use of a related verb in Gal. 3:13; 4:5.

38. The striking vision (Rev. 6:9–11) showing the souls of martyrs under the heavenly altar emphasizes the element of the "not yet." They cry out: "O Sovereign Lord, holy and true, how long before thou wilt judge and avenge our blood on those who dwell upon the earth?" They receive a white robe and are told to rest a little longer till the number of martyrs will be complete.

9. The Christology of the Gospel and the Letters of John

1. This introduction reflects the author's stand in the scholarly discussion on the many difficult problems connected with the literary history of the Fourth Gospel and the historical situation of the Johannine communities.

For further details see my *Jesus: Stranger from Heaven and Son of God.* I find myself in agreement with most of the lines drawn by R. E. Brown, *The Community of the Beloved Disciple.* I am very skeptical about the possibility of reconstructing earlier sources used by John and an earlier Christology contained in them. The author of the Fourth Gospel may, for instance, have had at his disposal a source relating conspicuous deeds of Jesus, and used them for his stories of the signs of Jesus. We can trace how he used the material in the course of his Christological argument—but we are unable to conclude from tensions and unevennesses in the stories that the original source had a different, more "primitive" Christology.

2. In a number of passages (John 13:21–30; 18:15–18; 19:25–27 (35); 20:1–10; ch. 21) "the disciple whom Jesus loved" occupies an important place. In 21:20–24 he is described as the authority behind the Fourth Gospel. The relation between this disciple as witness par excellence and the other disciples can not be discussed here, but see my "The Beloved Disciple and the Date of the Gospel of John."

3. The Pharisees are the only Jewish group to be mentioned. They are people with authority (John 1:24; 4:1; 7:32; 8:13; 11:46–47; 12:42). Sometimes, in the course of a story, "the Jews" alternates with "the Pharisees" (see, e.g., 8:13, 22 and 9:13, 15, 16, 18, 22, 40).

4. On this, see my *Jesus: Stranger from Heaven and Son of God,* 100–102. In John 4, Samaritans are said to come to believe in Jesus. According to 4:39–42 their reaction is that of true disciples. Yet in 4:31–38 the group of disciples who follow Jesus hear the central Christological truth in verse 34. They seem to continue playing a key role. All this may be a reflection of particular events in an earlier period of the history of the Johannine communities.

5. 1 John 2:7, 8 can only be fully understood against the background of John 13:34; the argument in 1 John 2:22–25 presupposes that the reader knows that the central Christological confession is that Jesus is the Christ, the Son of God (see John 20:30–31).

6. There is also John 12:34, where the Jews state that according to the law the Messiah will remain forever, but Jesus maintains that the Son of man must be lifted up. The last expression refers to his death, resurrection, and ascension as aspects of the return of the Son to the Father. We may also mention 4:25 (cf. 4:19), where Jesus claims to realize the Samaritan expectations concerning the Messiah. In 4:42 he is accepted as "the Savior of the world" (cf. 1 John 4:14). In 1:17; 17:3, we find the double name Jesus Christ.

7. Therefore the deeds that he performs are not simply prophetic "signs" but "the works of God"; see chapter 5, "Signs and Works in the Fourth Gospel," in my *Jesus: Stranger from Heaven and Son of God,* 141–168.

8. In his article "The Central Structure of Johannine Christology," W. R. G. Loader has argued that the Son of man cluster is used by the evangelist to highlight what from the perspective of the earthly ministry of Jesus is something greater yet to come. He points to John 1:50f.; 3:12ff.; 5:20; 6:62; and 7:39; 8:28; 12:16, 32 (and 14:12).

9. See note 6.

10. See J. A. Bühner, *Der Gesandte und sein Weg im 4. Evangelium,* and chapter 12, first section.

11. The term is used in John 1:6; 3:28 in connection with John the Baptist, and once of people sent by the Pharisees (1:24). In 9:7 it is used as translation of the name Siloam (and as clearly referring to Jesus' mission in the world). We should note in passing that the term *apostolos* is also not used of Jesus' disciples. We only find it in the general statement in 13:16, "nor is he who is sent greater than he who sent him."

12. John 3:14 adds, "And as Moses lifted up the serpent in the wilderness, so must the Son of man be lifted up"—a cryptic reference to the cross as a stage on the way to the Father.

13. In the case of the believers the terms "from/of above" and "from/of God" are linked with the verbs "to be" or "to be born" (or "to be begotten"—see John 1:12, 13; 3:3–8; 8:47; cf. 1 John 2:29; 3:9; 4:7; 5:1, 4, 18). The believers are always called "children" (1:12; 11:52; cf. 1 John 3:1, 2, 10; 5:2) as distinct from "the Son." The believers too are strangers in the world!

14. "The bread of life," John 6:35, 48 (cf. vs. 41, 51); "the light of the world," 8:12 (cf. 9:5); "the door," 10:7, 9; "the good shepherd," 10:11, 14; "the resurrection and the life," 11:25; "the way, and the truth, and the life," 14:6; "the (true) vine," 15:1, 5.

15. In John 4:26; 6:20; 18:5, 6, 8, the expression is used as an identification formula, but we may suspect overtones. As a revelation formula the phrase occurs in 8:24 (but see v. 23), 28, 58. RSV translates "I am he" in verses 24, 28; "I am" in verse 58. See also 13:19.

16. Compare chapter 12, last section.

17. I have here followed the RSV but adapted it to the reading chosen in the 26th edition of the Nestle-Aland text; compare RSV margin.

18. In John 13:13–16, "Lord" is used parallel with "Teacher." Important is verse 16, "Truly, truly, I say to you: a servant is not greater than his lord; nor is he who is sent greater than he who sent him" (RSV, alt.), which, however, is followed by 15:15, "No longer do I call you servants (slaves), for the servant (slave) does not know what his lord is doing; but I have called you friends" (RSV, alt.). In 1:23 we find a quotation from Isa. 40:3 (as in Mark 1:3; Matt. 3:3; Luke 3:4).

19. Compare John 12:32, "And I, when I am lifted up from the earth, will draw all men to myself." Note the emphasis on the defeat of Satan in 12:31 (cf. 14:30; 16:11; and 1 John 3:8).

20. Here (perhaps) Ex. 12:10 (LXX), 46 and Num. 9:12, enjoining that no bone of the Paschal lamb shall be broken, is referred to. But see Ps. 34:20, "He keeps all his bones; not one of them is broken."

21. Of course we do not know in what form the material that now makes up the Fourth Gospel was current in the Johannine circles in which the secession reflected in 1–2 John occurred. The present Gospel has antidocetic passages in John 6:51b–58 (cf. vs. 60–66) and 19:34–35. John 1:14 and 20:24–29 are not antidocetic in themselves but could be used in such a controversy. It is possible that the Gospel we have underwent a redaction reflecting the controversies which necessitated the letters.

22. Compare 1 John 3:5, "he appeared to take away sins, and in him there is no sin" (cf. John 1:29). Therefore, those who abide in him do not and cannot sin. The entire section 3:4–10 underscores the absence of sin among the children of God, effected by the Son during his presence on earth.

10. Jesus as Herald of a New Age

1. On what follows, see P. Stuhlmacher, *Das paulinische Evangelium*, I, section C, "Die religionsgeschichtlichen Wurzeln des neutestamentlichen Evangeliums," 109–206, now supplemented by remarks in his contributions to P. Stuhlmacher, ed., *Das Evangelium und die Evangelien*.

2. Though there is nowhere a clear opposition between the good news about Jesus Christ and the glad tidings about Caesar.

3. See now O. Camponovo, *Königtum, Königsherrschaft und Reich Gottes in den frühjüdischen Schriften*.

4. In this passage in his *Jewish War*, Josephus tells his readers that the sect founded by Judas had *nothing* in common with the others! Compare also *J. W.* 2.433: "Judas the Galilean—that redoubtable teacher who in old days, under Quirinius, had upbraided the Jews for recognizing the Romans as masters when they already had God."

5. See chapter 2, pp. 54f., and the section "Jesus and the Kingdom" in chapter 3.

6. See chapter 2, second section.

7. G. Vermes, *Jesus the Jew;* see especially 58–82 (also 89–90, 206–210).

8. See *M. Taan.* 3:8. He even corrects God when the rain only commences to trickle and, later, when it comes down with violence!

9. Again *M. Taan.* 3:8 (trans. G. Vermes); Prov. 23:25 is quoted.

10. On him, see also the two articles by G. Vermes, "Hanina ben Dosa: A Controversial Galilean Saint from the First Century of the Christian Era."

11. *B. Taan.* 24b; *B. Yoma* 53b.

12. *B. Taan.* 24b.

13. See *Jesus the Jew*, 210f. The anecdote is found in *B. Taan.* 23b.

14. Mark 14:36 (cf. Rom. 8:15; Gal. 4:6). See also the section on "Son of God" below.

15. On this subject, see R. Meyer, "Prophecy and Prophets in the Judaism of the Hellenistic-Roman Period"; G. Vermes, *Jesus the Jew*, chapter 4, "Jesus the Prophet" (86–102); R. A. Horsley and J. S. Hanson, *Bandits, Prophets, and Messiahs,* especially chapter 4, "Prophets and Prophetic Movements" (135–189); and R. A. Horsley, " 'Like One of the Prophets of Old.' "

16. *Tosephta Soṭa* 13:2; trans. G. Vermes, *Jesus the Jew*, 92. The following quotation is also from that page.

17. On 81f. Vermes mentions the anecdote about a legal debate between R. Eliezer ben Hyrcanus and his colleagues in which a miracle and even an utterance by a heavenly voice are ruled out of order (*B. Baba Mezia* 59b). The first chapter of the Mishnah tractate *Abot,* which mentions a succession

of revered teachers who transmitted and interpreted the law, begins with the words "Moses received the Law from Sinai and committed it to Joshua, and Joshua to the elders, and the elders to the Prophets, and the Prophets committed it to the men of the Great Synagogue" (trans. H. Danby, *The Mishnah,* 446). The latter body is portrayed as bridging the gap between the Prophets (clearly primarily seen as interpreters of Torah!) and the first historically tangible teacher Simeon the Just, probably the High Priest Simeon II living at the end of the third century B.C. and praised in Sirach 50:1–21; see E. Schürer, *The History of the Jewish People in the Age of Jesus Christ,* II, 359f.

18. Compare the story of Jesus' baptism by John (Mark 1:9–11 and par.).

19. In his *Against Apion* (1.40–41) Josephus comes close to the theory of the rabbis when he introduces the prophets as inspired chroniclers of the history between the death of Moses and Artaxerxes, the successor of the Persian king Xerxes, and adds: "From Artaxerxes to our own time the complete history has been written, but has not been deemed worthy of equal credit with the earlier records, because of the failure of the exact succession of the prophets."

20. When, later in the story, Josephus recounts his first address to the Jewish fighters in the city, standing before the walls of Jerusalem, he implicitly compares his message with that of Jeremiah in the dark days before the capture of Jerusalem by the Babylonians (*J. W.* 5.362–419). On these and other matters see also J. Blenkinsopp, "Prophecy and Priesthood in Josephus," and M. de Jonge, "Josephus und die Zukunftserwartungen seines Volkes." See also G. Delling, "Die biblische Prophetie bei Josephus."

21. Compare Jesus' lament over Jerusalem in Q (Matt. 23:37–39, par. Luke 13:34–35).

22. Compare Josephus' picture of himself in *J. W.* 3.352: "He was an interpreter of dreams and skilled in divining the meaning of ambiguous utterances of the Deity; a priest himself and of priestly descent, he was not ignorant of the prophecies in the sacred books."

23. Trans. G. Vermes, *The Dead Sea Scrolls in English,* 236, 239.

24. With 1QS 9:10f. one may compare Damascus Document 6:10–11, where the sect expects guidance from a man called "he who shall teach righteousness," a counterpart of the teacher of Righteousness. The passages in 1 Maccabees should be read in connection with 1 Macc. 9:27: "Thus there was great distress in Israel, such as had not been since the time that prophets ceased to appear among them." One should note that John Hyrcanus (135–104 B.C.) was regarded as a prophet in Hasmonean circles; see the idealized picture in Josephus, *Ant.* 13.299–309: "Now he was accounted by God worthy of three of the greatest privileges, the rule of the nation, the office of high priest, and the gift of prophecy" (cf. 282–283).

25. Josephus also mentions the case of the eunuch Bagoas, who had been carried away by their assurance "that he would be named father and benefactor in a pronouncement made by the future king who, since all would lie in his hands, would grant him the ability to marry and to father children—his own" (trans. in E. Schürer, *The History of the Jewish People,* II, 505). In this rather vague and not altogether clear report Josephus wants

to suggest that the Pharisees as interpreters of the law *and* prophets were no more than intriguers against Herod.

26. In John 1:19–23, however, John the Baptist denies that he is Elijah, just as he denies that he is the Messiah or the prophet. We should note that the idea that Elijah would be the forerunner of the Messiah was not widely known or accepted in the first century A.D. (if it was found at all); see M. M. Faierstein, "Why Do the Scribes Say That Elijah Must Come First?", with the reactions of D. C. Allison, Jr., in *JBL* 103 and J. A. Fitzmyer in *JBL* 104.

27. See Acts 5:36 (Theudas) and 21:38 (Paul mistaken for "the Egyptian").

28. Matthew 24:26 adds: "So, if they say to you, 'Lo, he is in the wilderness,' do not go out." Compare also John 6:14f., where the people welcome Jesus as "the prophet who is to come into the world" and are "about to come and take him by force to make him king."

29. For the Mount of Olives see Zech. 14:1–4, 9. Josephus only briefly mentions a similar incident under Felix's successor Festus (A.D. 60–62) with "a certain impostor who had promised them salvation and rest from troubles, if they chose to follow him into the wilderness" (*Ant.* 20.188). This man must have envisaged a retreat into the wilderness, where God would make a new start with his people.

30. See R. A. Horsley and J. S. Hanson, *Bandits, Prophets, and Messiahs,* 166, and R. A. Horsley, "Like One of the Prophets of Old," 457.

31. We may compare also a Mosaic prophet in Samaria under Pontius Pilate (A.D. 26–36) on whom Josephus reports in *Ant.* 18.85–87 and much later (c. 74) the action of Jonathan, a weaver, in Cyrene (*Ant.* 7.437–442). Jonathan "led them forth into the desert, promising them a display of signs and apparitions" (438).

32. See also 277: "Such was the great madness that settled upon the nation because they had no king of their own to restrain the people by his pre-eminence."

33. The brigand chief once captured by Herod with great difficulty; see *Ant.* 14.159.

34. *Bandits, Prophets, and Messiahs,* 116.

35. See ibid., chapter 3 (88–134), and R. A. Horsley, "Popular Messianic Movements Around the Time of Jesus."

36. See *Bandits, Prophets, and Messiahs,* 126–127; also R. A. Horsley, "Popular Messianic Movements," 490–491, who points to the account in Philo of the mocking of Agrippa I in Alexandria (*Flaccus* 36–39) and that of Jesus in Mark 15:16–20. Compare also the long note 20 on *J. W.* 7.29 in O. Michel and O. Bauernfeind, *De Bello Judaico* II, 2, 225f.

37. We have already met Jesus, son of Ananias.

38. Compare Tacitus, *Histories* 5.13, and Suetonius, *Vespasian* 4. Josephus does not specify the passage of scripture that he has in mind. See further my article, "Josephus und die Zukunftserwartungen seines Volkes," 209–210.

39. For further details, see my "The Earliest Christian Use of *Christos,*" especially 329–333.

40. And even Cyrus in Isa. 45:1.

41. In the Damascus Document we find the term "the anointed one of Aaron and Israel" (12:23–13:1; 14:19; 19:10–11; 20:1). Probably a single person is envisaged.

42. See also 4QFlor 7–13.

43. Compare the relatively unimportant role of the "Prince of all the Congregation" in the War Scroll (1QM 5:1) and 4Q 161:8–10, where "the Branch of David" is said to judge at the end of times in accord with the teaching of the priests.

44. In 1QM 11:7–8 and Damascus Document 2:12 and 5:21–6:1 the prophets of the past are called "anointed ones."

45. The use of "the anointed of the Lord" in *Pss. Sol.* 18 inscription, 5, 7, is already more stereotyped.

46. See the section on "Jesus the Son of Man" below.

47. All versions except the Latin add that he will spring from the seed of David.

48. See J. A. Sanders, *The Psalms Scroll of Qumran Cave 11*, 91–93. Compare Pseudo-Philo, *Biblical Antiquities* 59, 60.

49. See especially M. Hengel, *The Son of God*, and J. D. G. Dunn, *Christology in the Making*, 12–64.

50. See J. A. Fitzmyer, "The Contribution of Qumran Aramaic to the Study of the New Testament," especially 90–94 and the Addendum, 102–107.

51. Compare also Sir. 4:10 (Greek: "you will then be like a son of the Most High"; Hebrew: "and God will call you son"); 51:10; *Pss. Sol.* 13:8.

52. Mark 13:32 (par. Matt. 24:36) excludes the knowledge of "the hour" of God's final intervention on earth.

53. See the careful analysis of the evidence by J. A. Fitzmyer in *"Abba* and Jesus' Relation to God." Compare the use of *pater* (= father) in Luke 10:21 (par. Matt. 11:25–26) and Luke 11:2 (the simpler version of the Lord's Prayer), both from Q, and also Luke 23:46; John 11:41; 12:27, 28; 17:1, 5, 11, 21, 24, 25.

54. *Christology in the Making*, p. 39.

55. In Dan. 3:25, 28 it is king Nebuchadnezzar who calls an individual angel one "like a son of the gods."

56. See J. A. Bühner, *Der Gesandte und sein Weg im 4. Evangelium*, 191–206. On "son of the house" see also the story of Honi the Circle-Drawer, mentioned above.

57. An exception is John 5:27. Also *anthrōpou* has the article, in accordance with the rule in NT Greek that in cases where a noun is followed by another noun in the genitive both nouns have or omit the article.

58. Trans. M. A. Knibb, *The Ethiopic Book of Enoch*, II.

59. So, e.g., M. A. Knibb, "The Date of the Parables of Enoch."

60. See, e.g., G. Vermes, *Jesus the Jew*, chapter 7, "Jesus the *Son of Man*" (160–191); M. Casey, *Son of Man;* B. Lindars, *Jesus, Son of Man;* and J. A. Fitzmyer, "The New Testament Title 'Son of Man' Philologically Considered."

61. For this interpretation of the Markan "Son of man" see M. D.

Hooker, *The Son of Man in Mark* and "Is the Son of Man Problem Really Insoluble?"

62. In the second century the term "son of man" (without article) recurs to denote Jesus' manhood in Ignatius, *To the Ephesians* 20.2, and *Letter of Barnabas* 12.10.

11. Jesus' Death, Resurrection, and Exaltation

1. See chapter 1, notes 3 and 4.

2. See chapter 5, last section.

3. On what follows see especially the studies by L. Ruppert, *Der leidende Gerechte,* and *Jesus als der leidende Gerechte?,* now to be supplemented with K. Th. Kleinknecht, *Der leidende Gerechtfertigte.* Very helpful is also G. W. E. Nickelsburg, Jr., *Resurrection, Immortality, and Eternal Life in Intertestamental Judaism.*

4. See, e.g., Ps. 56:14 (13E), "For thou hast delivered my soul from death, yea, my feet from falling, that I may walk before God in the light of life," and compare Pss. 22:16 (15E); 30:4 (3E); 40:3 (2E); 86:13; 116:8; etc.

5. In the Song of the Three Young Men (inserted in the Greek Daniel between 3:23 and 24 together with the Prayer of Azariah), God is praised in verse 88 (66) "for he has rescued us from Hades and saved us from the hand of death, and delivered us from the midst of the burning fiery furnace; from the midst of the fire he has delivered us."

6. Compare John 2:17 in the context of Jesus' cleansing of the temple: "Zeal for thy house will consume me."

7. The next verse (Ps. 34:21 [20E]), "He keeps all his bones; not one of them is broken," may be referred to in John 19:36.

8. In H. F. D. Sparks, ed., *The Apocryphal Old Testament,* trans. R. H. Charles and L. H. Brockington. *Syriac Baruch* was written after the destruction of Jerusalem and the temple in A.D. 70.

9. See chapter 2. In his *Das Markus-evangelium,* II (13–15), R. Pesch has brought together a host of possible references and allusions to OT traditions about the righteous sufferer in Mark 14:1–16:8 and earlier parts of the Gospel that he considers to have belonged to the pre-Markan passion narrative.

10. Luke, who clearly wants to avoid misunderstanding, replaces the quotation from Ps. 22:2 by one from Ps. 31:6 (5E), another psalm of suffering and deliverance: "Into thy hands I commit my spirit!" (see Luke 23:46).

11. On Ps. 49:16 and Ps. 73:24 see above. Compare also among the hymns found at Qumran 1QH 15:14–17, where it is said about the just, "and that [Thou mightest show Thyself great] in the multitude of Thy mercies, and enlarge his straitened soul to eternal salvation, to perpetual and unfailing peace. Thou wilt raise up his glory from among the flesh" (trans. G. Vermes).

12. See chapter 10, last section.

13. L. Ruppert, in his *Jesus als der leidende Gerechte?,* 23–24, calls them a "diptych," comparing them to the two corresponding wings of medieval

altars; he is of the opinion that originally they formed a separate unit, composed in the first half of the first century B.C. when pious Jews suffered and were put to death during the reign of Alexander Jannaeus. In his view, the two passages were only later incorporated in the Book of Wisdom and used to illustrate a somewhat different view on suffering (see Wisd. of Sol. 2:10–11; 3:1–9).

14. On this see, e.g., K. Wengst, *Christologische Formeln und Lieder des Urchristentums*, 55–104, and M. Hengel, *The Atonement*. On 2 and 4 Maccabees I have learned much from the Leiden dissertation *De Joodse martelaren als grondleggers van een nieuwe orde* by J. W. van Henten.

15. So also L. Ruppert and K. Th. Kleinknecht in their studies mentioned in note 3.

16. We should note in passing that the Greek terms used in Isa. 52:13 for "exaltation" and "lifting up" are taken over in Johannine Christology (John 3:14; 8:28; 12:32, 34 and 7:39; 12:16, 23; etc.).

17. See, e.g., G. W. E. Nickelsburg, Jr., *Resurrection, Immortality, and Judgment: Eternal Life in Intertestamental Judaism*, 24–26, 62–66.

18. In Acts 3:13, 26 the expression is used, however, in the context of the contrast pattern: "whom you delivered up" (v. 13); "God, having raised up his servant" (v. 26).

19. Compare Matt. 20:28 and 26:28 (but not Luke 22:19, 20 or 1 Cor. 11:24, 25). In 1 Tim. 2:6 we find "all"; in Rom. 5:12–21 "all" and "many" alternate; "many" is not used exclusively but inclusively. For Mark 10:45 compare also Isa. 43:3–4 (see M. Hengel, *The Atonement*, 36, referring to Werner Grimm).

20. See, e.g., T. W. Manson in his *The Teaching of Jesus*, 230–236, and *The Servant-Messiah*, 64 and 73; J. Jeremias in many publications and in particular in his *New Testament Theology*, I: *The Proclamation of Jesus*, §24; and O. Cullmann, *The Christology of the New Testament*, I, §2. On the discussion around this topic, see H. Haag, *Der Gottesknecht bei Deuterojesaja*, 66–78.

21. For Eleazar see 2 Macc. 6:18–31 and 4 Macc. 5–7; for the seven brothers and their mother, see 2 Macc. 7 and 4 Macc. 8–18. 2 Macc. 14:37–46 adds the story of the suicide of Razis, which has a number of elements in common with the martyrdoms.

22. For a good survey see M. Hengel, *The Atonement*, 1–32, and J. W. van Henten, *De Joodse martelaren*, 129–130, 141–144, 158–169.

23. See Introduction, p. 27, referring to studies by M. Hengel. It is not surprising that also in his *The Atonement*, Hengel (against K. Wengst and others) refuses to draw a sharp distinction between Hellenistic and Palestinian Judaism (pp. 2–4, 60–61).

24. 2 Macc. 6:14; compare Matt. 23:32–33 and 1 Thess. 2:16, where, however, the expression is used in connection with the Jews (Jewish leaders).

25. The Greek verb used here in 2 Macc. 1:5; 5:20; and 8:29 is, with the related noun, also found in Rom. 5:6–11 and 2 Cor. 5:16–21. Note the parallel between "saved by him from the wrath of God" and "reconciled to God by the death of his Son" in Rom. 5:10–11.

26. The notion of suffering as punishment is found in Ps. 39:12 (11E) and Ps. 73:14. In *Pss. Sol.* 10:1–4 and 13:7–12 it is connected with "cleansing from sin" (10:1; cf. 13:10: "the Lord will wipe out their errors by means of discipline").

In 2 Maccabees the deaths of the martyrs affect the whole people. This shows acquaintance with notions found in classical Greek and Hellenistic literature, but it also ties up with ideas about noncultic atonement by Moses and Phinehas found in Ex. 32:30–34; Ps. 106:16–23 (cf. Ps. 78, esp. 17–22, 30–38, 56–64), Num. 25; Lev. 45:23; 1 Macc. 2:54; and Ps. 106:28–31 respectively. There is clear correlation between the sins of the people and God's anger and punishment. Time and again, however, God shows his mercy and reconciles himself to his people—see, e.g., Ps. 78:38, and especially Ps. 79:9–10.

27. *exhilaskesthai* beside *hilaskesthai.* The verbs are often used in a cultic context. Interesting here are verses 38–40 (15–17) in the Prayer of Azariah (among the additions to Daniel), where the author, after complaining that offerings have ceased ("there is no place to make an offering before thee or to find mercy") argues that "a contrite heart and a humble spirit" may be accepted as a sacrifice. "Such may our sacrifice be in thy sight this day, to make atonement before thee" (so the Septuagint; RSV follows the Greek translation of Theodotion). We may compare here the use of *hilasmos* in 1 John 2:2 and 4:10 and *hilaskesthai* in Heb. 2:17 (see chapter 8, p. 133). For a parallel to *hilastērion* in Rom. 3:25 (see chapter 6, pp. 117f.), see 4 Macc. 17:22 below.

28. See also Taxo and his sons in *Assumption of Moses* 9. In 9:6, 7 Taxo says: "let us die rather than transgress the commandments of the Lord of lords, the God of our fathers. For if we do this and die, our blood will be avenged before the Lord" (trans. R. H. Charles and J. P. M. Sweet in H. F. D. Sparks, *The Apocryphal Old Testament*). Compare Deut. 32:43 and Ps. 79:10.

29. The martyrs declare that the tyrant king will not escape divine punishment (2 Macc. 7:17, 19, 31, 34–37). In fact, 2 Macc. 9 relates Antiochus' death (and repentance!) at great length.

30. In 2 Macc. 15:12–16, Judas has a vision of Onias, the last high priest killed treacherously near Antioch years before (2 Macc. 4:33–38), and Jeremiah praying for the people of God in heaven. These two great men in Israel could be regarded as comparable to the Maccabean martyrs. In the difficult passage 12:39–45, however, the group of those expected to rise again seems to be larger. Judas prays for fallen soldiers punished by God for their idolatry, expecting that they would rise again. "If he was looking to the splendid award that is laid up for those who fall asleep in godliness, it was a holy and pious thought" (12:44–45).

31. Here and below I use the translation by H. Anderson in J. H. Charlesworth, ed., *The Old Testament Pseudepigrapha,* II.

32. Compare "for the Law's sake" (4 Macc. 13:9, cf. v. 13), "for the sake of God" (9:8; 16:25), with "for goodness' sake" (1:10) and "for the sake of their religion *(eusebeia)"* (9:6, 7; 18:3).

33. The word *katharsion* means "purificatory offering," "expiation."

34. The word for ransom used here and in 4 Macc. 17:21 is *antipsychon;* i.e., "life given for another life."

35. Here we find *hilastērion,* used by Paul in Rom. 3:25.

36. The story of Abraham's "binding of Isaac" in Gen. 22 has led to many Jewish traditions on the meaning of this event. Scholars differ in their reconstruction of the stages in the development of these traditions and their date, also in their answers to the question whether at the oldest stage they could have influenced early Christian interpretation of the death of Jesus. The incident is mentioned as an illustration of Abraham's faith in James 2:21 and Heb. 11:17–19. Perhaps Gen. 22:16 has influenced the beginning of Rom. 8:32: "He who did not spare his own Son (but gave him up for us all)." On this matter see M. Hengel, *The Atonement,* 61–63; K. Th. Kleinknecht, *Der leidende Gerechtfertigte,* 159–163, and the survey of the discussion up to 1977 in M.-L. Gubler, *Die frühesten Deutungen des Todes Jesu,* 336–375.

37. In 1 Thess. 4:13–18, "being with the Lord" of the living and the dead applies to the time after the *parousia.* We may compare here *4 Ezra,* which expects the arrival of the Messiah with his companions (7:28; 13:52) and (in 14:9) promises Ezra that he will be taken away from the world of men to remain with "my Son" and people like him (Ezra) until the end of time (see also 14:49, 50 in most of the oriental versions). If this applies to people conveyed to heaven without death, as in the case of Enoch or Elijah (see 6:26), the company of the Messiah is a very small one. We should, therefore, consider the possibility that Ezra is thought to belong to a wider group of departed righteous servants of God.

38. When in the Gospels of Matthew and Luke the respectful address *kyrie* ("sir") is used by disciples and people who hope he may heal and save, and when in Luke-Acts the expression "the Lord" is used freely to denote the earthly as well as the exalted Jesus, this too is the result of "retrojection."

39. See, e.g., W. Foerster, "Gods and Rulers as *Kyrioi.* "

40. See also Acts 25:26, where governor Festus declares, in connection with Paul's appeal to the emperor, "I have nothing definite to write to my Lord about him."

41. Tertullian, *Apology* 34.1, to be dated A.D. 197.

42. On this and on what follows, see J. A. Fitzmyer's excellent article "The Semitic Background of the New Testament Kyrios-Title."

43. See chapter 1, p. 46.

44. For details see Fitzmyer's article, 119–127.

45. See, e.g., D. M. Hay, *Glory at the Right Hand;* M. Gourgues, *A la Droite de Dieu;* W. R. G. Loader, "Christ at the Right Hand."

46. On Jewish and Christian interpretation of scripture see also J. L. Kugel and R. A. Greer, *Early Biblical Interpretation.*

47. For this exegesis of Mark 12:35–37 and 14:62 see above, chapter 2, second section.

48. In Acts 7:55–56, Jesus is portrayed as *standing* at the right hand of God.

49. On this passage see also chapter 5, p. 110.

50. See also *Letter of Barnabas* 12:10–11 and compare Mark 16:19: "So then the Lord Jesus . . . was taken up into heaven and sat down at the right hand of God." In the Greek version of Ps. 110:1a given in the NT texts mentioned, the same word *kyrios* is used twice. From this it may not be concluded that only Greek-speaking Christians (of Jewish or non-Jewish descent) could use this passage in their Christological discussions; see also J. A. Fitzmyer in his article mentioned in note 42 and also 87–90 of his "The Contribution of Qumran Aramaic to the Study of the New Testament."

51. A similar combination of texts is found in Heb. 1:13 and 2:6–8; compare 1 Peter 3:18 and Eph. 1:20–23.

12. Jesus Christ and God Before Jesus' Mission on Earth

1. There are some exceptions: Paul's attempts to explain the resurrection with the help of the image of the dying grain of wheat producing a new ear, and terms such as "physical body" and "spiritual body" (1 Cor. 15:35–57). Luke emphasizes the concrete reality of the risen Lord when he tells that he eats a piece of broiled fish (Luke 24:36–43).

2. See chapter 1, second section.

3. See chapter 6, last section.

4. See chapter 9, third section.

5. For John 1:1–18 see second section, below.

6. On this see, for instance—besides J. A. Bühner's *Der Gesandte und sein Weg im 4. Evangelium*—J. D. G. Dunn, *Christology in the Making,* 149–159, and the very instructive article by C. H. Talbert, "The Myth of a Descending-Ascending Redeemer in Mediterranean Antiquity."

7. The three divine messengers who visit Abraham and Sarah to announce the birth of Isaac (Gen. 18) appear as men and eat the food set before them (vs. 2, 8, 16, 22). In chapter 19 the story continues with a reference to two angels (v. 1).

8. Gal. 4:14 cannot be used as proof here (see Dunn, *Christology in the Making,* 155–156). We should note that in Heb. 3:1 Jesus is called "the apostle" (a title studiously avoided in the Fourth Gospel) but is repeatedly said to be superior to the angels (1:4–2:16). It would be very interesting to investigate why in the second century Jesus Christ is frequently spoken of in angelic categories; e.g., by Justin Martyr and in the *Shepherd of Hermas* (see C. H. Talbert, "The Myth of a Descending-Ascending Redeemer," 430–435).

9. See Dunn, *Christology in the Making,* 217–220; and Bühner, *Der Gesandte und sein Weg,* 97–100, who also points to Acts 10:36, "the word which he [God] sent to Israel, preaching good news of peace by Jesus Christ" (cf. 13:26).

10. So, in particular, E. Schweizer in a number of publications on the sending formula; see especially *TDNT* 8 (1972), 374–376 (cf. 383–384, 386).

11. On what follows, see C. H. Talbert's article cited in notes 6 and 8.

12. Compare also Wisd. of Sol. 7:22–27.

13. On the subjects treated in this subsection (and many related ones) see especially J. D. G. Dunn, *Christology in the Making,* 163–250.

14. In *1 Enoch* 42, Wisdom is said to have gone out to dwell among the sons of men but not to have found a dwelling. She returned to her place and took her seat in the midst of angels (cf. 94:5).

15. See RSV text and margin. In Prov. 3:19, "The LORD by wisdom founded the earth; by understanding he established the heavens" (cf. v. 20), Wisdom is not personified.

16. See also chapter 6, third section, where 1 Cor. 8:6 is discussed together with 1:24; 2:6–10; and 10:4.

17. Dunn, *Christology in the Making,* 176.

18. Ibid., 210.

19. See E. Schüssler Fiorenza, "Wisdom Mythology and the Christological Hymns of the New Testament." The term was used earlier by H. Conzelmann. The quotations in the text are from p. 29.

20. See Dunn, *Christology in the Making,* 241, quoting Philo, *On Dreams* 1.229–230.

21. Ibid., 241 and 248.

22. We should note that the expression "The Word dwelt *(eskēnōsen)* among us" may be compared to Sir. 24:8, "The one who created me assigned a place for my tent *(skēnē).* And he said, "Make your dwelling *(kataskēnōson)* in Jacob."

23. Compare also 1 Peter 1:20, "he was destined before the foundation of the world but was made manifest at the end of the times for your sake," and 1 Tim. 3:16 (RSV margin), "who was manifested in the flesh."

13. The One with Whom It All Began

1. For the formulation of this criterion and the following ones, see, e.g., N. Perrin, *Rediscovering the Teaching of Jesus,* 39, 43, 45.

2. See now E. P. Sanders, *Jesus and Judaism.*

3. In all other Christian writings (above all in Paul's letters) we find the "already" and the "not yet" side by side.

4. See chapter 1, p. 40.

5. See, again, chapter 1, p. 45.

6. N. A. Dahl, *The Crucified Messiah and Other Essays,* 10–36.

7. Ibid., 26.

8. In chapter 2, pp. 69f., I have argued that the strong emphasis on Jesus' kingship in Mark 15 may reflect dangerous misunderstandings of the confession "Jesus is the Messiah" in the years leading up to the Jewish war against Rome.

9. Dahl, *The Crucified Messiah,* 32–33.

10. See the chapter "Jesus as Revolutionary" in my *Jesus: Inspiring and Disturbing Presence,* 128–147, with, among other things, a discussion of S. G. F. Brandon, *Jesus and the Zealots.*

Epilogue

1. A. N. Wilder, *The Language of the Gospel: Early Christian Rhetoric,*
51.

2. On this matter see also the various essays in my *Jesus: Inspiring and
Disturbing Presence.*

Bibliography

Aland, K.[13]1985. *Synopsis Quattuor Evangeliorum.* Stuttgart: Deutsche Bibelstiftung.

————, et al. [3]1975. *The Greek New Testament.* United Bible Societies.

Allison, D. C., Jr., 1982. "The Pauline Epistles and the Synoptic Gospels: The Pattern of Parallels." *NTS* 28, 1–32.

————. 1984. "Elijah Must Come First." *JBL* 103, 256–258.

Attridge, H. W. 1985. "Gospel of Thomas." In *Harper's Bible Dictionary,* 355–356. San Francisco: Harper & Row.

Aune, D. E. 1987. *The New Testament in Its Literary Environment.* Library of Early Christianity 8. Philadelphia: Westminster Press.

Barrett, C. K. 1957. *A Commentary on the Epistle to the Romans.* HNTC. London: A & C. Black; New York: Harper & Row.

————. [2]1971. *A Commentary on the First Epistle to the Corinthians.* HNTC. London: A. & C. Black; New York: Harper & Row.

————. 1973. *A Commentary on the Second Epistle to the Corinthians.* HNTC. London: A. & C. Black; New York: Harper & Row.

Beardslee, W. A. 1969. *Literary Criticism of the New Testament.* Philadelphia: Fortress Press.

Beker, J. C. 1980. *Paul the Apostle: The Triumph of God in Life and Thought.* Philadelphia: Fortress Press; paperback ed. with new preface, 1984.

Best, E. 1969–70. "1 Peter and the Gospel Tradition." *NTS* 16, 95–113.

————. [3]1979. *A Commentary on the First and Second Epistles to the Thessalonians.* HNTC. London: A. & C. Black; New York: Harper & Row.

Betz, H. D. 1980. *Galatians.* Hermeneia. Philadelphia: Fortress Press.

Blenkinsopp, J. 1974. "Prophecy and Priesthood in Josephus." *JJS* 25, 239–262.

Brandon, S. G. F. 1967. *Jesus and the Zealots.* Manchester: Manchester University Press.

Brown, R. E. 1979. *The Community of the Beloved Disciple.* New York: Paulist Press; London: Geoffrey Chapman.

Bühner, J. A. 1977. *Der Gesandte und sein Weg im 4. Evangelium.* WUNT II, 2. Tübingen: J. C. B. Mohr.

Camponovo, O. 1977. *Königtum, Königsherrschaft und Reich Gottes in den frühjüdischen Schriften.* OBO 58. Freiburg: Universitätsverlag; Göttingen: Vandenhoeck & Ruprecht.

Casey, M. 1983. *Son of Man: The Interpretation and Influence of Daniel 7.* London: SPCK.

Charlesworth, J. H., ed. 1985. *The Old Testament Pseudepigrapha,* II. Garden City, N.Y.: Doubleday & Co.

Cranfield, C. E. B. 1975. *A Critical and Exegetical Commentary to the Epistle to the Romans,* I. ICC. Edinburgh: T. & T. Clark.

Cullmann, O. 1959, ²1963. *The Christology of the New Testament,* Philadelphia: Westminster Press. Trans. of *Die Christologie des Neuen Testaments.* Tübingen: J. C. B. Mohr, 1957.

Dahl, N. A. 1974. "The Crucified Messiah." In *The Crucified Messiah and Other Essays,* 1–36. Minneapolis: Augsburg Publishing House.

―――. 1974. "The Messiahship of Jesus in Paul." In *The Crucified Messiah and Other Essays,* 37–47.

Danby, H. 1933. *The Mishnah.* London: Oxford University Press.

Davies, W. D. 1964. *The Setting of the Sermon on the Mount.* Cambridge and New York: Cambridge University Press.

Delling, G. 1974. "Die biblische Prophetie bei Josephus." In O. Betz, K. Haacker, M. Hengel, eds., *Josephus-Studien* (Festschrift O. Michel). Göttingen: Vandenhoeck & Ruprecht.

Dibelius, M. ²1923. *An die Thessalonicher, I–II. An die Philipper.* HNT. Tübingen: J. C. B. Mohr.

Dunn, J. D. G. 1980. *Christology in the Making: A New Testament Inquiry Into the Origins of the Doctrine of the Incarnation.* Philadelphia: Westminster Press; London: SCM Press.

Edwards, R. A. 1976. *A Theology of Q: Eschatology, Prophecy, and Wisdom.* Philadelphia: Fortress Press.

Faierstein, M. M. 1981. "Why Do the Scribes Say That Elijah Must Come First?" *JBL* 100, 75–86.

Feld, H. 1985. *Der Hebräerbrief.* Darmstadt: Wissenschaftliche Buchgesellschaft.

Fitzmyer, J. A. 1979. "The Contribution of Qumran Aramaic to the Study of the New Testament." *NTS* 20 (1973–74), 382–407 = *A Wandering Aramean: Collected Aramaic Essays,* 83–113. SBLMonS 25. Missoula, Mont.: Scholars Press.

―――. 1979. "The Semitic Background of the New Testament Kyrios-Title." In *A Wandering Aramean,* 115–142.

―――. 1979. "The New Testament Title 'Son of Man' Philologically Considered." In *A Wandering Aramean,* 143–160.

―――. 1981. *The Gospel According to Luke, I–IX.* AB 28. Garden City, N.Y.: Doubleday & Co.

―――. 1985. *The Gospel According to Luke, X–XXIV.* AB 28A. Garden City, N.Y.: Doubleday & Co.

―――. 1985. "*Abba* and Jesus' Relation to God." In *A cause de l'évangile: Etudes sur les Synoptiques et les Actes offertes au P. Jacques Dupont O.S.B.,* 15–38. Lectio Divina 123. Paris: Editions du Cerf.

————. 1985. "More About Elijah Coming First." *JBL* 104, 292–294.

Foerster, W. 1966. "Gods and Rulers as *Kyrioi.*" *TDNT* 3, 1046–1058.

Fohrer, G. 1972. *"Ben (bar)* as a Term for Relationship to God." *TDNT* 8, 347–353.

Francis, F. O. 1977. "The Christological Argument of Colossians." In J. Jervell and W. A. Meeks, eds., *God's Christ and His People: Studies in Honour of Nils Alstrup Dahl,* 192–208. Oslo-Bergen-Tromsö: Universitetsforlaget.

Friedrich, G. 1964. Art. *euaggelizomai,* etc. *TDNT* 2, 707–737.

Fuller, R. H. 1965. *The Foundations of New Testament Christology.* London: Lutterworth; New York: Charles Scribner's Sons.

Goppelt, L. 1978. *Der erste Petrusbrief.* KEK. Göttingen: Vandenhoeck & Ruprecht.

Gourgues, M. 1978. *A la droite de Dieu: Résurrection de Jésus et actualisation du Psaume 110.1 dans le Nouveau Testament.* Paris: J. Gabalda.

Gubler, M.-L. 1977. *Die frühesten Deutungen des Todes Jesu. Eine motivgeschichtliche Darstellung aufgrund der neueren exegetischen Forschung.* OBO 15. Freiburg: Universitätsverlag; Göttingen: Vandenhoeck & Ruprecht.

Guelich, R. 1983. "The Gospel Genre." In P. Stuhlmacher, ed., *Das Evangelium und die Evangelien. Vorträge vom Tübinger Symposium,* 183–220. WUNT 28. Tübingen: J. C. B. Mohr.

Haag, H. 1985. *Der Gottesknecht bei Deuterojesaja.* Darmstadt: Wissenschaftliche Buchgesellschaft.

Hahn, F. 1969. *The Titles of Jesus in Christology: Their History in Early Christianity.* London: Lutterworth; New York: World Publishing Co. Trans. of *Christologische Hoheitstitel. Ihre Geschichte im frühen Christentum.* FRLANT 83. Göttingen: Vandenhoeck & Ruprecht, 1963.

————, ed. 1985. *Zur Formgeschichte des Evangeliums.* Wege der Forschung 81. Darmstadt: Wissenschaftliche Buchgesellschaft.

Hartman, L. 1973–74. "Into the Name of Jesus." *NTS* 20, 432–441.

————. 1974. "Baptism 'Into the Name of Jesus' and Early Christology." *ST* 28, 21–48.

Hay, D. M. 1973. *Glory at the Right Hand: Psalm 110 in Early Christianity.* SBLMonS 18. Nashville: Abingdon Press.

Hengel, M. 1964. *Judaism and Hellenism: Studies in Their Encounter During the Early Hellenistic Period.* London: SCM Press; Philadelphia: Fortress Press. Trans. of *Judentum und Hellenismus.* WUNT 10. Tübingen: J. C. B. Mohr, 1959.

————. 1976. *The Son of God.* Philadelphia: Fortress Press; London: SCM Press. Trans. of *Der Sohn Gottes. Die Entstehung der Christologie und die jüdisch-hellenistische Religionsgeschichte.* Tübingen: J. C. B. Mohr, 1975.

————. 1980. *Jews, Greeks, and Barbarians: Aspects of the Hellenization of Judaism in the Pre-Christian Period.* London: SCM Press; Philadelphia: Fortress Press. Trans. of *Juden, Griechen, und Barbaren. Aspekte der Hellenisierung des Judentums in vorchristlicher Zeit.* SBS 76. Stuttgart: Katholisches Bibelwerk, 1976.

————. 1981. *The Atonement: The Origins of the Doctrine in the New Testament.* Philadelphia: Fortress Press; London: SCM Press.

————. 1983. "Between Jesus and Paul." In *Between Jesus and Paul: Studies in the Earliest History of Christianity,* 1–29. London: SCM Press; Philadelphia: Fortress Press. Trans. of "Zwischen Jesus und Paulus," *ZTK* 72 (1975), 151–206.

————. 1983. "Christology and New Testament Chronology." In *Between Jesus and Paul,* 43–67. Trans. of "Christologie und neutestamentliche Chronologie," in *Neues Testament und Geschichte* (Festschrift O. Cullmann). Tübingen: J. C. B. Mohr, 1972.

————. 1983. "Hymns and Christology." In *Between Jesus and Paul,* 78–96. Trans. of "Hymnus und Christologie" in W. Hanbeck and M. Bachmann, eds., *Wort in der Zeit* (Festschrift K. H. Rengstorf). Leiden: E. J. Brill, 1980.

Henten, J. W. van. 1986. *De Joodse martelaren als grondleggers van een nieuwe orde. Een studie uitgaande van 2 en 4 Makkabeeën.* Dissertation. Leiden.

Hoffmann, P. 1972. *Studien zur Theologie der Logienquelle. Neutestamentliche Abhandlungen,* N.F. 8. Münster: Aschendorf.

Holtz, T. ²1971. *Die Christologie der Apokalypse des Johannes.* Texte und Untersuchungen 85. Berlin: Akademie Verlag.

Hooker, M. D. 1967. *The Son of Man in Mark.* London: SPCK.

————. 1979. "Is the Son of Man Problem Really Insoluble?" In E. Best and R. McL. Wilson, eds., *Text and Interpretation: Studies in the New Testament Presented to Matthew Black,* 155–168. Cambridge and New York: Cambridge University Press.

Hoppe, R. 1977, ²1985. *Der theologische Hintergrund des Jakobusbriefes.* Forschung zur Bibel 28. Würzburg: Echter Verlag.

Horsley, R. A. 1984. "Popular Messianic Movements Around the Time of Jesus." *CBQ* 46, 471–495.

————. 1985. " 'Like One of the Prophets of Old': Two Types of Popular Prophets at the Time of Jesus." *CBQ* 47, 435–463.

————, and Hanson, J. S. 1985. *Bandits, Prophets, and Messiahs: Popular Movements at the Time of Jesus.* Minneapolis: Winston Press.

Huck, A., and Greeven, H. ¹³1981. *Synopse der drei ersten Evangelien: Synopsis of the First Three Gospels.* Tübingen: J. C. B. Mohr.

Jeremias, J. 1971. *New Testament Theology,* Vol. 1: *The Proclamation of Jesus.* New York: Charles Scribner's Sons. Trans. of *Neutestamentliche Theologie,* I: *Die Verkündigung Jesu.* Gütersloh: Gerd Mohn.

Jonge, H. J. de. 1983. "Traditie en exegese: De hogepriesterchristologie en Melchizedek in Hebreeën," *NedTTs* 37, 1–19.

Jonge, M. de. 1974. *Jesus: Inspiring and Disturbing Presence.* Trans. and ed. by J. E. Steely. Nashville: Abingdon Press.

————. 1974. "Josephus und die Zukunftserwartungen seines Volkes." In O. Betz, K. Haacker, M. Hengel, eds., *Josephus-Studien* (Festschrift O. Michel), 205–219. Göttingen: Vandenhoeck & Ruprecht.

————. 1975. "The Use of HO CHRISTOS in the Passion Narratives." In

J. Dupont, ed., *Jésus aux origines de la christologie,* 169–192. BETL 40. Gembloux: J. Duculot; Louvain: Leuven University Press.

———. 1977. *Jesus: Stranger from Heaven and Son of God.* SBLSBS 11. Missoula, Mont.: Scholars Press.

———. 1979. "The Beloved Disciple and the Date of the Gospel of John." In E. Best and R. McL. Wilson, eds., *Text and Interpretation: Studies in the New Testament Presented to Matthew Black,* 99–114. Cambridge and New York: Cambridge University Press.

———. 1980. "The Use of the Expression *ho Christos* in the Apocalypse of John." In J. Lambrecht, ed., *L'Apocalypse johannique et l'apocalyptique dans le Nouveau Testament,* 267–281. BETL 53. Gembloux: Duculot; Louvain: Leuven University Press.

———. 1986. "The Earliest Christian Use of *Christos:* Some Suggestions." *NTS* 32, 321–343.

Kim, S. 1981, ²1984. *The Origin of Paul's Gospel.* WUNT II, 4. Tübingen: J. C. B. Mohr.

Kingsbury, J. D. 1975. *Matthew: Structure, Christology, Kingdom.* Philadelphia: Fortress Press; London: SPCK.

———. 1983. *The Christology of Mark's Gospel.* Philadelphia: Fortress Press.

Kleinknecht, K. T. 1984. *Der leidende Gerechtfertigte. Die alttestamentlich-jüdische Tradition vom 'leidenden Gerechten' und ihre Rezeption bei Paulus.* WUNT II, 13; Tübingen: J. C. B. Mohr.

Knibb, M. A. 1978. *The Ethiopic Book of Enoch,* II. Oxford: Clarendon Press.

———. 1978–79. "The Date of the Parables of Enoch: A Critical Review." *NTS* 25, 345–359.

Koester, H., and Lambdin, T. O. 1977. "The Gospel of Thomas." In J. M. Robinson, ed., *The Nag Hammadi Library in English,* 117–130. San Francisco: Harper & Row; Leiden: E. J. Brill.

Kramer, W. 1966. *Christ, Lord, Son of God.* Naperville, Ill.: Alec R. Allenson. Trans. of *Christos Kyrios Gottessohn. Untersuchungen zu Gebrauch und Bedeutungen der christologischen Bezeichnungen bei Paulus und den vorpaulinischen Gemeinden.* ATANT 44. Zurich and Stuttgart: Zwingli Verlag, 1963.

Kugel, J. L., and Greer, R. A. 1986. *Early Biblical Interpretation.* Library of Early Christianity 3. Philadelphia: Westminster Press.

Kümmel, W. G. 1975. *Introduction to the New Testament,* rev. ed. Nashville: Abingdon Press. Trans. of *Einleitung in das Neue Testament.* Heidelberg: Quelle & Meyer, ¹⁷1973.

Lambrecht, J. 1980. "A Structuration of Revelation 4,1–22, 5." In J. Lambrecht, ed., *L'Apocalypse johannique et l'apocalyptique dans le Nouveau Testament,* 77–104. BETL 53. Gembloux: Duculot; Louvain: Leuven University Press.

Lindars, B. 1983. *Jesus, Son of Man.* London: SPCK.

Loader, W. R. G. 1977–78. "Christ at the Right Hand—Ps. CX.1 in the New Testament," *NTS* 24, 199–217.

―――. 1981. *Sohn und Hohepriester. Eine traditionsgeschichtliche Untersuchung zur Christologie des Hebräerbriefes.* WMANT 53. Neukirchen-Vluyn: Neukirchener Verlag.

―――. 1984. "The Central Structure of Johannine Christology." *NTS* 30, 188–216.

Lohse, E. 1981. *The Formation of the New Testament.* Nashville: Abingdon Press. Trans. of *Die Entstehung des Neuen Testaments.* Stuttgart: W. Kohlhammer.

Manson, T. W. ²1935. *The Teaching of Jesus.* Cambridge and New York: Cambridge University Press.

―――. 1953. *The Servant-Messiah.* Cambridge and New York: Cambridge University Press.

Marshall, I. H. 1978. *The Gospel of Luke.* NIGTC. Exeter: Paternoster Press.

Martin, R. P. 1983. *Carmen Christi: Philippians ii.5–11 in Recent Interpretation and in the Setting of Early Christian Worship.* 2nd enlarged ed. Grand Rapids: Wm. B. Eerdmans Publishing Co.

Matera, F. J. 1982. *The Kingship of Jesus: Composition and Theology in Mark 15.* SBLDS 66. Chico, Calif.: Scholars Press.

Mayor, J. B. 1897. *The Epistle of James.* London: Macmillan & Co.

McKnight, E. V. 1969. *What Is Form Criticism?* Philadelphia: Fortress Press.

Meeks, W. A. 1974. "The Image of the Androgyne: Some Uses of a Symbol in Earliest Christianity." *HR* 13, 165–208.

―――. 1977. "In One Body: The Unity of Humankind in Colossians and Ephesians." In J. Jervell and W. A. Meeks, eds., *God's Christ and His People: Studies in Honour of Nils Alstrup Dahl,* 209–221. Oslo-Bergen-Tromsö: Universitetsforlaget.

―――. 1983. *The First Urban Christians: The Social World of the Apostle Paul.* New Haven: Yale University Press.

Meyer, R. 1969. "Prophecy and Prophets in the Judaism of the Hellenistic-Roman Period," *TDNT* 6, 812–828.

Michel, O., and O. Bauernfeind. 1969. *De Bello Judaico. Der jüdische Krieg* II, 2. Darmstadt: Wissenschaftliche Buchgesellschaft.

Moule, C. F. D. 1977. *The Origin of Christology.* Cambridge and New York: Cambridge University Press.

Murphy-O'Connor, J. 1983. *Saint Paul's Corinth: Texts and Archaeology.* Wilmington, Del.: Michael Glazier.

Mussner, F. 1964. *Der Jakobusbrief.* HTKNT XIII, 1. Freiburg-Basel-Vienna: Herder.

Nestle, E., and K. Aland, eds. ²⁶1979. *Novum Testamentum Graece.* Stuttgart: Deutsche Bibelstiftung.

Nickelsburg, G. W. E., Jr. 1972. *Resurrection, Immortality, and Eternal Life in Intertestamental Judaism.* HTS 26. Cambridge, Mass.: Harvard University Press.

Perrin, N. 1967. *Rediscovering the Teaching of Jesus.* New York: Harper & Row; London: SCM Press.

Pesch, R. 1977. *Das Markus-evangelium* II. HTKNT II, 2. Freiburg-Basel-Vienna: Herder.

Polag, A. 1977. *Die Christologie der Logienquelle.* WMANT 45. Neukirchen-Vluyn: Neukirchener Verlag.

———. 1979. *Fragmenta Q. Textheft zur Logienquelle.* Neukirchen-Vluyn: Neukirchener Verlag.

———. 1983. "Die theologische Mitte der Logienquelle." In P. Stuhlmacher, ed., *Das Evangelium und die Evangelien. Vorträge vom Tübinger Symposium 1982,* 103–111. WUNT 28. Tübingen: J. C. B. Mohr.

Rese, M. 1984. "Die Aussagen über Jesu Tod und Auferstehung in der Apostelgeschichte—ältestes Kerygma oder lukanische Theologumena?" *NTS* 30, 315–353.

Ruppert, L. 1972. *Der leidende Gerechte. Eine motivgeschichtliche Untersuchung zum Alten Testament und zwischentestamentlichen Judentum.* Forschung zur Bibel 5. Würzburg: Echter Verlag.

———. 1972. *Jesus als der leidende Gerechte? Der Weg Jesu im Lichte eines alt- und zwischentestamentlichen Motivs.* SBS 59. Stuttgart: Katholisches Bibelwerk.

Sampley, J. P. 1971. *"And the Two Shall Become One Flesh": A Study of Traditions in Ephesians 5:21–33.* SNTSMS 16. Cambridge and New York: Cambridge University Press.

Sanders, E. P. 1977. *Paul and Palestinian Judaism.* Philadelphia: Fortress Press; London: SCM Press.

———. 1983. *Paul, the Law, and the Jewish People.* Philadelphia: Fortress Press.

———. 1985. *Jesus and Judaism.* Philadelphia: Fortress Press; London: SCM Press.

Sanders, J. A. 1965. *The Psalms Scroll of Qumran Cave 11.* DJD IV. Oxford: Clarendon Press.

Schenke, L. 1982. "Die Kontrastformel Apg 4,10^b." *BZ,* N.F. 26, 1–20.

Schneider, G. 1980. *Die Apostelgeschichte,* I. HTKNT V,1. Freiburg-Basel-Vienna: Herder.

Schulz, S. 1972. *Q. Die Spruchquelle der Evangelisten.* Zurich: Theologischer Verlag.

Schürer, E. 1979. *The History of the Jewish People in the Age of Jesus Christ,* II, revised by G. Vermes et al. Edinburgh: T. & T. Clark.

Schüssler Fiorenza, E. 1975. "Wisdom Mythology and the Christological Hymns of the New Testament." In R. L. Wilken, ed., *Aspects of Wisdom in Judaism and Early Christianity,* 17–41. Notre Dame, Ind.: University of Notre Dame Press.

Schweizer, E. 1971. *Jesus.* London: SCM Press; Richmond: John Knox Press. Trans. of *Jesus Christus im vielfältigen Zeugnis des Neuen Testaments.* Munich and Hamburg: Siebenstern, 1968.

———. 1972. "The Sending of the Pre-Existent Son of God." *TDNT* 8, 374–376.

Sparks, H. F. D., ed. 1984. *The Apocryphal Old Testament.* Oxford: Clarendon Press.

Stambaugh, J. E., and Balch, D. L. 1986. *The New Testament in Its Social Environment.* Philadelphia: Westminster Press.

Stanton, G. N. 1975. *Jesus of Nazareth in New Testament Preaching.* SNTSMS 27. Cambridge and New York: Cambridge University Press.

———. 1973. "On the Christology of Q." In B. Lindars and S. S. Smalley, eds., *Christ and the Spirit in the New Testament* (Festschrift C. F. D. Moule), 27–42. Cambridge and New York: Cambridge University Press.

Steck, O. H. 1967. *Israel und das gewaltsame Geschick der Propheten. Untersuchungen zur Überlieferung des deuteronomistischen Geschichtsbildes im Alten Testament, Spätjudentum und Urchristentum.* WMANT 23. Neukirchen-Vluyn: Neukirchener Verlag.

Stuhlmacher, P. 1968. *Das paulinische Evangelium,* I: *Vorgeschichte.* FRLANT 95. Göttingen: Vandenhoeck & Ruprecht.

———. 1983a. "Zum Thema: Das Evangelium und die Evangelien." In P. Stuhlmacher, ed., *Das Evangelium und die Evangelien. Vorträge vom Tübinger Symposium 1982,* 1–26. WUNT 28. Tübingen: J. C. B. Mohr.

———. 1983b. "Das paulinische Evangelium," *Das Evangelium und die Evangelien.* 157–182.

Talbert, C. H. 1975–76. "The Myth of a Descending-Ascending Redeemer in Mediterranean Antiquity." *NTS* 22, 418–440.

Theissen, G. 1978. *Sociology of Early Palestinian Christianity.* Philadelphia: Fortress Press; = *The First Followers of Jesus.* London: SCM Press. Trans. of *Soziologie der Jesusbewegung. Ein Beitrag zur Entstehungsgeschichte des Urchristentums.* Munich: Chr. Kaiser Verlag, 1977.

———. 1982. *The Social Setting of Pauline Christianity: Essays on Corinth.* Philadelphia: Fortress Press. Partial trans. of *Studien zur Soziologie des Urchristentums.* WUNT 19. Tübingen: J. C. B. Mohr, 1979.

Tödt, H. E. 1965. *The Son of Man in the Synoptic Tradition.* Philadelphia: Westminster Press. Trans. of *Der Menschensohn in der synoptischen Überlieferung.* Gütersloh: Gerd Mohn, 1959, ²1963.

Vermes, G. 1972–73. "Hanina ben Dosa: A Controversial Galilean Saint from the First Century of the Christian Era." *JJS* 23, 28–50, and *JJS* 24, 51–64.

———(trans.). ²1975. *The Dead Sea Scrolls in English.* Harmondsworth: Penguin Books.

———. 1973, ²1977. *Jesus the Jew: A Historian's Reading of the Gospels.* London: Collins.

Wengst, K. 1972. *Christologische Formeln und Lieder des Urchristentums.* SNT 7. Gütersloh: Gerd Mohn.

Wilckens, U. 1961, ³1974. *Die Missionsreden der Apostelgeschichte.* WMANT 5. Neukirchen-Vluyn: Neukirchener Verlag.

———. 1978. *Der Brief an die Römer,* I. EKKNT VI/1. Cologne: Benziger; Neukirchen-Vluyn: Neukirchener Verlag.

Wilder, A. N. 1964. *The Language of the Gospel: Early Christian Rhetoric.* New York: Harper & Row.

Subject Index

"Abba, Father": as acclamation, 42f., 168f., 208; and Jewish prayers, 218n22, 237n53
Abraham: as example of faith, 116; and Isaac, 183, 241n36
acclamations, 23
Acts, 17, 97-111; elements reflecting ancient traditions, 108-111, 175; speeches, 108
Adam and Christ, 109f., 121
Alpha and Omega, 231n34
angels: as heavenly messengers, 191-194; and powers subjected to Christ, 119, 125ff., 131, 136, 230n24
Anointed with the Spirit, Jesus as the, 57, 74, 99f., 104, 156, 166f.; see also Christ/Messiah
Antichrist; see opponents of Jesus Christ at the *parousia*
antidocetism in the Johannine writings, 144, 149ff., 192, 233n21; see also flesh and spirit
apocalyptic imagery in Rev., 137
apostle, Jesus as, 132, 242n8
ascension of Jesus, 98, 230n24
ascent and descent, 146
Athronges, 164
atonement; see expiation
authors and communities, 15-17, 18, 23, and passim

baptism: formulas, 16, 23f., 46, 218n29; into Christ, 41f., 116f., 217n17; and confession of Jesus as Lord, 46; in the name of Father, Son, and Holy Spirit, 93; in the name of Jesus Christ/the Lord Jesus, 103; in

Col., 125; baptismal hymn in Eph., 127
Beatitudes, 74, 91, 175ff., 206
blood: and cleansing of sins, 133f., 139, 149f., 229n7; and purification in 4 Macc., 183
body of Christ, 41, 217n17; with Jesus Christ as head, 125ff.
bride: the church as, 127; New Jerusalem as, 138

catechetical teaching, 23
catholic epistles, 18
charismatics, Jewish, 159f.
Christ/Messiah
    Jesus as Christ: in Mark, 57-63, 68ff., 155, 165; not in Q, 83f., 208; in Matt., 94; in Luke-Acts, 100, 104f.; in Paul, 114, 226n4; in the Gospel of John, 143, 144f.; in the letters of John, 149f.; see also Anointed with the Spirit
    Christ and the millennium in Rev., 137f.
    Messiah in *Pss. Sol.*, 157f.
    "Anointed One/Messiah" in OT and Jewish sources, 28, 166f.
    Jesus and the designation "Christ/Messiah," 208-211
    "of Christ," 41f., 63
    "in Christ"; see corporate notions
Christianity as a variety of communities in a network, 19f.
Christians, as designation, 105
Christological titles, 19, 28, 207
Christology: always in context, 15-17, 214; continuity and development, 19,

Index of References

Index of References